LITERACY FOR A CHANGING WORLD

Theme monograph series

To ensure that its research and development program is focused and sustained, ACER has adopted five themes upon which to concentrate for a period of at least three years. The themes for 1988–90 are:

1. The Compulsory Years — The Common Experience
2. Beyond Compulsory Schooling
3. Cognitive Processes and Education
4. Education and Technology
5. Teachers in Australian Society

Because there is much more to be said on each theme than will emerge from ACER's own program, ACER has established five series of *theme monographs* to provide a forum for the expression of a wide range of views on the significant issues involved. Each series is co-edited by a member of ACER staff and a distinguished academic from outside ACER, who together are commissioning monographs from an impressive array of scholars.

Barry McGaw
Director

Other titles in this series:

Being numerate: what counts? edited by Sue Willis

A FRESH LOOK AT THE BASICS

LITERACY FOR A CHANGING WORLD

Edited by
Frances Christie

ACER

First published 1990
by The Australian Council for Educational Research Ltd
Radford House, Frederick Street, Hawthorn, Victoria 3122, Australia

Cover by Ogden Art & Design Pty Ltd
Typeset by Savage Type Pty Ltd
Printed in Australia by Globe Press Pty Ltd

National Library of Australia
Cataloguing-in-Publication data:

Literacy for a changing world.

Includes index.
ISBN 0 86431 059 5.

1. Literacy — Australia. 2. Curriculum planning — Australia. I. Christie, Frances, 1939- . II. Australian Council for Educational Research.

302.22440994

Foreword

This volume is the first in the series of monographs on Australian studies in compulsory schooling, designed to complement the Australian Council for Educational Research's program of research on the compulsory years of schooling. A major focus of that program has been core areas of learning such as language, number, and social education, and in particular the reconceptualization and redefinition of what is meant by *competence* in these areas. It is therefore fitting that the series should begin with three volumes that take a fresh look at the basics, starting with the concept of literacy, so central to learning during the compulsory years of schooling.

Our primary intention in planning the series was to provide a resource for teacher education, both pre-service and in-service, which would provide an Australian focus on issues central to the debate on the future of education in Australia, but it is hoped that particular volumes will also be of interest to practising teachers, policy makers and researchers, the wider educational community, and those members of the general public who have a direct involvement in education, for example through membership of school councils. So, too, in specifying an Australian focus for the series there is no intention of excluding overseas contributors where such contributions are seen as illuminating the issues, nor is it intended that Australian education will be examined in isolation from trends and developments in other countries.

Inevitably an invitation to reconceptualize the basic and familiar is also an invitation to controversy, and in taking up that invitation Frances Christie and her fellow contributors have produced a volume that is both provocative and challenging. Needless to say the views expressed are those of the contributors, and are not necessarily endorsed by either the Australian Council for Educational Research or the series editors. What we would endorse, however, is the commitment and enthusiasm with which the contributors to this volume have challenged both the old and the new orthodoxies in language education to produce a genuinely *fresh* look at the concept of literacy. We commend the volume to you as a significant contribution to the ongoing debate on the future of language education in Australian schools.

MALCOLM SKILBECK
KEVIN PIPER
Series Editors

Contents

Acknowledgements

The volume editor, the individual authors and the publishers would like to express their gratitude and appreciation to all the students and teachers whose contributors have given this study its special vitality. Without their generosity in allowing us to reproduce their various modes of expression — written, spoken and drawn — the book would have lost much of its immediacy and value. Wherever possible, individual contributors have been acknowledged, although in one or two cases they are not known, and in some others anonymity has been requested.

Thanks are also due to the following publishers for granting permission to reproduce copyright material:

All Rights Reserved, London for the *Masters of the Universe* comic strip example; Longman Cheshire Pty Ltd for the extracts from *The World of Science Book 2* by D. A. Heffernan & M. S. Learmonth; Jacaranda Wiley for the material from *Science for Living Book 1* by R. Cull & G. Comino; Rigby Education for the extracts from *Science for Secondary Schools 2* by K. E. G. Heading, D. F. Provis, T. D. Scott, J. E. Smith & R. T. Smith; The Science Foundation for Physics within the University of Sydney for the extracts from *Science for High School Students* edited by H. Messel, R. L. Crocker & E. N. Barker; and the *Sydney Morning Herald* for the article on hospital staff resignations.

Preface

The task of editing a volume such as this involves, among other matters, the exercise of choosing the themes worth pursuing. There are no doubt several possible avenues one might follow in the interests of developing some new perspectives on literacy, and no attempt has been made here to exhaust the full range of issues that might be taken up. Indeed, one would hope that the publication of this volume will stimulate discussion and debate about literacy, thereby leading to the identification of themes not explored in the book.

It seems appropriate to say a little about the choices made in preparing this particular volume, and about the sequence of chapters. No attempt is made to explore the matter of literacy in all areas of the curriculum, though all the contributors would, of course, argue that literacy development, like spoken language development, is a responsibility for teachers of all subjects at all levels. Instead, the opening chapter (which I have written myself) sets a context for considering contemporary issues in literacy, and subsequent chapters take up some of the themes introduced in the first chapter in greater detail.

Thus, in chapter 1 I examine the notion of literacy in the world of the late twentieth century. That involves consideration of not only the demands for literacy in a complex western society such as Australia, but also of the nature of the changed and still changing perceptions of language itself, and of literacy in particular. A new look at literacy, I argue, will focus, much more than in the immediate past, on teaching explicitly *about* language, as an enabling process for the learner. To make much important knowledge about language explicit to young learners, the new programmes for literacy will have to overcome many of the inequalities currently suffered by various groups — the economically disadvantaged, girls and second-language learners, to name just three.

The second chapter is by Jennifer Hammond, who examines in greater detail at least one of the matters introduced in the first chapter. Specifically, she addresses the nature of literacy, and contrasts it with speech, the better to develop a sense of what is involved in learning to become literate. An awareness of the differences between the spoken and written modes, Hammond suggests, should inform all educational programs.

Chapters 1 and 2 having laid a broad foundation for thinking about literacy, both as a socially valuable tool and as a linguistic phenomenon, the following three chapters pick up selected themes in three familiar areas of the curriculum — English language studies, the natural sciences and the social sciences. Thus, in chapter 3, Pam Gilbert turns to some of the concerns of the English classroom, most notably issues of creativity and authorship, both qualities often sought in the teaching of English, yet frequently misunderstood and needlessly elusive in terms of definition.

The discussion turns to literacy in the science classroom in chapter 4, and J. R. Martin explores the ways in which the resources of language are used to build up the specialist language of the natural sciences. He examines in some detail both the development of technical language for dealing with scientific concepts and some of the more important generic structures which are used to construct the contents of science.

In the fifth chapter, Bill Cope and Mary Kalantzis consider literacy in the social sciences. They argue for a greater clarity about the purposes of teaching the social sciences than is often found in schools, and for more explicit attention to the linguistic resources in which the various discourses of the social sciences are developed.

In the sixth and seventh chapters, discussion turns away from a direct consideration of particular subject areas as Janet White and Lynn Wales respectively consider issues of literacy and gender, and of literacy and the second-language learners so familiarly a part of contemporary classrooms in multicultural Australia. In the learning of literacy, as in any other area of school performance, there are significant gender differences, and teachers need to be alert to their disadvantaging effects not only for girls but also for boys. As there can be few if any classrooms left in Australia in which there are not some second-language learners, it behoves all teachers to have an appropriate sense of the literacy needs of such students. Like the other contributors, White and Wales both argue for teachers to be explicit about the manner in which language is used, and for corresponding programmes which enable students to develop appropriate control of their language.

The final chapter, written by Joan Rothery and myself, considers some of the implications of the discussions throughout the book for curriculum planning and assessment, as well as the perennially vexed questions of 'standards' in literacy. Literacy assessment, we argue, is intimately linked to the overall goals of the literacy programme, so that curriculum planning and assessment are to be understood as aspects of the same process — one in which, ideally, students and teachers alike have a clear understanding both of the goals for learning and of the criteria for assessment.

Each author has provided an annotated list of follow-up reading to assist those readers who wish to pursue any issue that interests them further. For convenience these lists are grouped together at the back of the book.

Throughout the various contributions several themes emerge as constantly valued and important. One is the concern for an explicit appreciation of the nature of language and its role in learning. For most contributors this involves a commitment to understanding the various genres or text types associated with the different subjects, and with the manner in which the discourses of the subjects are built up in these genres. It is because of this interest in the nature of language that most chapters discuss selected texts:

samples of classroom discourse, or genres written by children, or genres and sometimes illustrations from textbooks used in schools.

I hope that the concern to build much of the argument from a careful examination of actual texts gives this book one of its most distinctive characteristics. Another characteristic — indeed another theme of overall concern — is the manner in which the book draws upon aspects of the history of literacy teaching in order to develop its arguments. My first chapter makes the most overt use of history, but several other chapters also offer reflections on 'where we have been' in the recent past in English language work, in science and the social sciences, and 'where we might need to go' in the light of these reflections. History is not perhaps as valued these days as it once was, and I hope that this book makes a modest contribution towards correcting that attitude.

In closing this prefatory note, I should like to record my thanks firstly to the several contributors of this book who cooperated so willingly in its preparation, and secondly to Professor Malcolm Skilbeck and Dr Kevin Piper, who invited me to edit the volume.

F.C.

1 The changing face of literacy

FRANCES CHRISTIE

A 'FRESH LOOK' AT LITERACY: WHAT'S INVOLVED?

A great deal has been written over the years about literacy — about what it is, about why it should be valued, and about how to teach it. Indeed, interest in literacy is as old as education itself, and from the very earliest times, simple reading materials — often merely the letters of the alphabet or the Lord's Prayer on wooden tablets known as horn-books (Davies, 1973) — were produced for teaching young children at least sufficient literacy to pen their names and to read simple religious tracts. Historically, literacy and numeracy have been the oldest and most valued of the prizes an education can confer. When the earliest schools in nineteenth-century colonial Australia were established, for example, a fundamental expectation was that they should teach basic literacy as well as basic numeracy. Literacy was valued both because it taught capacity to read the Bible and other improving works, and because it was said to develop sober, law-abiding workers, and later, after the vote was extended to all, responsible citizens. In the nineteenth century, literacy and numeracy, together with a little 'general knowledge', constituted the main elements of the emerging mass education, though it is a matter of some note that they were often badly taught, and that many children did not actually attend school to gain such benefits (Christie, 1976).

In fact, mass education as we know it dates from the nineteenth century. It was during that century that most western countries moved steadily towards adopting the principle that an elementary education (later called a primary education) should be freely available to all children. In the Australian colonies, state-sponsored education had been introduced in the 1850s, and by the 1870s and 1880s the colonial governments passed legislation making an elementary education 'free, compulsory, and secular'. By

This is a considerably enlarged and revised version of an address, 'Literacy in a changing world: educating for proficiency', which was presented as the John Smyth Memorial Lecture in Melbourne, 21 October 1987.

the mid-twentieth century the principle of a free compulsory secondary education had been generally adopted in the various English-speaking countries (Connell, 1980). Today, as the century draws to a close, increasing numbers of students complete not merely a secondary education, but go on to undertake tertiary studies of some kind as well. Whether by the end of this century tertiary education will be free and compulsory, in Australia at least, is at this stage in doubt. What is not in doubt, however, is that more and more people will feel the pressure to obtain tertiary qualifications of some kind, given the changing nature of the contemporary world.

In what sense, then, in the late twentieth century, might we take a 'fresh look' at the nature of literacy? What does it mean to be literate at this stage in Australian and world history? Should the education system attach the same significance to literacy as it has in the past? On the one hand, a view is sometimes expressed that the advent of twentieth-century communications media has made literacy less relevant, less important, for so much of the knowledge of the age is now made available in ways other than the printed word: Why not then, goes this argument, teach children through the auditory and visual impact of radio, television and film? On the other hand, another view often heard is that since contemporary industrial societies like Australia have so many social problems, most born of poor oral communication between persons, between governments, industrial leaders, trade unionists, professional groups and the like, it is imperative that spoken language capacities be given greater significance than in the past: it will be upon effective development of oral language capacities more than on the development of literate capacities, goes this argument, that the future harmony and well-being of society will depend.

While not totally unmoved by such arguments, I want nevertheless to adopt a somewhat different position. I want to suggest that literacy is, if anything, more important now than it has been in the past. In fact, I want to argue that literacy is in itself a more complex thing than it was, say, one hundred or even fifty years ago, and that schools have a major responsibility today in teaching literacy in all areas of the curriculum and at all levels of schooling. So diverse and so numerous are the instances of literacy, and so fundamentally important are its uses in many, many areas of our lives, that it is impossible to imagine contemporary life without it. Not only is the volume of books, newspapers, journals and magazines today greater than it has been in the past, but the very nature of what constitutes literacy has been transformed by the appearance of the microfiche, the computer and the word processor. Their emergence has changed the ways we build and store knowledge, the ways we conduct government, commerce and banking, the ways in which we administer the law and conduct the affairs of the law courts, even the ways in which many sporting, recreational and community groups handle their bookkeeping, correspondence, meeting reports, membership lists, and so on. There is in fact virtually no area of contemporary life in which literacy is not involved in some way, and it is imperative that all people understand the many kinds of literacy which collectively have such an impact on their lives.

Changes in literacy, like changes in spoken language, are in themselves measures of the constantly changing nature of society. As a society changes, so too must its language, as a necessary resource within which change is encoded, promoted and explained. While the two language modes of speech and writing are of course equally important in different ways, literacy has achieved a special significance in cultures such as ours. That is because late twentieth-century western societies like Australia have actively built so much of their habits of thinking, of working and of dealing with experience in the written mode. Where we deny our children proper access to literacy at this stage in our history, we deny them capacity to develop as fully rounded persons, able to participate effectively in the workforce and to engage fully in democratic processes.

To be literate in the contemporary world is to understand the very large range of written forms, text types or — as I shall call them here, *genres* — which we all need for both the reading and the writing essential to participation in the community. Incidentally, the term *genre* is used here, and elsewhere in the book, to refer, much as in the conventional sense, to the manner in which different patterns of language are built up to establish different kinds of meanings. Genres may thus be the relatively 'prestige' ones found in literary pursuits, but in addition the term is used to refer to the many 'non-prestige' genres of both speech and writing which are so essential to much of our lives as human beings, functioning in all kinds of situations. Genres of speech include job interviews, casual conversations, public speeches, to name a few obvious ones, but since this is a book about literacy, they will not detain us here. Genres of writing include items as various as recipes, reports, newspaper articles, different types of essays, and so on.

To learn to recognize and create the various genres found in one's culture is to learn to exercise choices — choices in building and ordering different kinds of meaning and hence, potentially, choices in directing the course of one's life. Learning to control such genres, with their patterned uses of language, is a matter of practice and opportunity, and here the schools have a major responsibility to provide good educational programmes for the teaching and learning of literacy. The more students can be encouraged to enter with real understanding into the ways the written language works in creating the many written genres, the more enriched and independent they will actually become.

We need to develop resistant and critical readers as well as challenging and fluent writers. The most effective way to achieve this will be through educational programmes that cause students to examine the ways language works for the building and ordering of meanings. Such programmes will, by their nature, involve examination of both the spoken and the written modes, and they will teach explicitly the ways in which language operates. Knowing how language works in one's culture is important, I suggest, not only because it enables the individual to operate effectively in the culture, but also because it enables the individual to work for changes within the culture, where that is deemed a desirable thing.

What might be some of the features of the literacy programmes thus envisaged, and in what ways might they differ from the programmes of the past? In fact, this whole book is an attempt to provide some answers to these two questions, the former in particular. While I propose to say something about the first question, I want to consider the second question in more detail. I shall argue that the attempt to define our current needs in a literacy programme can be better illuminated by a selective examination of past practices, where I shall have interests in at least two related themes. One theme concerns the changed and still changing nature of society, and the kinds of literacy such a society needs: about this I have already said a little. The other theme concerns practices for teaching language, including some examination of the limitations of past practices as well as of the kinds of practices which might be adopted instead. Briefly, I shall suggest that older models of literacy, regrettably with us still in some cases, have tended not to focus upon language as a resource with which to build meaning: rather, such models have focused upon sets of discrete and simple skills in letter, sentence and paragraph recognition which, once learned, are somehow expected to provide the individual with sufficient capacities to become an effective reader and writer. The literacy programmes of the future, while not denying the importance of spelling, punctuation and so on, will primarily teach about the unit that is the text type or the genre and its function as a socially created tool for the building and communication of meaning.

I shall commence my detailed discussion by turning to the first of my two chosen themes, and I shall briefly examine the relevance of literacy to the Australian people in the nineteenth and early twentieth centuries.

LITERACY FOR AN EARLIER AGE

It was possible for young people in Australia to leave school largely unlettered as recently as the 1930s, and to enter gainful employment, taking up economically useful lives. For those who did stay at school, especially in the first quarter of this century, the level of literacy obtained was often of a pretty minimal kind, though it normally equipped them with sufficient skills to enter the workforce and lead reasonably satisfactory lives. In so far as it was taught in schools and valued in the workforce, literacy was represented by the capacity, for example, to read and copy simple passages, or to write the occasional short text, quite often a personal or a business letter, but sometimes a passage on an approved theme. It was a limited and limiting view of literacy at best, and at worst it left many people effectively unable to operate with real independence either as writers or as readers. It was a view of literacy whose origins were quite old, dating back some centuries, but which had been particularly influential from the early years of the nineteenth century (Christie, 1981).

As I have already indicated, from the earliest attempts to provide education in colonial Australia, the teaching of literacy had sought to do no more than develop very basic capacities indeed. The truth was that those responsible for providing education had not reckoned that the majority of children required more than this, a view with which many parents had appeared to agree, as the patterns of school attendance actually revealed. In fact, for a significant number of the jobs available to the poorer colonial classes throughout the nineteenth century, literacy was largely irrelevant (Christie, 1976). Long after the passage of the Victorian *Education Act 1872* and the New South Wales *Public Instruction Act 1880*, for example, both ostensibly making an elementary education compulsory for all in the two colonies, many children, actively encouraged by their parents, did not attend school at all, or if they did, their patterns of attendance were so erratic as to render their schooling a waste of time (Christie, 1976; Bessant, 1982).

In fact, down to and well beyond the turn of the century, in many occupations and industries, both rural and urban, literacy was not required, and significant numbers of child labourers were gainfully employed. Throughout the First World War and into the 1920s, many Australian children continued to be employed either by their parents, as for example often happened on farms, or by others in the various situations in towns and cities, such as tanneries, brick yards, clothing factories, woollen mills, collieries, tobacco factories, blacksmiths, and domestic situations, to name only a few (Christie, 1976).

Children made significant contributions to the economic well-being of their families, and they simply could not be spared from gainful employment for long periods of education. Many parents therefore either had no interest in education at all, or wanted their children to obtain no more than a minimal ability to read simple texts and to write, if anything, even simpler texts. Those who did want their children to acquire such basic literacy expected it to be gained in quite short periods of time, after which the children would become full-time members of the workforce.

Of those who did obtain an education during the first two decades of the twentieth century, in some cases staying on to obtain a minimal secondary education, most, like my father who attended Sydney Boys High School during the First World War, had nonetheless left school by about the age of 15. In this the Australian experience was very similar to that in other western societies of the period, according to Davey (1982: 446–7). 'Success in school', he notes 'was simply not important for future work chances'.

Until the 1920s, of the occupations available in which literacy was relevant, most were in banking, commerce and the branches of government service. Copying of documents and bookkeeping appear to have been among the commonest of tasks available to young people entering such occupations. Capacity to draft and write in 'a fair hand' various letters, memos and statements of accounts was essential. Persons were still being employed as copy clerks certainly into the first decade of this century (as a glance at the Engagement Book of J. H. Farmer and Company for 1900–1910, in the New South Wales state archives, will show), though the gradual introduction of typewriters must have caused their eventual disappearance by the end of the First World War.

How might proficiency in literacy have been described in the first quarter of this century, at least in so far as the educational system appeared to define it, and as the various occupations appeared to require it? Much as in the nineteenth century, it consisted firstly of the ability to read one of the several series of school readers approved for use in the state primary schools such as *The Victorian Readers 1929*, which have been republished in facsimile by the Victorian Ministry of Education (1968). Secondly, literacy consisted of the ability to write neatly, normally one of several 'hands', though as the years progressed the functional upright 'hands' favoured by commerce were the most extensively taught. One measure of the significance of handwriting to commerce, banking and government well into this century was the introduction, in Sydney at least, of annual handwriting competitions sponsored by the publishers Angus & Robertson. (The annual reports of these competitions are held in the New South Wales State Library.)

In addition to the ability to write a fair hand, literacy consisted of the ability both to parse a sentence, recognizing its various parts of speech and their relationship one to another, and to analyse a sentence, identifying its various clauses and their relations as well. Knowledge of such matters was held to offer a training in 'logical thinking', and it was also expected to contribute in some unexplained way to the capacity to write. Finally, literacy consisted of the ability to write, where that might include writing a model letter of the kind used in commerce, or dealing with some improving 'theme' such as what constituted good manners or, as students grew older, with subjects such as the virtues of honesty. The first years of a primary education were devoted to copying first letters, then words, then simple phrases and sentences. Once children had learned these, they graduated to learning the parts of speech and to parsing, while sentence analysis, considered an advanced activity appropriate to the later stages of cognition, belonged to the upper primary school and the secondary school. Where students did take up a secondary education, they normally read a little Shakespeare, learning to write paraphrases of major speeches, and sometimes writing essays on themes, again on various allegedly moral and improving subjects.

English language textbooks which were representative of what was required in teaching language and whose principles were followed in setting public examinations included, among others, that by Conway (1899), who was for a time headmaster of the Cleveland Street Superior Public School, Sydney and whose textbook continued to be used for many years, and those by Nesfield (1926), whose works, imported from Britain, were used in Australia well into this century, even as late as the years of my own education in the 1950s. Though scholars occasionally questioned the patterns of language teaching found in such books, and had done so even well back in the nineteenth century, they were on the whole endorsed, both by the various educating authorities responsible for public examinations, and by employing organizations such as Chambers of Commerce.

Overall, literacy was developed through a series of measured stages in school learning, so that the learner could move from the smaller to the larger units of language. Learning to read involved learning to recognize the alphabet and exercising the various letters firstly in monosyllabic, later polysyllabic, words before graduating to reading phrases and/or sentences more remarkable for their lack of sense than otherwise. The class readers constituted the major reading material even for those students who stayed at primary school for the full period, enjoying the relative advantages in control of literacy that this conferred. For most of the primary school years, writing consisted of copying improving expressions, chosen both for their moral uplift and for the opportunity they afforded to perfect handwriting skills. Composition, to the extent that children practised it at all, involved writing formal letters or short improving pieces on moral themes.

Many of the features of literacy teaching and learning that I have described continued long after the 1920s and 1930s, certainly until the days of my own schooling in Sydney in the 1950s and, as I have already indicated, some at least prevail to this day (Piper, 1983, 1984). That they have survived at all is most regrettable, since they are increasingly irrelevant in a world in which literacy and the needs of people generally have changed so much. They survived for so long because of a particularly crippling view of the nature of language and literacy which has bedevilled a great deal of nineteenth- and twentieth-century language educational practice.

However, before I turn to those matters, I should like to recapitulate: literacy, arguably the most prized of the benefits an education might confer, was until quite recent times simply not relevant to many of the occupations available to young people. To be sure, there was always a proportion of children, mainly from the middle classes, which did complete a secondary education and in some cases even go on to university, but it was a minority. That Australian politicians in the late nineteenth and early twentieth centuries were very conscious of the employment opportunities available to young people without education was apparent in their reluctance to alientate the electorate by obliging people to send their children to school. This explains the failure of the governments in both New South Wales (Christie, 1976) and Victoria (Bessant, 1982) to tighten the Education Acts so that children might be compelled to attend school, until well into this century. Moreover, the pattern by which children took up a secondary education after about 1920 remained patchy, so that many received little if any formal secondary schooling even as late as the Second World War.

However much we might deplore such a state of affairs on the grounds of the rights of all individuals to receive a good education, the point I want to stress is that one reason many people for so long achieved little more than a minimal degree of literacy, was undoubtedly that gainful employment was available without much education. It is true that during the Depression years of the 1930s many people were unemployed for long periods, though that was due less to a lack of appropriate skills for working than to the state of the economy. Today's world is a very different one, however, so that anyone not possessed of a considerable education, and of the considerable proficiency in literacy which such an education requires, is disadvantaged indeed. For that reason alone, we should all feel an urgency to do better in providing relevant literacy programmes for young Australians at school now, and in the future.

Now I would like to turn to a fuller consideration of language and literacy. In particular, I want to consider the origins of the model of literacy I have sketched above, for it is based upon some serious misconceptions about the nature of language, of a kind which continue to do harm in much educational practice. At heart, such a model views language and meaning as independent of each other, whereas, as I shall argue, the two are so intimately related that we cannot usefully consider the one without the other. Two models of language are actually in contest here: on the one hand, there is the model of language as a kind of 'conduit', whose role is to 'carry' information and meaning; on the other hand, there is the model of language as a symbolic system, one of a number of symbolic systems humans have evolved with which to build meaning.

LANGUAGE: CONDUIT OR SYMBOLIC SYSTEM?

A very old tradition of thinking about language often finds expression still in English-speaking cultures such as Australia. It sees language as a rather neutral commodity which, once learned, simply becomes a kind of carrier — what Reddy (1979) has called a *conduit* — by means of which various forms of content or information are 'conveyed'. In this view, knowledge, content, ideas, are held to have an existence independently of the various behavioural modes, including language, in which they 'find expression'. In this sense language merely 'clothes' the ideas, content or knowledge of concern at any time. It is because this view is still commonplace that distinctions are often created in language education between such things as 'form and content', 'form and function', or 'process and product'.

Such distinctions — or *dichotomies*, to use the term Gilbert employs in chapter 3 — have had unfortunate results for a great deal of teaching practice. That is because they serve to direct teachers' attention away from the manner in which language patterns are built up to organize and shape meaning, in writing as well as in speech, and cause teachers instead to focus upon the relatively surface features of spelling, punctuation, sentence structure, and so on. The point to be stressed here is that far from being a neutral commodity which merely conveys information in some way, language is in fact centrally involved in the construction of meaning, a matter of great importance for all educational practice to acknowledge properly.

To be sure, there are many ways available for making meaning apart from language: music, dance, painting, photography all come to mind immediately. In fact, all of these are instruments evolved by human beings to build meaning: in that sense they are actually symbolic systems or, to use another term often invoked today, they are *semiotic systems*. But the oldest of the instruments humans have evolved to build meaning and to impose some kind of order upon experience must surely be language. Just as language evolved first in the species, so too, it is learned first by developing children. It is the principal resource, in fact, through which young children learn about their world, developing many of the attitudes, values and beliefs which will remain with them all their lives. Striking testimony to the manner in which children learn to construct a sense of their world in language, including the building of values, attitudes and beliefs, has been provided in studies by Halliday (1975, 1985), Painter (1985), Hasan (1986), Brice Heath (1983) and Cloran (1989).

Symbolic systems are never neutral for they are always centrally involved in the ways in which information, thought, feeling, attitude, are established, as several of the contributors to this volume amply demonstrate. White, for example, examines the ways in which ideologies and values about gender are built up quite substantially through the very literacy programmes that apply in schools. It will be by coming to terms with the very intimate relationship between the language patterns chosen and the ideologies of gender found in them that we can begin to bring about changes in our attitudes to boys and girls in schools and, hopefully, in their behaviour both while at school and in later life. Martin, looking specifically at literacy in science, examines the ways the language patterns of scientific genres build the knowledge and the habits of thinking and of dealing with experience that give scientific discourse its distinctive character. Examining the science curriculum guidelines of two Australian states, he is able to show what is involved in developing both the scientific knowledge and the habits of thinking and of enquiry that the science programme ideally seeks to have children learn. Gilbert, reflecting upon some of the difficulties of the English classroom examines aspects of the ideologies of authorship and of creativity, and the ways in which these are constructed in language; she proposes that if as teachers we recognize the ways in which creativity is both learned and constructed in language, then we will pursue somewhat different strategies from those that often prevail in the English classroom.

Once we turn our attention to the manner in which language is patterned in different contexts for the creation or the *realization* of different meanings, then we can begin to come to terms not only with the notion of language as a symbolic system, but also with developing some sense of how we might teach about language. In order to develop such a sense, I suggest, we need to look both forward and back: forward, in the manner suggested in several chapters of this book, to articulation of clearer goals for teaching about language; and back to some of the lessons of older language educational traditions and practices, most of which predate the nineteenth century patterns of literacy teaching to which I have alluded. I shall now turn to some discussion of those older practices and traditions, and in examining them I hope to throw a little more light on the question of why the model of literacy I examined above came to have such a grip on language education for so long.

THE RHETORICAL TRADITION

The very much older tradition of language study to which I allude was that of rhetoric, itself as old as the Greeks. Rehetoric, born of oral traditions of working in language, involved examination of the ways to use language for a series of powerful social purposes — persuasion, argument, analysis and explanation, for example. It took as its focus the nature of language as a social phenomenon, and its concerns were always with the ways one selected from one's total language system those linguistic patterns through which one might construct and organize meaning (Christie, 1981). Above all, it invited the learner to focus primarily upon the totality of the text one sought to create, and upon the kinds of purposes such a text might serve: that is to say, one must always begin with a sense of the overall organization of the text and of the meanings to be built up in it. For each of the many purposes one might wish to satisfy in creating a passage of language, a possible form (what today we would call a genre) could be identified. It was this which students would study, relying initially in particular upon the models of good practice as exemplified in the works of experts and, as competence developed in the students, it was intended that they would learn to modify, indeed to play with and to adapt, the generic forms, necessarily also on occasions producing new ones.

Rhetorical studies, which were strong in the English-speaking tradition, particularly among the Scots, still flourished in the eighteenth century, but they effectively disappeared in the nineteenth century, the period of the expansion of mass education. In fact, by the twentieth century, as slowly more and more children began attending school, at least for the completion of a primary school education, the model of literacy which schools had to offer them had become increasingly impoverished. It was a model, one might argue, which challenged children to become proficient readers and writers despite its influence, rather than because of it. Small wonder, then, since the model survives in many places in some form to this day, that significant numbers of students leave school reluctant and poor writers, and quite often reluctant and poor readers as well.

In 1921, Ballard, an authority on the teaching of English in England, referred to the decline of interest in rhetorical studies over the previous century, noting the comparative ineffectiveness of the patterns of teaching traditional school grammar which had by then come to dominate the school programmes for teaching *literacy*. He also noted a tendency that had developed among many to dismiss rhetoric as a somewhat dishonest method for developing arguments and opinions. I am interested to note, incidentally, that even today the term *rhetoric*, which appears quite often in fields as dissimilar as journalism and academic discourse, is more often than not used in a disparaging sense. For example, a student drew my attention to a letter written to the *Age* in which reference was made, disparagingly, to the 'democratic rhetoric' of the French, and to the terrorism they displayed in the *Rainbow Warrior* affair in New Zealand (Wootton, 1987).

It is a lamentable commentary upon our present collective awareness of language and literacy that a study traditionally devoted to exploring how language is used for the development of judgement, argument and opinion has become so misunderstood over time.

Why did scholarly and educational interest in rhetoric decline so much in the nineteenth century? Vernacular rhetorics had appeared in England as early as the sixteenth century, and as I have noted, rhetoric was still studied in the eighteenth century. Rhetorics by Campbell (1838, first published 1776), Blair (1783) and Whately (1968, first published 1828) were all influential. The eighteenth century was also the period of the development of a series of grammars, the most famous of which was that of Lindley Murray (1968, first published 1795). Now it is important to note here that for the eighteenth-century scholar and teacher, the relationship between the studies of rhetoric and of grammar was clear, as Murray himself certainly acknowledged. Rhetoric concerned the overall organization of the discourse while grammar concerned the syntax of the sentence. Without a primary interest in the purposes of creating a text, and in the particular linguistic demands to be borne in mind in organizing such a text, the study of grammar was a barren thing — as both rhetoricians and grammarians, at least in the eighteenth century, would have acknowledged.

Where a tradition of language studies abandons a primary interest in the uses of language as a social phenomenon, most notably its role in the creation and negotiation of meaning, then the interest in its grammar becomes weakened and impoverished as well, as nineteenth- and twentieth-century history demonstrates all too well. While I cannot claim to have surveyed all the grammars written for schools over the nineteenth and twentieth centuries, I can claim to have examined a large number of those most widely used in both Britain and Australia (Christie, 1976, 1981). The most remarkable observation I would make about them is that, with the steady passage of time they became increasingly wretched and ill informed. A narrow pursuit of the parts of speech — nouns, verbs and adjectives in particular — and an occasional foray into selected rules of syntax are about all that remain. In short, contemporary approaches to school grammar bear little relationship to the principles as taught by Murray, for example, or, as it happens, those offered by most schools of contemporary linguistics, though I am not suggesting that all such schools of linguistics are relevant to educational practice: many certainly are not. In a recent study that examines the models of grammar available to school students in a representative sample of textbooks used in Australian schools, Huddleston (n.d.) has concluded that these books present a model of the language which is as outdated as it is wrong.

Where teachers do teach the old models of traditional school grammar, they know that such activities are ineffectual, as a study in Australian schools by Piper (1983, 1984) has revealed. But teachers lack any better alternative, since studies which focus upon broader purposes in using language, and upon the ways in which linguistic choices are made to create the different genres that serve such purposes, have largely disappeared from our educational tradition. That is because interest in such studies has largely disappeared in the wider culture, though the indications are that we are poised to see a turn to a renewed interest in such matters, fostered alike by semiotic studies with their interests in how we *sign* (Culler, 1981) or make meaning, and by certain traditions of linguistics — specifically those which see language in functional terms and which propose that language itself is the principal resource with which we 'sign' (Halliday, 1985).

SOME FACTORS RESPONSIBLE FOR THE DECLINE OF RHETORIC

It is appropriate to say a little about the factors responsible for the decline in the study of rhetoric, for the light this will throw upon our developing understanding of the kinds of patterns of literacy teaching that have become such an entrenched part of our cultural tradition. The factors responsible, like those for any major movement in history, were many and complex, though I shall focus on only two of them because of their particular relevance to the educational themes that concern me here. The first concerns the loss of interest in oral language which began, probably, in the late eighteenth century; the other concerns the related pedagogical requirement that children be educated in large numbers and disciplined to work in silence, a requirement which became commonplace in the nineteenth century, the period of the growth of mass education.

To take the former first, it is worth reminding ourselves that rhetoric, sometimes referred to as the study of oratory, concerned itself originally with the spoken mode, since it predated the invention of writing. Schools for the study of rhetoric had flourished in ancient Greece and, much as many people today view the invention of the pocket calculator and the computer with suspicion, so too did many ancient Greeks view the invention of writing with alarm, on the grounds that people would become mentally lazy (Ong, 1982). In oral societies the spoken word was necessarily the medium in which knowledge, information and ideas were passed from one generation to another, as indeed it still is to this day in many parts of the world. It is very difficult now for those of us reared in literate cultures even to imagine a world in which the printed word has no place. Yet it is a fact that most of the world's languages have never been written down, and even today there are many peoples functioning successfully in cultures without a literate tradition.

Elaborate and skilled are many of the traditions of rhetorical style associated with most oral cultures. Quite commonly, only certain chosen persons — elders, priests, those said to be able to exercise healing powers — are allowed to learn and pass on the features of such styles, whose function is to move, excite or persuade people, as well as to inform them. Great orators in the western tradition were valued for many centuries, as Shakespeare was certainly aware when, for example, he wrote his play *Julius Caesar*, in which Mark Antony makes his celebrated speech to the Roman crowds after the death of Caesar.

Spoken language is patterned in all sorts of ways to suit the human ear, for listeners must process what they hear as it is spoken, normally at reasonable speed. The more skilled orators are, the better they are at using spoken language, exploiting its characteristic features in a variety of ways. They will, among other things, make effective use of rhythmical and rhyming devices, of judicious repetition, of deliberately staged pauses (Ong, 1982), of formulaic expressions either heard before or at least adapted from those heard before; all these devices are intended to aid the memory in varying ways, and hence to assist comprehension. Of all these things at least, the early orators in Europe appear to have been aware, though in addition — a matter of which the orators were not aware — the very grammar of a spoken language reflects the fact that it is spoken out loud to be heard. Recent linguistic research (Tannen, 1982; Halliday, 1985) has had a great deal of value to say about this, as Hammond demonstrates in chapter 2. Suffice to note here that written language is 'denser' than speech, carrying more 'content words' per clause than speech, which by contrast makes more use of the various grammatical or 'function' items that serve to hold language together. Furthermore, as Hammond shows, the very patterns by which we create a sequence of clauses in talk tend to be different from those that apply in writing.

The invention of writing, in itself a remarkable thing, was to change the character of human experience, leading to the capacity to process knowledge and information in new ways, though by its nature such a capacity was available only to the privileged elites in those cultures which became literate. For many centuries, while making copies of manuscripts was a laborious process, necessarily done by hand, relatively few people learned to read and write. The invention of printing, which was almost as remarkable as that of writing, would eventually change this, for in time it would extend the possibility of literacy to an increasingly large number of people. When, in the fifteenth century, the first printing press was set up in England, a new age in the history of the English-speaking people was heralded, the legacies of which are with us still.

The interest in rhetoric in the oral mode led to an interest in rhetoric in the written mode and, as I have already noted, books on rhetoric in English date at least from the sixteenth century; important books on the subject appeared in the eighteenth century, though it is notable that those published in the nineteenth century (e.g. Bain, 1887) were increasingly inferior, eventually disappearing altogether. Moreover, by the eighteenth century, because of the increasing use of printing presses, it was written, not spoken language which became the principal repository of knowledge and of ideas. Today the new technologies of computer and word processor are revolutionizing the publishing industry, transforming the ways in which we deal with experience, process and build information, and so on.

The process of changing from an oral to a literate culture had been so gradual that its significance was no doubt easy to overlook: yet it represented a truly remarkable step in the development of the human species. In fact, from about the eighteenth century on, it was written language which became authoritative, and which remains so today: so powerful is it, indeed, that its very dominance in our culture tends to blind us to the significance and value of speech, a point to which I shall return a little later.

Firstly, however, I want to say a little more about the effect of the invention of printing, and the consequent spread of what became, over time, reasonably inexpensive print materials. I have said already that those who worked in an oral culture, those at any rate who learned to be orators, knew a great deal about the features of style they needed to employ to be successful: they were to that extent very conscious of many aspects of their language, and its power in people's lives. But the act of writing down a language, and of producing larger and larger communities of people who become familiar with the printed word, produces a new kind of consciousness about language: in particular, it causes a people to focus upon the grammar of their language in a way that the oral tradition does not require (Ong, 1982; Halliday, 1985). That is because, once the language is written down, it becomes a kind of 'product', something whose pieces can be taken apart, as it were, and analysed quite closely.

Before the eighteenth century, the only grammars studied in England had been those of the classical languages, Greek and Latin — languages which had flourishing traditions of oratory before being eventually written down. It was to these models that the eighteenth-century English grammarians first went (e.g. Lowth, 1969, first published 1762; Priestley, 1969, first published 1761; Murray, 1968, first published 1795) with what were unfortunate long-term consequences, since the languages differed more than was appreciated, though there were, as we shall see, other reasons why the first English grammars had limitations.

It was no accident that the first English grammars developed in the eighteenth century, and that they then proliferated in the nineteenth. The former century in particular was the period in which the English-speaking people sought to regularize their language (McKnight, 1928) and to determine, among other matters, the patterns of acceptable spelling and syntax that should apply in English writing. More than one scholar has since noted that Shakespeare, educated in another and in some senses less regulated age, not only spelt his name in several ways during his life, but that he often used patterns of syntax which the eighteenth-century grammarians were to 'outlaw'. Those with interests in such things were from the leisured and cultivated classes, it should be noted, who could afford to be interested in such niceties as spelling and syntax, and who, enjoying all the benefits of life in a print age, were fascinated to learn about their language by studying it on the printed page.

Such a fascination led to some important discoveries of course, not least to the recognition that English does have a syntax — a set of rules which determine much of the pattern of the written English sentence. Murray, who wrote by far the best of the eighteenth-century English grammars, identified twenty-four rules of English syntax. It must be pointed out, however, that despite the great achievements of scholars like Murray, their grammars referred only to the syntax of the written English sentence, and this brings me to another of the limitations of their work. Murray never considered the grammatical patterns of speech, which are quite different from those of writing. Furthermore, as he himself acknowledged, he never saw his study of grammar as taking the place of the study of rhetoric, or 'style' as he called it: he intended only to teach something of the rules by which the written English sentence should be constructed with 'propriety'. It was an important intention in one sense, but nonetheless quite a modest one, for wider questions of meaning in language were not addressed in his model of grammar. Murray must have winced in his grave more than once at the manner in which his view of grammar has been corrupted and misunderstood by so much educational practice.

As the technology of printing improved, increasing numbers of relatively inexpensive books appeared, many of them school grammar books, paralleling the development of mass education. In fact, mass education as we know it would have been quite impossible without the proliferation of print materials — grammars, spelling books, reading books and composition books, as well as the many other textbooks of the twentieth century. So steeped in literacy is the present generation (including all the readers of this book, by the way) that we have become accustomed to judging written language as the 'correct' mode, so that we tend to view examples of written-down speech as 'disjointed', 'fragmented', and difficult to follow. The truth is that speech is not difficult to follow in the main, and furthermore that it is not in general either disjointed or fragmented. One teacher I encountered recently even dismissed a transcript of students' talk as 'ungrammatical': she was judging it, of course, by the standards of written language. It is an interesting commentary on the distance we as a people have moved from a primarily oral culture to a literate one, that we do not on the whole have appropriate means of talking about speech except in the relatively negative terms the teacher used. I can testify from my own experience that it takes a considerable effort to overcome the effects of being so steeped in literacy and to look afresh at the grammar of speech. Yet, as Hammond argues, it is important that we teachers do look again at the grammar both of speech and of writing, and consider the important consequences for our teaching practices.

The teaching of literacy, which allegedly was one of the principal benefits to be conferred by mass education, became increasingly preoccupied with the breaking down of the language into its various parts. Attention to meaning, and to the overall organization of the text, simply disappeared. At the same time, and for what I am sure are related reasons, children were increasingly enjoined to silence, and this brings me to the second of the two reasons I gave in explanation of the gradual disappearance of rhetoric from the English-speaking cultures and their schools.

Brice Heath has recently noted (1986) that writing rather than speaking became the valued mode in the nineteenth-century schools: children were encouraged to talk less and less, while their progress was measured more and more through the written mode, a practice which survives to this day. Among the complex of factors responsible for this, discipline and the need teachers felt (and often still do) to manage and keep children under control led to a preoccupation with reading and writing rather than with talking. But the reading and writing involved have often been no more than 'busy work' — exercises in reading isolated and meaningless words, phrases or even sentences; exercises in identifying parts of speech and the clauses of a sentence; exercises in copying; exercises in writing relatively meaningless passages and themes. Nineteenth-century practices such as the monitorial method of teaching large numbers of children (see, for example, Gosden, 1969, or Goldstrom, 1972), whereby under a teacher's general supervision, student monitors — sometimes 'assistant teachers' — were set to drill and rehearse children in reading and/or copying their letters, to chorus the various parts of speech, to correct 'faulty sentences' (actually sentences which broke one of the rules of syntax as proposed by Murray and others), served to both institute and legitimize the views firstly that the written language was the 'correct' or 'superior' form of language, and secondly that the appropriate object of language study was the written English sentence and its various parts. Such views trivialize what should be an important and exciting pursuit: the exploration of language both in terms of its different modes, spoken and written, and in terms of its many genres, serving significant personal and social ends.

What is far worse about such views, however, is that they serve to disempower those who learn, leaving them effectively deprived of any of the insights so essential to a proper capacity to use language, especially in writing, to construct knowledge, attitude and opinion. Inevitably, numbers of children have always succeeded in becoming appropriately literate despite the worst educational practices, capable of using their language in the pursuit of important personal and social goals. But such children, as we are all aware, are those who are advantaged anyway. They are the children whose family background or wider sociocultural experience prepare them to master many of the patterns of language required for successful learning and for subsequent participation in the community. Brice Heath (1983) in her recent studies, and Bernstein and his colleagues (1973) some years ago, have both sought to show the ways in which the processes of schooling serve to reward the students whose patterns of linguistic behaviour most closely match those required for school learning. Literate behaviour is clearly very much involved here.

Think of the significant disadvantage suffered today in Australia by the adult illiterates we are told about, including many Aboriginal people in both traditional and urban situations, as well as by the many children currently failing to become functionally literate. Of the children disadvantaged because of difficulties in coming to terms with written English, we must include those for whom English is a second language who, as Wales argues in chapter 7, must often struggle to make sense of both the spoken and the written modes. For educationally good reasons, such children are entering more and more fully into 'mainstream' classrooms, where they are often taught by teachers who claim no specialist interest in the needs of second-language learners. It is essential then, that all teachers do develop such an interest, recognizing that they are responsible for the language needs of mother-tongue and second-language learners alike, where that will involve some explicit teaching about language to both groups. In fact, as Wales also suggests, a proper examination of the matter will often reveal that many of the desirable patterns for teaching about language to mother-tongue speakers are relevant for the second-language learner as well. Houston (1986), for example, has demonstrated the relevance to both mother-tongue and second-language speakers of thoughtfully based language-across-the-curriculum programmes in the secondary school, involving teachers in a wide range of subjects.

LITERACY AND CONTROL

Historically, so ineffective have many of the traditional patterns of teaching been in developing genuine capacity to read and write with confidence and skill, that we are forced to consider why such patterns have persisted for as long as they have. We must conclude, I believe, that the relative disempowerment of children from the nineteenth century onwards is part of a wider social pattern by which mass education has been used as an instrument of social control. The function of the patterns of teaching I have described was to develop at best a very limited kind of literacy in most students: that is to say, these patterns were not calculated to develop persons equipped to challenge the *status quo*, or to participate very vigorously in political and democratic processes. For, as I noted early in this discussion, capacity in literacy is very much involved in developing individuals able to operate effectively in a democracy, appropriately challenging and exploring aspects of their world, and skilled at changing it where they see social change as a desirable thing. If schools were places in which students were genuinely encouraged to talk in well-directed ways, and if schools did pursue programmes that engaged students in actively exploring the written word, especially its role in building the contents of the various school subjects, then they would be demonstrably different kinds of places from many of the schools of today. Moreover, the students found in such schools would operate in demonstrably different ways, as Lemke (1985: 30–35) has pointed out in a somewhat different context.

Since the 1960s we have seen a number of initiatives in language education, both in Australia and overseas, aimed at interesting teachers in language and its role in learning. Those responsible for such initiatives (e.g. Dixon, 1967, 1985; Britton, 1970; Britton *et al.*, 1975; Barnes, 1976; Barnes, Britton and Rosen, 1971; Barnes, Britton and Torbe, 1986; Moffett, 1968, 1981; Graves, 1981, 1983) have often argued the importance of empowering children through development of their language, both spoken and written. The influence of these ideas did have an impact upon Australian language curriculum guidelines, as a review by Christie and Rothery (1979) showed very clearly, and in varying ways language initiatives since the 1970s have continued to reflect a concern around the Australian states with the role of language in learning. The Commonwealth Curriculum Development Centre, for example, sponsored a Language Development Project (LDP) and a National Working Party on the Role of Language in Learning. More recent initiatives like the Early Literacy Inservice Course (ELIC) have been influential, as have been the numerous language curriculum guidelines which continue to be produced through the various state curriculum directorates or boards.

All these moves have brought about important reassessments of the significance of language in learning, and among other things have drawn teachers' attention to the need to respect children's own language uses in their learning: to that extent these moves represent an important departure from the model of language which played such a fundamentally important and unfortunate role in the teaching of literacy for so long. Like a great deal else that has emerged in curriculum theory since the 1960s however, the newer initiatives in language have had more useful things to say of 'processes' than of 'products', to take up an unhappy dichotomy of the kind that conduit notions of language always create (Christie, 1988). In all but a very limited sense, it is meaningless to draw a distinction between 'process' and 'product', either in general curriculum and learning theory, or in language curriculum theory. That is because in the act of using language, either spoken or written, one necessarily engages both in process and in product building: but, and this is the important point here, unless one's attention is properly directed towards the 'product' — upon the kind of text type or genre which the occasion requires — then the activity of using language is merely unfocused in a very unhelpful way.

Contemporary interest in so-called 'process writing', for example, of the kind fashionable in many parts of Australia following the influential work of Graves (1981, 1983) in particular, but also of Walshe (1981: 5–16), Turbill (1983) and others, is but one recent manifestation of a very old tendency in western cultures to separate 'form' from 'function', or 'form' from 'content' (Christie, 1988). Another manifestation of the same phenomenon was evident a few years ago in Dixon's proposal (1967) that teachers should promote 'growth' through language. The dilemma such a proposal creates is that it never addresses directly the issue of growth for *what*? Australian language curriculum guidelines of the 1960s and 1970s stressed the wisdom of promoting growth through the four language 'modes' or 'skills' — listening, speaking, reading and writing — but they neglected the wider issue of purposes in using. I ask the question: Listening, speaking, reading and writing — about what, to whom, and what for?

Interests in growth and process in language have discouraged teachers from intervention in their children's language learning, particularly in the writing programme, on the grounds that children must be left 'to find their own way', or 'to make their own choices' in using language. More than one teacher I have encountered has spoken shamefacedly of intervening in their children's language learning, reluctant to acknowledge what they have seen as a betrayal of their responsibilities as teachers. It is a sorry situation indeed when teachers feel so compromised, their authority so confused. The only children who really cope in classrooms where they are left to 'work it out for themselves' are those who are already advantaged, though even they will benefit from more direct intervention than often occurs. Those who suffer from policies of being left to find their own way and their own models in language are the seriously disadvantaged: those from backgrounds where literacy is less highly visible and valued and/or those for whom English is a second language.

Returning for a moment to the older traditions of rhetorical study, with its fundamental commitment to the notion of language as systematically fashioned to create different meanings, you will recall that serious interest in such a study died over the nineteenth and twentieth centuries. With its death came a preoccupation with what has become known as 'traditional school grammar' — these days reduced to not much more than a faltering examination of the major parts of speech. Those who initiated the new wave of thinking about language in the 1960s quite properly rejected such a model of language and literacy. But in the end they have proposed no alternative model, focusing instead upon 'growth' and 'process' at the expense of any coherent interest in language at all.

Such a state of affairs represents in one sense the end of a long journey in the English-speaking cultures, yet in another sense it leaves the way open for the start of a new journey. It is the end of a journey which started firstly with the loss of an understanding of oral language as a rich resource with which persons build meanings, and secondly with the associated failure to understand written language. Yet a new journey is already commencing, one in which a revitalized interest in language, both spoken and written, is beginning to shape our professional understanding of what to teach in schools. This book aims to make some contribution to the development of such an understanding among teachers, language curriculum consultants, and others interested in language and its role both in school learning and in the community at large.

I referred earlier to one of the initiatives in language education of the 1970s, namely the Curriculum Development Centre's Language Development Project. The project adopted Halliday's model of language development (Language Development Project, 1979), which proposed that language development involves learning language, learning through language, and learning about language. Curriculum teams in all states sought to develop language curriculum materials, but the work of the project was never really finished because of the federal government's intervention in 1980–81. However, its model of language development is worth noting here, for whatever the achievements of the project (and it did have some), it failed to address the question of what to do in the name of teaching and learning about language. An important task of the 1980s will be to set that problem straight.

The new model of the 1980s, I suggest, will use a functionally relevant grammar, and will employ it to explore the characteristics of speech and writing, where the object will be primarily to focus upon the ways in which linguistic items are used to build up meaning. Far from leaving children to 'find it out for themselves', it will make frequent use of exemplars in developing competence in literacy. If, for example, as Gilbert suggests in chapter 3, the object is to develop certain stylistic qualities valued in writing literary–type genres, then teachers will teach for an understanding of what these qualities are rather than leaving them clouded in the mystery that often surrounds discussion of 'creativity' in writing. In only a special and limited sense indeed is anyone 'creative' or 'original', for we all learn to function in the world by mastering the necessary patterns of working — of dealing with experience in socially relevant ways — and here language is critically important as the principal resource with which we learn to deal with experience (Lemke, 1988). To learn to use the language of one's culture is to learn a basic resource both for functioning within it and for changing it. The use of models in language is therefore quite vital in a literacy programme, for it will be through effective study and use of models that our students will acquire the confidence and the 'know-how' with which to move on, experimenting with the models, in time developing new ones.

Turning to the other areas of the curriculum, the new programmes of literacy teaching and learning will similarly take seriously the use of models. In particular, they will acknowledge the very intimate relationship between literacy and 'content', and will have students explore what it is to construct knowledge in, for example, the various sciences — natural and social —

which concern Martin and Cope and Kalantzis in this volume, as well as in the other school subjects. And since school subjects, like any other area of enquiry, are in themselves social inventions, open to adaptation and change, the new models of literacy will encourage students to examine the very character of the subjects and to question their purposes in varying ways, including the interests they serve in the wider society.

Finally, and by no means least, the new literacy programmes, because they will be sensitive to the ways in which ideologies, attitudes and values are subtly built in language, will address the various gender imbalances to which White draws attention.

Overall, because they will aim to develop in students a much greater consciousness about language than has been the case in education for a long time now, the new literacy programmes will develop individuals who are in control of their language, rather than, as often happens today, merely controlled by it.

LITERACY IN THE LATE TWENTIETH CENTURY

All this brings me back to some of the themes with which I commenced this chapter, in particular to the kinds of literacy valued quite recently in Australia, as in other western countries, and to the very marked contrast between that state of affairs and what prevails today. While it was possible not so very long ago to be either totally illiterate or at least merely possessed of the most minimal literacy and still able to function quite adequately in the community, working in one of a number of possible occupations, that plainly is not the case now. On the contrary, anyone not possessed of very considerable literacy in the contemporary world will be indeed dispossessed and unhappy, for such a person will be effectively 'locked out' from so much of the knowledge, information and ideas which are part of a literate culture. I earlier noted that the inventions of writing and later of printing were both of great significance in their impact on human history, and to this point I should like briefly to return.

In several very interesting discussions of the differences between oral and literate traditions, Ong (1977, 1981, 1982) has argued that the inventions of writing and thence of printing brought about fundamental changes in the nature of human consciousness, making it possible not only to store and pass on knowledge and information in new ways, but also to create new kinds of knowledge, new modes of thinking and of intellectual enquiry. Literacy is in this sense a tool whose invention has both marked one step in the evolution of human cultures and made possible the further evolution of those cultures. Just as the invention of the printing press unlocked capacities in undertaking new enquiries and in passing on the fruits of those enquiries, so too, in the late twentieth century, Ong argues, the inventions of the computer and of the many other technologically sophisticated communication media have made possible both new kinds of thinking and intellectual effort and new kinds of knowledge. Ong even speaks of a 'secondary literacy' made possible by such technological advances, and itself rapidly transforminng our societies. The primary tool which human beings invented, as both Vygotsky (1934) and Halliday (1985) have argued, was oral language. Having invented language, human beings and their cultures evolved for many centuries before taking the giant evolutionary step of inventing writing. The development of writing, as Ong suggests, was 'consciousness raising' (1982:179) for it made possible genuinely new modes of thinking and experience.

Now, the relevance of this to the contemporary Australian situation should be clear. Literacy in today's world is a very different thing from what it was either at the turn of the century or even mid-century. The contemporary world demands a level of sophistication in literacy greater than at any time in the past. It demands a people capable not only of handling the awesome range of print materials now a feature of a technologically advanced society, but also of creating and responding to new ones, for we do keep generating new kinds of writing, new kinds of genres, as a necessary part of generating new knowledge and new ways of thinking.

To leave school today without an appropriate level of literacy is to be impoverished indeed, for those without the capacity to go on and secure some kind of additional education or training will be competing for a rapidly diminishing pool of unskilled jobs, and in other ways effectively disempowered and prevented from participating fully in community life. It is in this sense, I suggest, that illiterate persons will be 'shut out'. The relationship between illiteracy, social alienation, failure and poverty is too acute to be ignored. A recent enquiry into causes of unemployment among young people in Commonwealth countries (Kirby *et al.*, 1987) showed that in developed countries like Australia, the higher the levels of educational attainment achieved, the greater the likelihood of finding work.

Where persons do attain reasonable levels of literacy at school, qualifying them to enter other educational programmes and/or occupations of various kinds, they need to recognize that whatever they do, and whatever new ways of thinking and forms of knowledge they aspire to master, language will always be centrally involved. Thus, the pursuit of proficiency — indeed of excellence — in literacy, is necessarily bound up with the pursuit of learning ever more varied and complex ways of working in the late twentieth-century world. This has particular implications for literacy learning, for so much of the complex work of business, government, commerce and industry as well as of academic and scholarly enquiry is now found in a veritable flood of printed documents of many kinds.

Much earlier I noted that it is sometimes suggested that the various communication media such as television, film and radio are now the important sources of new information and in consequence the need to teach children to be literate in print is declining. This is a quite dangerous myth, for the evidence indicates that many forms of writing have proliferated throughout the nineteenth and twentieth centuries. Internationally, the publishing industry, stimulated by such developments as the production of relatively cheap paperback books, had already spawned very large numbers of books by the Second World War (Barnes, 1985). Since that war, the volume of publications has increased every year. In the United Kingdom, for example,

11 924 publications were produced in 1949, whereas in 1984 there were 40 246 new titles (Hodgkin, 1986: 153). Figures for Australia (*Australian Book Scene 1987–88*: 10) over the last two decades show a similar pattern: the volume of print materials increases year by year.

But the issue is not merely one of the increasing volume of publications produced over the years. It is also, and perhaps more importantly, a matter of both the increasing range of written genres a complex culture such as ours produces, and the increasingly varied uses of written language through those genres. The computer and the word processor, as well as the fax machine, currently make possible a very complex series of activities of a kind not possible even ten years ago, let alone fifty or a hundred years ago. In the world of commerce and banking, for example, major projects such as the merging of various companies, the planning of significant investment initiatives, the development of programmes of work, both national and international, all involve generating great quantities of written language at considerable speed. Interviews with a management consultant and a banker indicate that, because of the sheer quantity of the relevant written materials, such commercial activities would simply not be possible without the speedy capacity for text generation that the modern computer and word processor provide. Add to that the quite remarkable capacity of the fax machine to communicate texts from one part of the world to another within the space of five minutes, and we have some measure of the significantly changed world in which we live — a world in which those we teach will soon be seeking work!

While the computer, the word processor and even the fax machine certainly have had an impact in educational settings (I regularly use all three), they are probably still less a feature of daily life there than they are in other parts of our society, and consequently many teachers know less about them than they might. Considerably more might be done to build bridges between schools and the wider society, to better inform both teachers and students of the ways written language in particular is continuing to change the pattern of the contemporary world.

As yet, no reliable data have been amassed about the range of written genres people are required to write to participate in the modern world, and major research work is needed here. As our culture evolves, so too do the many forms of language within which its ways of thinking, of working, and of negotiating and dealing with experience are encoded.

The new technology, as well as the complex society it has helped create, demands a greater degree of conscious reflection upon its ways of working — particularly its ways of working in language — than have earlier periods of history. To be alert to the ways one's language works for creating and organizing meaning is to be conscious of how to manipulate and use it. Schools should encourage capacity for conscious reflection upon language, not only because that develops desirable skills with which to enter the workforce, but also because it is essential to fully developed persons, capable of conducting their lives with some independence, and capable of participating effectively in a democracy.

REFERENCES

Australian Book Scene 1987–88. (Supplement to *The Australian Bookseller and Publisher.*) The year in review. Melbourne: D. W. Thorpe.

Badham, C. (1890). *Speeches and lectures delivered in Australia by the late Charles Badham, D.D.* Sydney: Dymocks.

Bain, A. (1887). *English composition and rhetoric, revised in two parts: Part I, Intellectual elements of style; Part II, Emotional qualities of style*. London: Longman, Green and Co.

Ballard, P. (1921). *Teaching the mother tongue*. London: Hodder and Stoughton.

Barnes, D. (1976). *From communication to curriculum*. Harmondsworth, Middlesex: Penguin.

Barnes, D., Britton, J., & Rosen, H. (1971). *Language, the learner and the school*. Harmondsworth, Middlesex: Penguin.

Barnes, D., Britton, J., & Torbe, M. (1986). *Language, the learner and the school*. (3rd ed.). Harmondsworth, Middlesex: Penguin.

Barnes, J. (1985). Depression and innovation in the British and American booktrade, 1819–1939. In R. Myers & M. Harris (Eds.), *Economics of the British booktrade 1605–1939*. Publishing History Occasional Series No. 1. Cambridge/Alexandria, Va: Chadwyck-Healey.

Bernstein, B. (Ed.). (1973). *Class, codes and control, Vol. 2*. Applied Studies Towards a Sociology of Language. London: Routledge & Kegan Paul.

Bessant, B. (1982). The school — The institute and its controlling bureaucracy. *Educational research in the 1980s: Conference papers Vol. 2*. Paper presented at the Annual Conference of the Australian Association for Research in Education, Brisbane, November.

Blair, H. (1783). *Lectures on rhetoric and belles lettres, Vols I and II*. London: W. Strahan and T. Cadell.

Brice Heath, S. (1986). Literacy and language change. In D. Tannen & J. Alatis (Eds.), *Languages and linguistics: The interdependence of theory, data, and application*. Georgetown University Round Table on Languages and Linguistics, 1985. Washington, DC: Georgetown University Press.

Brice Heath, S. (1983). *Ways with words: Language, life, and work in communities and classrooms*. Cambridge: Cambridge University Press.

Britton, J. (1970). *Language and learning*. Harmondsworth, Middlesex: Penguin.

Britton, J., Burgess, T., Mcleod, A., & Rosen, H. (1975). *The development of writing abilities (11–18)*. London: Schools Council Research Studies and Macmillan Education.

Cambourne, B. (1986). Provide natural learning conditions. In R. D. Walshe, P. March, & D. Jensen (Eds.), *Writing and learning in Australia*. Melbourne: Dellasta Books and Oxford University Press.

Campbell, G. (1838). *The philosophy of rhetoric*. London: T. Tegg and Son. (First published 1776.)

Christie, F. (1976). *The teaching of English in elementary schools in New South Wales 1848–1900: An enquiry into social conditions and pedagogical theories determining the teaching of English*. Unpublished M.Ed. thesis, University of Sydney.

Christie, F. (1981). *The 'received tradition' of English language study in schools: The decline of rhetoric and the corruption of grammar*. Unpublished M.A. thesis, University of Sydney.

Christie, F., & Rothery, J. (1979). English in Australia: an interpretation of role in the curriculum. In J. Maling-Keepes & B. D. Keepes (Eds.), *Language in education: The LDP phase 1*. Canberra: Curriculum Development Centre.

Christie, F. (1988). Language development in education. In R. Hasan & J. R. Martin (Eds.), *Learning language: Learning culture*. Norwood, New Jersey: Ablex Publishing Corporation.

Cloran, C. (1988). Learning through language: The social construction of gender. In R. Hasan & J. R. Martin (Eds.), *Learning language: Learning culture*. Norwood, New Jersey: Ablex Publishing Corporation.

Connell, W. F. (1980). *A history of education in the twentieth century world*. Canberra: Curriculum Development Centre.

Conway, J. (1899). *English grammar, composition and precis writing* (2nd ed.). Sydney: Angus & Robertson.

Culler, J. (1981). *The pursuit of signs: Semiotics, literature, deconstruction*. London: Routledge & Kegan Paul.

Davey, I. (1982, November). Past and present: The transformation of age relations. *Educational research in the 1980s. Collected Papers, Vol. 2.* Paper presented at the Annual Conference of the Australian Association for Research in Education, Brisbane.

Davies, F. (1973). *Teaching reading in early England*. Bath: Pitman Publishing.

Dixon, J. (1967). *Growth through English*. London: National Association for the Teaching of English and Oxford University Press.

Dixon, J. (1985). Teaching English 1984. In S. N. Tchudi (Ed.), *Language, schooling and society*. Proceedings of the International Federation for the Teaching of English Seminar, Michigan State University, November 1984. New Jersey: Boynton/Cook Inc.

Goldstrom, J. M. (1972). *Education: elementary education, 1780–1900*. Newton Abbot: David & Charles.

Gosden, P. H. J. H. (1969). *How they were taught*. Oxford: Basil Blackwell.

Graves, D. H. (1981). In R. D. Walshe (Ed.), *Donald Graves in Australia: Children want to write*. Sydney: Primary English Teaching Association.

Graves, D. H. (1983). *Writing: Teachers and children at work*. London: Heinemann Educational Books.

Halliday, M. A. K. (1975). *Learning how to mean: Explorations in the development of language*. London: Edward Arnold.

Halliday, M. A. K. (1985). *Spoken and written language*. Geelong, Victoria: Deakin University Press.

Hasan, R. (1986). The ontogenesis of ideology: An interpretation of mother child talk. In T. Threadgold, E. A. Grosz, G. Kress, & M. A. K. Halliday (Eds.), *Semiotics, ideology and language*. Sydney: Sydney Association for Studies in Society and Culture.

Hodgkin, A. (1986). New technologies in printing and publishing: The present of the written word. In G. Baumann (Ed.), *The written word: Literacy in transition*. Wolfson College Lectures, Oxford, 1985. Oxford: Oxford University Press.

Houston, C. (1986). *English language development across the curriculum*. Queensland: Division of Special Education, Department of Education.

Huddleston, R. (n.d.). The presentation of English grammar in primary and secondary schooltexts. Mimeo, Department of Linguistics, University of Queensland.

Kirby, P., Diejomaoh, V. P., Ghai, D., Khan, A. R., O'Brien, R., Fairbairn, T. I. J., Juneau, A., Massiah, J., Roy, P., & Wright, C. (1987). *Jobs for young people: a way to a better future*. Marlborough House, London: Commonwealth Secretariat.

Language Development Project. (1979). *LDP Occasional Paper No. 1*. Canberra: Curriculum Development Centre.

Lemke, J. L. (1985). *Using language in the classroom*. Geelong, Victoria: Deakin University Press.

Lemke, J. L. (1988). Towards a social semiotics of the material subject. In T. Threadgold (Ed.), *Working Papers Vol. 2, Nos. 1–2*. Sydney: Sydney Association for Studies in Society and Culture.

Lowth, R. (1969). *A short introduction to English grammar*. Facsimile Reprint No. 18. Menston: Scolar Press. Originally published 1762.

McKnight, G. H. (1928). *Modern English in the making*. New York: Appleton Century Crofts.

Ministry of Education, Victoria. (1968). *The Victorian Readers, 1929*. Melbourne: Schools Division, Victorian Ministry of Education.
Moffett, J. (1968). *Teaching the universe of discourse*. Boston: Houghton Mifflin Company.
Moffett, J. (1981). *Active voice: A writing program across the curriculum*. New Jersey: Boynton/Cook Publishers.
Mumby, F. A. (1956). *Publishing and bookselling: a history from the earliest times to the present day* (4th ed.). London: Jonathan Cape.
Murray, L. (1968). *English grammar*. Facsimile Reprint No. 106. Menston: Scolar Press. Originally published 1795.
Nesfield, J. S. (1926). *Aids to the study and composition of English*. London: Macmillan.
Ong, W. J. (1971). *Rhetoric, romance, and technology: Studies in the interaction of expression and culture*. Ithaca, NY: Cornell University Press.
Ong, W. J. (1977). *Interfaces of the word: studies in the evolution of consciousness and culture*. Ithaca, NY: Cornell University Press.
Ong, W. J. (1982). *Orality and literacy: the technologizing of the word*. New Accent Series. London: Methuen.
Painter, C. (1985). *Learning the mother tongue*. Geelong, Victoria: Deakin University Press.
Piper, K. (1983). *Curriculum style and English language*. Hawthorn, Victoria: ACER.
Piper, K. (1984). The teaching of writing. In F. Christie (Ed.), *Children writing* (B.Ed. course Study Guide). Geelong, Victoria: Deakin University Press.
Priestley, J. (1969). *The rudiments of English grammar adapted to the use of schools with observations on style*. Facsimile Reprint No. 210. Menston: Scolar Press. Originally published 1761.
Reddy, M. J. (1979). The conduit metaphor — A case of frame conflict in our language about language. In A. Ortony (Ed.), *Metaphor and thought*. Philadelphia: Cambridge University Press.
Tannen, D. (1982). The oral/literate continuum in discourse. In D. Tannen (Ed.), *Spoken and written language: exploring orality and literacy*. Vol. IX in Roy O. Freedle (Ed.), *Advances in Discourse Processes*. Norwood, New Jersey: Ablex Publishing Corporation.
Turbill, J. (1983). *Now we want to write*. Sydney: Primary English Teaching Association.
Vygotsky, L. (1934). *Thought and language* (Translation newly revised and edited by Alex Kozulin, 1986). Cambridge, Massachusetts: MIT Press.
Walshe, R. D. (Ed.). (1981). *Donald Graves in Australia: children want to write*. Sydney: Primary English Teaching Association.
Whately, R. (1968). In J. L. Golden & E. P. J. Corbett (Eds.), *The rhetoric of Blair, Campbell, and Whately*. New York: Holt, Rinehart & Winston. Originally published 1828.
Wootton, R. F. (1987, 1 September) The *Age*. Letter to the editor.

2 Is learning to read and write the same as learning to speak?

JENNIFER HAMMOND

INTRODUCTION

The question which concerns this chapter is an important one in any book attempting to offer a fresh look at literacy. Like spoken language, writing is easily taken for granted, both in that its character is often not fully understood, and in that its particular demands in learning are frequently underestimated. Literacy is one of the most valued of the skills that schooling offers children, and it is clear that children will make little progress in their school learning unless they achieve considerable levels of proficiency in literacy.

In recent years it has often been suggested that the most appropriate approaches to the teaching of literacy will be those that attempt to parallel the natural processes by which children learn to talk. Just as children learn to talk because of the need to interact with others, mastering the various features of their mother tongue in largely unconscious ways, so too, it is suggested, literacy will best be learned through a mainly unconscious adoption of the features of the written mode. Spelling, handwriting and punctuation all need to be learned, but, it is argued, these will best be learned while children have various encounters with print materials and engage in a number of writing activities.

Such arguments, often based upon close observation of young children learning to talk, have had the merit of causing teachers to reflect upon the ways speech is learned in use, and to plan for the most desirable contexts in which children can learn to read and write. In these senses, such arguments have been very helpful. However, they are also misleadingly simple. I shall argue that as they fail to acknowledge just how different from the spoken mode writing actually is, for related reasons they also fail to acknowledge that the written mode is not learned in the same ways as speech.

In order to address properly the question of what the basics of literacy entail, we need to have information about the nature of language, especially its spoken and written modes and their relationship to each other. In this chapter I shall consider firstly both the similarities and differences between speech and writing and, secondly, focus on students' developing awareness of these differences. I shall argue that where teachers have an appropriate sense of the nature of language and of the significant differences between speech and writing, they will be in a better position to teach literacy, developing the kinds of capacities valued and discussed in detail in several other chapters of this book. In developing my discussion, I shall draw on systemic functional linguistics, developed by Halliday and others (e.g. Halliday, 1978, 1985b; Halliday and Hasan, 1976, 1985), to provide both a theoretical framework and a means of analysing language.

A COMPARISON OF SPEECH AND WRITING

To explore the question of the relationship between learning to speak and learning to read and write, I shall begin by examining spoken and written language used by some year 9 students in one of their English lessons. This year 9 class had been studying the novel *Z for Zachariah* by Robert O'Brien. The lesson from which the following texts were taken consisted of a discussion of the two major characters in the novel, Ann and Mr Loomis. Following the oral discussion which took place during the English lesson, the students were asked to write a summary of the two characters. Most of the writing was done during a subsequent lesson. The oral discussion, and the writing that followed, were part of the normal routine of the class English lessons. Text 2.1 is part of the recorded discussion about the two characters that took place during the lesson, and texts 2.2 and 2.3 (pages 28–31) are examples of the written work produced by the students following the class discussion.

Text 2.1

(At this point the discussion is about the character of Mr Loomis.)

Student: He's got that sort of attitude, like he seems so used to a life of power and glory and now that he's with Ann and he sees how creative and nice she is, he doesn't, he sort of rejects her, doesn't want to open up his own feelings, and it's probably why he seems so dominating.

Teacher: Yes, J . . . ?

J: Umm.

Teacher: Well, think about it. K . . . ?

K: He's sort of got a hangup, sort of . . .

Teacher: About what?

K: About power, he's got to have it or else he's nowhere.

Teacher: Yes?

Student: Like, I reckon he would have been really like nice and like good and that, but now he's been to all the towns and seen, like there's no life or anything, and he comes into, um, the valley and sees Ann, and sees life, and he sort of, um, you know, was the only one, he just wanted the power over her because, um, he's never had power or anything before.

Teacher: It's also possible that all the things, all the death and all the ghastly things that he must have seen, have made him so determined to survive, that it's made him sort of blind to anything and anyone else's feelings. But there is a suggestion in the novel, isn't there, that there is a softness in him, the way he responds to Ann's playing? What else does he respond to when he's very ill and unconscious?

Student: Her reading.

Teacher: Her reading. Her reading. So what suggests that there is a sensitivity in him, but very deeply buried? Yes?

Student: Well, I think he is just like the people who dropped the wall because (laughter) dropped the bomb, because they dropped it because they wanted something, and so he's doing things because that's the way he wants it.

Teacher: Mmm. And in the process of that, what is he also doing?

Student: He's just changing everything.

Teacher: Well, what did the people do in the process of getting what they wanted, what did they do?

Student: They hurt and killed people.

Teacher: They destroyed what they wanted. They left nothing. Yes, J . . . ?

J: Umm, also we know that he's sensitive because how he dreams about when he's killed Edward, it's haunting him, like it's not as if he doesn't give it a second thought.

Teacher: Yes, he's got a conscience about killing Edward.

Text 2.2 Character summary of Mr Loomis written after classroom discussion (reduced size)

Mr Loomis

Mr Loomis is totally opposite in character to Burke. He has a light complexion & reddish brown hair which is quite long & has a beard.

Character

Mr Loomis never lets anyone stop him if he wants to do something. He's a very insecure person who needs to have power & control to keep him going.
Underneath, deep down there is somebody who's kind & compassio-nate, we see this side of Mr

Loomis character when he thanks Anne for reading to him, playing the piano & holding his hand.
When Mr Loomis doesn't have power he becomes very insecure like when Anne confronts him & tells him she's leaving, he keeps asking her to stay & becomes frightened. When Anne mentioned to Mr Loomis right at the end that if he had already killed Edward, he might as well kill her, he falls to pieces & says how she doesn't know that for sure, so we also know that Mr Loomis has feelings of remorse about killing Edward & that he didn't really think of the consequences.
He wants to control Anne but when Anne doesn't let him have his own way, he tries all sorts of ploys to make her come back to the house & be his "slave." He's always thinking of realistic, practical things whereas Anne loves to think about fantastic things & imagining happy, carefree things. I don't think Mr Loomis enjoys doing things for himself, he prefers to have Kate do all the dirty work while he sits back & relaxes.

Text 2.3 Character summary of Ann written after classroom discussion (reduced size)

Ann Burden.

Ann Burden, physically, is a slim, ~~tanne~~d girl with short, roughly cut, mousy blonde hair. She has a tanned complexion from working in the sun and wears mens clothes, for they are the most practical for farming.

At only sixteen, Ann is a mature and affectionate young lady. She values many things of the spirit, including going to church and reading the bible, along with reading creative novels and poetry. Ann likes to ~~kee~~ collect flowers and places them in the church to keep alive the ~~spirit~~ spiritual life and hope, out of all the nuclear destruction and deadness outside the valley. Ann is a very strong person, in that she is able to survive alone in the valley without profound fear and without anyone to turn to for company or advice. She is also strong minded with a great sense of creativity which I find unique, because being able to ~~uphold~~ uphold a creative and optimistic attitude is almost courageous after what has happened.

Ann is not a withholding person. She is very deeply sensitive to Mr Loomis in the novel. She also displays a great amount of affection and love for him. It quite surprised me, how Ann had this attitude towards him (which is also another display of her courage), because he was a total stranger from a different place and mainly, different values and Ann made herself vunerable to be injured & hurt.

She also a very fair and considerate person. Even when she was driven out of her own home by Mr Loomis, Ann left half of the farm produce for him, when really he did not deserve it.

I think that Ann was a bit too sensitive in the novel to Mr Loomis. She could not think ill of anyone, probably because she was brought up that way and valued human life so much.

Overall, to finish off, Ann is an admirable character to anyone, who is kind and sensitive and a healthy minded person who valued many things of the spirit. She was also a independent person with a great sense of creativity and consciousness. Ann is also a level headed person. who has hope and thinks of her future well being.

SIMILARITIES BETWEEN THE SPOKEN AND WRITTEN TEXTS

The spoken and written texts broadly have the same purpose in that both attempt to describe and analyse the characters from the novel *Z for Zachariah*. Consequently there are a number of obvious similarities. For example, both the spoken and written texts contain many of the same vocabulary items, such as Mr Loomis, Ann, character, power, control, reading, playing the piano, etc.; and they both contain frequent use of the pronouns *he* and *she* to refer to Mr Loomis and Ann. Because their purposes are to describe and analyse character, rather than to recreate the activities in which the characters engaged, both contain frequent use of verbs such as *is* and *has* rather than action verbs, and so on.

A more general point is that both spoken and written texts draw on the same underlying linguistic systems of English. That is, they both draw on the same systems of vocabulary items and grammar in order to make meaning. While this may seem to be an obvious point, I believe it is a very significant one. It means that the underlying similarities of speech and writing are important — more important than the differences. This point also provides the context for the subsequent discussion in this chapter. That is, there are real and significant similarities in spoken and written texts in English. These arise because spoken and written texts draw on the same linguistic systems. Choices made in the creation of any English text are choices within the available systems of vocabulary and grammar.

However, having stressed the importance of the similarities between spoken and written language, I would also like to point out that there are significant differences between them. Much of the rest of this chapter will be an exploration of these differences and a consideration of their educational implications.

DIFFERENCES BETWEEN SPOKEN AND WRITTEN LANGUAGE

Probably the most obvious difference between spoken and written texts is that the former are normally jointly constructed by two or more participants, while the latter are essentially monologues. Spoken texts, with few exceptions, are created by speakers in conjunction with other speakers, within the same physical context. Although one person may do most of the talking, as when someone delivers a lecture, the physical presence of the people being addressed is important in that they share the same context of situation with the speaker. In the majority of situations, they also contribute in some way to the construction of the text, even if their contribution is only a non-verbal one. Written texts, on the other hand, are typically produced in contexts removed by time and distance from those in which they are read. Consequently the writer cannot depend on a shared context to convey any of the meaning. The meaning must be contained within the text itself. The fact that spoken texts are jointly constructed while written texts are produced by writers in isolation from their readers has a significant influence on their organization and development. For example, the spoken and written texts from the year 9 class, presented above, are quite different in this regard.

The spoken text is dialogic in nature, and the discussion moves from one aspect of the topic to another in a flexible manner. It began with a description of Ann's character (not reproduced here). The discussion moves to what Mr Loomis had done to Ann, what Ann had done for Mr Loomis, Mr Loomis's need for power and control, a description of Mr Loomis's character, how Ann planned for the future (also not reproduced here), and so on. While the discussion remains on the overall topic of the two characters, it ranges freely from one point to another. Within this discussion, the teacher is in a position of power. She introduces the topic of the discussion, determines who has the right to speak by nominating individual students, and closes the discussion at the end of the lesson. The teacher has an idea of the overall direction she wants the discussion to take. Frequently the content of the students' contributions relates to questions posed by the teacher. For example:

Teacher: Do you think she thought Mr Loomis was bad when he first arrived?

Student: Yes, even though he was only trying to scare her.

However, on other occasions, the responses given by the students clearly influence the direction of the discussion. For example:

Student: Like when he's very sick, he's always telling Ann what to do, say plan if you must think of the future.

Teacher: Do you think she was not thinking of the future?

Occasionally the students give unexpected responses and these alter the direction of the discussion:

Student: I think he thrives on it, he likes to have control.

Teacher: He thrives on it, doesn't he, yes. He needs it almost as a kind of incentive, as a stimulus. Yeah, you're right, I hadn't thought of that, I think that's a very good point.

Because of the dynamic nature of the classroom dialogue, it is impossible to predict the precise direction the discussion will take. It is the interaction occurring between teacher and students that creates the text, and while the teacher has the greatest influence, she can determine only the general direction of the discussion, not its every move.

The students' written texts are very different. They consist of sustained monologues, each produced by one pupil working by herself. Text 2.2 begins with a physical description and then moves on to an analysis of Mr Loomis's character. He is described as, among other things, insecure and needing power and control. Text 2.3 also begins with a physical description and then moves on to a description of Ann's character. Fewer points are made about the character in this text, but each is developed more fully. Ann is described as mature, affectionate, strong and sensitive. The writer refers back to the novel for evidence to support each point. The organization of this second text, I suggest, makes it a more successful written text than the one about Mr Loomis. In text 2.3 the writer has presented a number of points about Ann's character and has developed and dealt with one point at a time. The author of text 2.2 has tended to some extent to do what is typical of speech rather than of writing — to touch on a point, move on to something else, and then come back to the first point again. For example, she has referred to Mr Loomis's need for control and to his insecurity at three different places in her text.

While there are some important differences between the two written texts in terms of the success of their organization and development, they are much more like each other than they are like the spoken text. That is, there are real and significant differences between the organization and development of the spoken text in comparison with the organization and development of the two written texts.

NATURE AND PURPOSE OF SPEECH AND WRITING

The reason why the spoken and written texts shown above are organized differently has to do with the very nature of speech and writing, and the purposes for which they have evolved in a literate society. In the history of human evolution, speech was the primary language mode. It evolved to fulfil the communicative and social needs of people who lived in nomadic communities, and for many thousands of years spoken language fulfilled these needs adequately. It was not until people began living in settled communities that language functions began to change. People needed to be able to count their livestock, to keep records of exchanges of money, to record taxes etc., and hence the need for a means of keeping more permanent records arose. Writing evolved to fulfil these needs. (See Halliday, 1985a, for a more comprehensive account of the evolution of writing.) Thus literacy gradually developed many millennia after the evolution of speech to serve human needs which the spoken mode did not satisfy. The different functions for which the spoken and written modes of language evolved can be seen in the purposes for which the two modes are used today. Speech is typically used where participants are face to face, as in conversations, service encounters, recounts of personal experiences, or in formal and informal learning situations. Writing is used where some kind of permanent record of facts, information or ideas is required. The situation in regard to speaking and writing within a literate society is somewhat analogous to a bilingual community, where different languages are used in different contexts by the people of that community. If separate contexts and separate purposes for the use of the two languages disappear, the society becomes monolingual. There is no need to have two languages that fulfil the same functions and purposes. Similarly, in literate societies the written mode exists because it fulfils functions and purposes that the oral mode cannot. Oral and written modes are used for different purposes and occur in different contexts.

As spoken language and written language fulfil different purposes in society, it is hardly surprising that their natures are different. Speech is dynamic in the sense that it is created at the moment of speaking and, unless it is recorded with twentieth-century recording equipment, exists only for that moment. Typically (as in the texts shown above) it is created jointly by two or more people and thus it develops fluidly as each participant contributes. It is not preplanned in most cases, and it cannot be drafted and edited. The participants are together in the context in which the speech is being constructed. Because of this they quite frequently share knowledge and background information. Even if their shared knowledge is minimal, participants in most speech situations can request clarification if they have not understood something. They can ask for more details, for clarification of time and place, identity of the participants, sequence of events, or points in an argument. That is, because speech is constructed jointly by participants in a particular context, the context itself contributes to the meaning being created. The context includes the actual physical location, any non-verbal gestures, intonation used, and so on.

Writing, on the other hand, by its nature is not dynamic but fixed. A written text is a relatively permanent record, in that it can be reflected upon and analysed. It can be read by someone who is not in the same geographical or time location as the writer, and it can be read as many times as the reader wishes. A written text has an existence beyond the moment in which it is created. It can therefore be planned and it can be edited and drafted in a way that a spoken text can never be. In a different way, we draft and redraft in speech all the time — with hesitations, false starts, and self corrections. However, in speech we cannot throw away the drafts as we do in writing. It is essential for written texts to be planned and edited and carefully developed so that the writer can be sure the intended message is the one actually conveyed. The writer must ensure that all details of participants, sequence of events, sets of arguments, bodies of information are provided in a way that enables the reader to understand the message of the text. The reader, because she or he is not in the same context as the writer, cannot request clarification of any points that are not clear from the text itself. That is, a written text must be independent of the context in which it is created. It must be decontextualized so that it makes sense in another time and place for a reader who may never meet the writer.

In summary, speech and writing are used in different contexts because they have evolved to satisfy different human needs. With the steady evolution of human societies, language has had to serve increasingly complex purposes. Hence, as the spoken and written modes have developed, they have drawn differently upon the various aspects of the linguistic system, particularly the grammatical system. In the next section I shall attempt to explain some of these different grammatical aspects.

ASPECTS OF GRAMMAR IN SPOKEN AND WRITTEN LANGUAGE

Lexical density

To begin the discussion of grammatical differences between speech and writing, I shall introduce the expression *lexical item*. This is a technical term used by many linguists to refer to sets of vocabulary or content items as they are typically found clustered in different texts. Lexical items are the words that carry the content of the text. They are the words that are found in dictionaries, as they can be easily defined. They belong to an open set of linguistic items, in the sense that any language continually adds to its store of available lexical items for reference to new technology, new objects or new ideas.

In the following example, I have underlined the lexical items in a short extract from the beginning of text 2.3:

> Ann Burden physically is a slim girl with short, roughly cut, mousy blonde hair.
> She has a tanned complexion from working in the sun
> and wears men's clothes
> for they are the most practical for farming

The words which are not underlined are grammatical items. The main function of grammatical items in a text is not to provide the message, but to establish and maintain the relationships between the lexical items. Grammatical items help to hold the text together — that is their job. As Halliday (1985a:61) points out, grammatical items include:

> articles: e.g. a, the
> pronouns: e.g. he, she, you, me
> most prepositions: e.g. in, beside, under
> conjunctions: e.g. and, because, while
> some classes of adverbs: e.g. usually, often
> finite verbs: e.g. have, was, is (as in 'have eaten', 'was running', etc.)

Grammatical items belong to a closed system in the language in the sense that we do not keep inventing new articles and prepositions. There is a fixed number of such items in any language, and they are part of the system of grammar that is utilized in the making of meaning.

Halliday in his book *Spoken and Written Language* (1985a:67) has suggested that a useful way of comparing the distribution of lexical and grammatical items in any text is to establish a measure of lexical density. This can be done by simply dividing the number of lexical items by the number of clauses in the text. If we follow this system of measuring lexical density, we find that the above extract from text 2.3 has 19 lexical items spread across 4 clauses, thereby giving it a lexical density of 5.

Compare this with an extract from text 2.1, the spoken text:

> *Student:* Like I reckon he would have been really nice but now that he's been to all the towns and seen like there's no life or anything and he comes into the valley and sees Ann and sees life and he just wanted power over her because he's never had power or anything before.

In this extract, there are 14 lexical items distributed across 10 clauses, thus the text has a lexical density of 1.4. The spoken text has a considerably lower lexical density per clause than the written text. As Halliday points out (1985a:61), this is a characteristic difference between spoken and written language. Written language typically is more lexically dense than spoken language. This is not because the topics of written texts are necessarily different. In the above extracts from texts 2.1 and 2.3, the topics are similar, that is both texts are descriptions of the characters from the novel *Z for Zachariah*. The difference lies in the mode of organizing and presenting information. Written language is relatively dense: more information is packed into a single clause. Spoken language is relatively sparse.

How does this happen? What makes the written text more lexically dense than the spoken? What different aspects of the grammar are utilized in the construction of spoken and written texts?

Consider the first clause in the extract from text 2.3, one of the written texts:

> Ann Burden physically is a slim girl, with short, roughly cut, mousy blonde hair.

The structure of the clause itself is very simple. Like many clauses in English, the structure is subject ('Ann Burden'), followed by verb ('is', part of the verb 'to be'), followed by a complement to the subject ('a slim girl, with short, roughly cut, mousy blonde hair'). However, if we look at the group of words that make up the subject and complement in the clause, we get an idea of what makes the written text lexically dense. The complement in particular consists of a long and complex nominal group. Nominal groups (Halliday, 1985a:72) are groups of words organized around a noun which forms the head of the group. A nominal group may consist of only one noun:

Ann Burden
(head)

he
(head)

It may consist of the head noun, preceded by one or more modifying elements:

a	withholding	person
(modifier)	(modifier)	(head)

a	mature	and	affectionate	young	lady
(m)	(m)		(m)	(m)	(h)

Or it may consist of the head noun, preceded by modifiers, and followed by either phrases or clauses which qualify the head:

many	things	of the spirit
(m)	(h)	(qualifier)

an	admirable	character	who is kind and sensitive
(m)	(m)	(h)	(qualifier)

Since qualifiers consist of phrases and clauses, they may contain additional nominal groups themselves, as in the nominal group which makes up the complement referred to above, from text 2.3:

a	slim	girl	with short roughly cut mousy blonde hair
(m)	(m)	(h)	(qualifier)

short	roughly	cut	mousy	blonde	hair
(m)	(m)	(m)	(m)	(m)	(h)

It is the composition of this nominal group which makes the clause lexically dense. This composition enables a list of Ann's physical attributes to be presented in one clause.

A comparison of other nominal groups in text 2.1 (the spoken text) and text 2.3 (the written text) reveals some of their differences:

Written text	*Spoken text*
a mature and affectionate young lady	I
a tanned complexion from working in the sun	he
the spiritual life and hope	the towns
the nuclear destruction and deadness	life
	Ann

While the spoken text contains a few longish nominal groups, such as 'that sort of attitude', 'life of power and glory', overall the written text contains many longer and more lexically dense nominal groups than the spoken text. Longer nominal groups enable a written text to compress information, to convey more content within its clauses. Spoken language can convey the same amount of 'content', but it employs more clauses to do so.

The differences in lexical density found in these two short extracts are representative of differences that occur across the whole of texts 2.1, 2.2 and 2.3. Text 2.1 (the spoken text), for example, has an overall lexical density of 1.5, while text 2.2 (Mr Loomis) has a lexical density of 2.7, and text 2.3 (Ann Burden) has a lexical density of 3.8. Both written texts have a considerably higher lexical density than the spoken text.

It is interesting to pursue the investigation of nominal groups a little further. The texts that we have been discussing are those produced by year 9 students who, although clearly competent students, are still developing as readers and writers. In order to gain some idea of the direction in which they are heading, it is instructive to examine some written texts that adults are expected to deal with. Consider the following extracts, texts 2.4 and 2.5.

Text 2.4 Extract from newspaper article

Shutdown Nearer as More Hospital Staff Resign

Further staff resignations from Sydney's only repatriation hospital may force it to close later this month. Following a meeting on Thursday, the majority of the 47 medical specialists and administration officers at Concord Repatriation and General Hospital have decided to resign, joining the 112 medical officers who resigned last Monday in support of a better pay deal.

Sydney Morning Herald, 4 April 1988, p. 3.

Text 2.4 is from a newspaper article and thus is written with the general public in mind. That is, it does not assume any prior knowledge or particular technical skill. Nominal groups in this text include:

1	Further	staff resignations	from Sydney's only repatriation hospital
	(modifier)	(head)	(qualifier)

2 the majority (head) of the 47 medical specialists and administration officers at Concord Repatriation and General Hospital (qualifier)

Because newspaper articles have to be short and to the point, they pack as much information as possible into a short space, typically through the use of long nominal groups such as those quoted above.

Another extract, this time from a textbook on policy, is in text 2.5:

Text 2.5 Extract from tertiary textbook

> **The Policy Process in the Modern Capitalist State**
>
> This familiarity sprang in part from the long standing interest in the operation of government and in policy issues among academics and researchers. Studies which had originally developed out of the work of political scientists, economists and others were now embraced by the emerging policy analysis perspective. (Ham and Hill, 1984:2)

In this extract, the nominal groups include:

1 the (m) long (m) standing (m) interest (h) in the operation of government and in policy issues among academics and researchers (qualifier)

2 studies (h) which had originally developed out of the work of political scientists, economists and others (qualifier)

In texts such as this, there is another interesting process in operation within the nominal groups.

Nominalization in written texts

The use of long nominal groups does something else besides increasing the lexical density of a text. It enables much of the content of written texts to be coded as nouns. That is, it *nominalizes* much of the content. In spoken texts, the content is coded in lexical items which may be verbs and adjectives as well as nouns, whereas the tendency in writing is for much of the content to occur as 'things'. For example, text 2.5, the policy text, contains a number of nominalizations. These are listed below, and the likely spoken version is shown beside each item:

Nominalizations in text 2.3	*Likely spoken version*
familiarity (noun)	something which is familiar (adjective)
studies (noun)	studying (verb)
the work (noun)	working (verb)
analysis (noun)	analysing (verb)

What has happened is that the actions have been nominalized: they have been turned into things. This process of nominalization is relevant to the nature of speech and writing referred to earlier. The actions of speech, which help to build its character as dynamic, become the nominalizations or 'things' of the written mode, which help to build the character of being 'fixed'. Once actions have been turned into things in written texts, they can do what other nouns can do; that is, they can act on other things or they can themselves be acted upon. As the text becomes increasingly nominalized, there are fewer people doing the actions. In the policy text, for example, it is 'familiarity', 'studies' and 'emerging policy analysis perspective' that are acting and being acted upon. This process of nominalization is a feature of many written texts, especially those of academic genres, and usually is associated with the build-up of abstraction within the text. This means that the abstract concept itself is the focus of discussion and the doer of the action, rather than people. If we 'translate' the policy text into a spoken version, the role of people becomes more obvious. For example:

> It was familiar, because academics and researchers had been interested for a long time in how governments operate, and how people decide on policy. Political scientists, economists, and other people had studied these things, and now they were taken up by people who were interested in analysing policy.

What such a 'translation' does is to change some of the nominalizations into verbs and qualities:

Written version		*Spoken version*
familiarity	becomes	it was familiar
long standing interest	becomes	had been interested for a long time
operation of government	becomes	how governments operate
policy issues	becomes	how people decide on policy
studies	becomes	people who had studied
policy analysis	becomes	people who were interested in analysing policy

The translation 'unpacks' some of the nominalizations that occur in the written text. This is why it appears a little easier to understand. However, it also makes the text more cumbersome: 'policy analysis' is much more succinct than 'people who were interested in analysing policy'. Nominalization, and the abstraction that results from it, is functional in that it enables abstract concepts to be discussed. It enables complex arguments to be summarized and then used as a basis for further discussion or argument.

Much of the language of subjects like history and English is characterized by nominalization and abstraction. Science, geography and economics all utilize nominalization in the build-up of the technical lexis which forms the basis of their taxonomies of the world. In chapter 5, Cope and Kalantzis take up some of these matters in the social sciences, while Martin considers the technical language of the natural sciences in chapter 4.

Grammatical intricacy

The discussion of lexical density could be interpreted as indicating that written language is more complex than spoken. While in one way this is true, it is quite untrue in another very important sense. I shall return to the brief extracts from the year 9 spoken and written text to explain what I mean. These extracts are presented again, this time set out clause by clause:

Written version (text 2.3)

1. Ann Burden physically is a slim girl with short roughly cut mousy blonde hair
2. She has a tanned complexion from working in the sun
3. and wears men's clothes
4. for they are the most practical for farming

Spoken version (text 2.1)

1. Like I reckon
2. he would have been really nice
3. but now that he's been to all the towns
4. and seen
5. like there's no life or anything
6. and he comes into the valley
7. and sees Ann
8. and sees life
9. and he just wanted the power over her
10. because he's never had power or anything before

The written extract consists of two sentences. The first contains just one clause, while the second contains three clauses. In the second sentence, clause 4 is in a dependency relationship with clause 3, and both add to clause 2 to form the sentence. Now compare the spoken extract. Here the relationships between the clauses are much more intricate. The entire extract forms one sentence (or *clause complex*, to use the linguistic term). There are three levels of relationship as indicated by the brackets beside the clauses. At the first level are clauses 1 and 2, 4 and 5, then 6, 7 and 8, and then 9 and 10. At the second level, clauses 4 and 5 are added to clause 3, and at the third level, clauses 1 and 2, then 3, 4 and 5, then 6, 7 and 8, and then 9 and 10 add to form the total clause complex. Other sections of the spoken text reveal even more intricate clause complexes.

This situation is characteristic of spoken and written texts. That is, spoken language is typically more grammatically intricate than written language. So, while written language is more complex than spoken language in terms of lexical density, it is also true that spoken language is more complex than written language in terms of its grammatical intricacy. Each is complex in its own way, and each serves the purposes for which it evolved in different ways.

A brief return to text 2.5, the extract from the book on policy, confirms this. The text is now presented again with the lexical items underlined:

Lexical items in textbook extract (text 2.5)

> This familiarity sprang in part from the long standing interest in the operation of government and in policy issues among academics and researchers.
>
> Studies [[which had originally developed out of the work of political scientists, economists and others]] were now embraced by the emerging policy analysis perspective.

The extract comprises two sentences consisting of one clause each, although the second contains an embedded clause ('which had originally developed out of the work of political scientists, economists and others'). However, when this extract is translated into a spoken version, we find the following:

Lexical items in spoken version of text 2.5

> It was familiar
> because academics and researchers for a long time had been interested in
> how governments operate
> and how people decide on policy.
> Political scientists, economists and other people had studied these things
> and now they were taken up by people [[who were interested in analysing policy]]

There are still two sentences, but instead of a total of two clauses there are now six, one of which contains an embedded clause. The sentences of the spoken version are considerably more complex than those in the written text. While the written text has 23 lexical items spread across 2 clauses giving a lexical density of 11.5, the spoken version has 21 lexical items, 6 clauses, and hence a lexical density of 3.5. The written text is lexically denser, while the spoken version is grammatically more intricate.

It should be pointed out that differences in lexical density, nominalization and grammatical intricacy which occur between spoken and written language are not absolute differences. In some contexts the distinctions become rather blurred. This is likely to occur, for example, in texts which are written to be spoken, as for radio, television or public lectures. Such texts will have features of both oral and written language. The differences referred to above represent clusters along a continuum. Generally, however, purposes and contexts in which oral and written language are used are separate, and their linguistic realizations reflect this separation.

STUDENTS' EMERGING CONTROL OF LITERACY

Thus far, I have attempted to describe the similarities and differences between spoken and written modes of language. I have suggested that, while the underlying similarities between the two modes are significant in that each draws on the same linguistic system to make meaning, there are also important differences. These differences lie principally in the areas of lexical density and grammatical intricacy. Written language tends to be lexically dense in comparison to spoken language, and spoken language tends to be grammatically intricate in relation to written language. I have also suggested that these differences exist because of the different natures of spoken and written language, and because of the different purposes each mode fulfils.

It follows that an important part of becoming literate is learning about these differences. How do children become aware of mode differences? How do they learn that when they write, they need to organize meanings in a different way from when they speak?

I shall now examine various stages in emerging control of literacy, by reference to data collected from children of different ages. In doing so, I shall draw on aspects of the comparison of spoken and written language presented above — in particular, the notions of lexical density and grammatical intricacy. I shall suggest that, as children mature as writers, the differences between their spoken and written language become increasingly obvious, and increasingly important. Further, I shall suggest that if students do not develop effective control of the features of written mode described above, their chances of academic success are minimal.

Beginning literacy development

When children begin learning to read and write, the first important thing they learn is that they can make meaning through the written mode. In order to do so, they must learn the conventions of writing, which include, in English, left-to-right progression, word spacing, letter formation, spelling and punctuation. In the very early stages of writing development, what the child actually produces on paper will depend, at least while at school, on the kind of approach to literacy development that is used. Approaches that provide opportunities for frequent reading to children, and opportunities for children to write about their own experiences, are likely to teach that written language is an agency of making meaning. In such circumstances children are able to draw on what they already know about language; that is, they draw on their knowledge of spoken language and whatever information they have of how literacy operates. At this stage what children 'write' is very similar to their spoken utterances. Thus children in kindergarten produce the kinds of text shown in Figures 2.1 and 2.2 (pages 44–5), representing their earliest attempts to come to terms with the written mode.

Both these figures were produced by young children from non-English-speaking backgrounds. Such children clearly have a more difficult task in becoming literate in English than first language users, in that they are learning the oral mode at the same time as they are beginning to learn the written one. However, for such children the underlying processes of becoming literate closely resemble those of children whose mother tongue is English. Fatmir spent a considerable part of his first year at school producing figures like the one shown here in figure 2.1. He regularly drew a series of apparently unrelated objects, such as the house, the boy, the rabbit and the caterpillar in figure 2.1, and then neatly labelled each one. Vlatko, who produced figure 2.2, on the other hand concentrated mainly on drawing

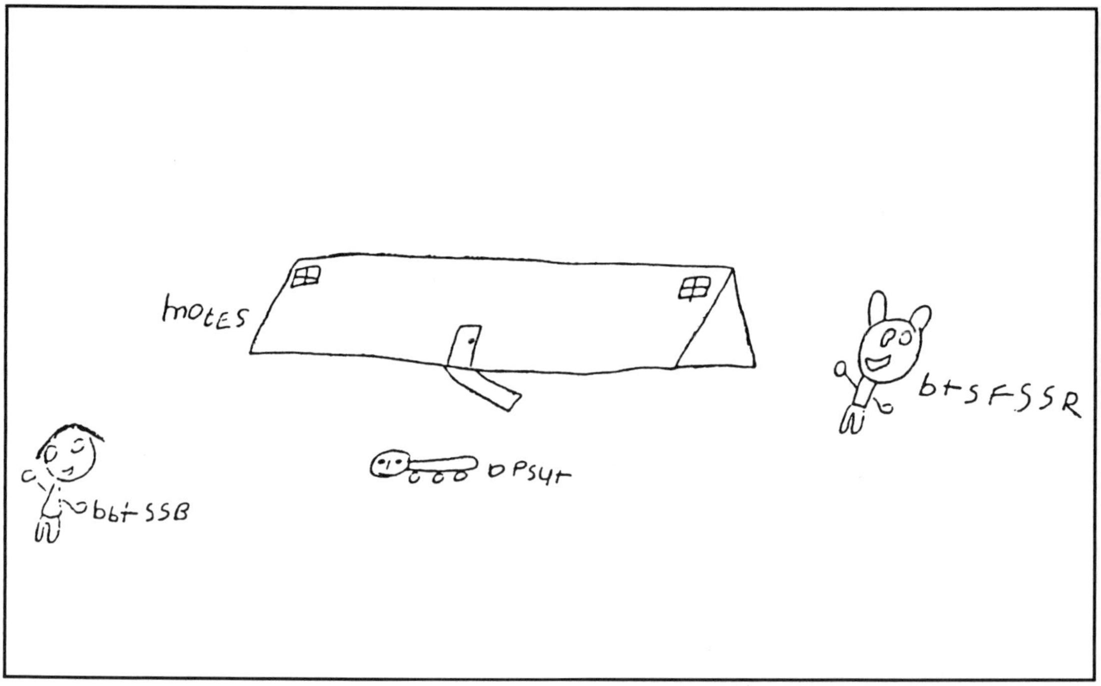

Figure 2.1 Beginning 'writing', by Fatmir, year 1 (reduced size)

elaborate pictures such as the one here, with Indians, cowboys, teepees, horses in a circle, and so on. His writing was of secondary consideration.

In these early attempts, the children were encouraged to move from drawing to writing, so that the drawing became a possible bridge helping them into the written mode. In such situations, the children's efforts to represent experience on paper clearly included the accompanying drawing. For example in figure 2.1, Fatmir's comments 'This is a house', 'This is a boy', etc. make sense only with reference to his drawing. While it is certainly possible for children to learn to write without drawing first, the drawing and attempted writing involve students and teacher in a negotiation of meaning. Such negotiations occur as the teacher reads to the children, and discusses the text being read. They occur when the child shows his or her attempts at producing written texts and then 'reads' to the teacher. These interactions between teacher and students mirror the interaction that occurs between adult and young child as the child begins to learn the mother tongue (Painter, 1986). In the same way as the adult supports and guides the child's early attempts at making meaning in the oral mode, the teacher supports and guides the children in their early attempts at developing control in the written mode. These interactions between student and teacher offer opportunities for discussion of the child's attempts at writing, and opportunities for the teacher to model written language in a way which is relevant to the individual child, and which demonstrates that writing makes meaning. This modelled writing also provides important opportunities for reading for the individual child, as well as for other children in the class.

Figure 2.2 Beginning 'writing', by Vlatko, year 1

Early literacy development lags behind oral language development

In the early stages of literacy development (for most children this includes the first few years at school), young children are considerably more proficient at speaking than at writing. This is partly due to the physical effort involved in producing written texts. But more importantly, young children simply know more about speech than about writing. They have, after all, been learning spoken language for a longer period of time than written language. Halliday, in his book *Spoken and Written Language* (1985a, chapter 1), points to an analogy between the development of the individual and the development of the species. He suggests that in many ways the individual recapitulates the history of the species. Thus, just as the use of the oral mode of language evolved in the human species long before the written mode so, in the development of the individual, the child learns to talk before learning to read and write. When the child begins to read and write, early attempts at written language parallell the kind of spoken language used by a much younger child. Children regress, as it were, to an earlier stage of language development as they begin to develop control of the written mode.

Even in the case of young children from non-English-speaking backgrounds such as Fatmir and Vlatko, control of oral English clearly develops at a much faster rate than that of written English. For example, while in year 1, Fatmir produced text 2.6.

Text 2.6 Beginning 'writing', by Fatmir, year 1

In producing text 2.6, Fatmir drew his picture and then gave his teacher a lengthy oral recount about riding his bike on the footpath near the water and seeing a shark in the water. When the teacher suggested he should write a recount of all these events, he replied that he couldn't, and instead he wrote:

> I bike and the stker [shark].

He read this to his teacher and, in doing so, he realized that it did not make sense. He next wrote:

> I waz riding my bike in the park.

He used some of the print available in the classroom environment to assist him to write this sentence. Thus a rich and quite detailed oral recount became a very simple and considerably less interesting written text.

The gap between Fatmir's control of the oral and the written modes of language is typical of other young children, whether from English-speaking or non-English-speaking backgrounds. Young children, in learning to read and write, are learning a new mode of making meaning. This involves learning the conventions of writing, but it also involves learning the mode differences that exist between spoken and written language, referred to earlier in this chapter. That is, it involves learning the decontextualized nature of written language, learning the structure of different written genres, learning to sequence events in an explicit linear fashion, learning to organize information, and learning to utilize the resources of grammar in different ways. All these aspects of written language are different from spoken language, so it is not surprising that children regress in their use of language for a time while they are developing control of the written mode.

Developing awareness of mode differences

The differences in proficiency between speaking and writing are apparent in the language development of young children for many years. However, primary school children demonstrate an increasing awareness of mode differences in their own use of spoken and written language, largely as a result of their language experiences both at school and at home. Christie (e.g. 1984a, 1985a), in her work on children's writing development, argues that it is context rather than stage of development that shapes children's growing awareness of oral and written modes of language. She demonstrates that the patterns of interaction occurring in the class between teacher and student are reflected in the written genres produced by children at school. For example, the patterns of the Morning News session and other such activities provide opportunities for a rehearsal of several early written genres of personal experience. As well, the reading that children engage in, both at home and at school, contributes to their developing awareness of the written mode of language. The more children read, and the greater the range of genres they encounter, the more they will learn about how written language works. However, as well as being involved in classroom activities that provide a rehearsal for written genres, and having opportunities for reading, children themselves need to engage in writing for specific purposes. If children receive support and guidance from their teachers in how to go about writing effectively in a range of genres, they can demonstrate increasing control of the mode features, referred to earlier, from quite a young age.

The following texts are part of the classroom discourse recorded in a year 3 class. The class had been engaged in a unit of work on traditional Aborigines. In the lesson in which this recording was made, teacher and students wrote a class-negotiated report about the kinds of food that traditional Aboriginal people ate. The classroom discourse that preceded the writing focused on what the children knew about food eaten by traditional Aborigines. The children contributed freely, either by recounting a relevant experience or by offering information. An example is given in text 2.7.

Text 2.7 Class discussion

Student: When we were in Queensland
my dad had some friends up there
and he asked
if we could borrow some guns for hunting and everything
and as we were all going there
we could see their paintings
like rocks and things got patterns on them and everything

Teacher: Good. Yes?

Student: When they find them in trees
sometimes they cut the roots off
and if they're strong roots
they put rocks around them
and they put the poison mixed in the water
and the fish lay down dead.

When it came to negotiating the written report, again the children participated freely, but the nature of their contributions was somewhat different. Here they were offering sentences that would form part of the written text. That is, in text 2.7 the children's contributions were oral statements that added to the shared class knowledge on the topic of the food eaten by traditional Aboriginals, while in text 2.8 the children's contributions, although spoken, were spoken to be written, that is, to add to the shared class report.

Text 2.8 Spoken contributions for written report

Student: Aborigines usually eat fish seafood as their main meal.

Teacher: (*writing*) Aborigines usually eat seafood. Okay. Yes?

Student: Aborigines used to cook their food in hot open fires
and they used to put in hot coals.

Teacher: (*writing*) Aborigines cooked their food, yeah, on hot open fires.
Okay, what else? Come on.

Student: Aborigines catch fish in nets
and when it was high tide
they would come
and get the fish.

Teacher: (*writing*) Fish in nets. Is that what you said? Yep?

Student: Aboriginals hunt for their food.

Student: Aboriginals spear ducks and birds by hiding in the reeds.

Student: Aboriginals eat emus, snails and eggs.

(Parts of the teacher's responses have been omitted in this text for the sake of brevity.)

If we compare the lexical density and grammatical intricacy of these two sections of the class discourse, we find similar patterns to those described earlier in the comparison of spoken and written language. Text 2.7 has the typical features of a spoken text. It contains 25 lexical items (e.g. Queensland, dad, friends). These are spread over 13 clauses and hence the whole text has a lexical density of 2. Text 2.8 on the other hand, contains 38 lexical items (e.g. Aborigines, fish seafood, main meal) spread over 10 clauses, and has a lexical density of 3.8, almost double that of text 2.7.

The nominal groups in text 2.8 are somewhat longer than those in text 2.7 although the differences here are not as great as those between the spoken and written texts produced by the year 9 students. For example:

Nominal groups in text 2.8	*Nominal groups in text 2.7*
fish seafood	we
ducks and birds	some friends
emus, snails and eggs	their paintings

However, text 2.8 is notably different in its use of circumstantial information, which provides additional details of how activities are undertaken, or of where they take place. For example:

Circumstantial information in text 2.8

> eat fish seafood <u>as their main meal</u>
> cook their food <u>in hot open fires</u>
> spear ducks and birds <u>by hiding in the reeds</u>

Such details are not necessary in spoken texts, as the context in which the spoken text is created typically provides this kind of information. It would appear that the students have a good sense of the need for written texts to be 'decontexualized'.

When we compare the grammatical structure of the sentences, we find that those in text 2.7 are considerably more intricate than the sentences in text 2.8. For example:

Grammatical structure of text 2.7

> When they find them in trees
> sometimes they cut the roots off
> and if they're strong roots
> they put rocks around them
> and they put the poison mixed in the water
> and the fish lay down dead.

Grammatical structure of text 2.8

> Aborigines usually eat fish seafood as their main meal.
> Aborigines used to cook their food in hot open fires,
> and they used to put in hot coals.

Thus, although the children are clearly still developing as writers, these texts reflect the patterns discussed previously, where spoken texts are lexically sparse but grammatically intricate, and written texts are lexically dense but grammatically less intricate. Such patterns contribute to the different qualities of the spoken and written texts.

The differences between texts 2.7 and 2.8 are interesting in that both were taken from the same class discourse on the same day and are about the same topic. The major difference between them is one of mode. Text 2.7 is typical spoken classroom discourse, while text 2.8, although spoken, was spoken to be written. The children knew that their contributions were to be used in the written class report, and consequently the differences between their contributions in the two texts clearly indicate the extent of their awareness of mode differences.

The role of the teacher

The role of the teacher in providing information about the written mode of language was a particularly significant feature of the lesson in which texts 2.7 and 2.8 were recorded. She had ensured, through work done in previous lessons, that the children had adequate information about the topic on which they were to write their report. She began this lesson by asking the children for relevant information and listing their contributions on the board. This information was used as a basis for negotiating the appropriate structure and organization of the shared class report. The discussion which followed focused on the purpose and structure of a report, as well as a suitable means of organizing the available information. At this stage of the school year, the children were familiar with terms like 'narrative' and 'report', as well as with those referring to text structures, so they had a shared class language which enabled them to discuss the construction of this report in quite explicit detail. For example, the discussion covered the need for a general introduction, comparison of introductions of various reports written by the class, the contrast between the structure of reports and the structure of narratives, and ways of organizing the information around the notions of hunting, fishing and gathering. The teacher and students together negotiated the writing of the text. Thus the report not only provided a model for the children to use in their own writing, but a model which the children themselves had actively constructed. The support and guidance provided by the teacher, which was a regular feature of this class, contributed in no small way to the children's developing awareness of mode differences, revealed through the analysis of texts 2.7 and 2.8.

Development of mode awareness: an ongoing process

Analysis of texts 2.7 and 2.8 indicates that the year 3 children who produced the texts already have a developing understanding of mode differences and of the requirements of writing texts for specific purposes. However, development of awareness of mode differences, and particularly development of awareness of requirements of written genres, continues for many years. We find evidence of this ongoing development of mode awareness if we return to texts 2.2 and 2.3, the two written texts produced by the year 9 students.

The lexical density of both texts 2.2 and 2.3 varies somewhat from section to section within the texts. This is particularly noticeable in text 2.2 in sections such as:

When Ann mentioned to Mr Loomis right at the end
that if he had already killed Edward
he might as well kill her
he falls to pieces
and says she doesn't know that for sure
so we also know Mr Loomis has feelings of remorse
about killing Edward
and that he didn't really think of the consequences.

In the student's text all of the above is one sentence, which consists of seven clauses. The lexical density of this section is 2.2, that is, it is lower than the average (2.7) for the whole text. Grammatically, the sentence is considerably more intricate than many of the others in the same text. Compare, for example, the following sentences, which appear in the same text:

Mr Loomis is totally opposite in character to Ann.
Mr Loomis never lets anyone stop him
if he wants to do something.

Here, the writer is using a more 'spoken' way of expressing herself. This section of the text indicates that, like the children in the year 3 class, she is still developing control of the written mode.

CONCLUSION

In this chapter, I have addressed the question of whether learning to read and write is the same as learning to speak. In doing so, I have compared the spoken and written modes of language. I have suggested that, because each evolved to fulfil different purposes, they draw differently from the underlying linguistic systems of English, and that the differences are most clearly reflected in patterns of lexical density and grammatical intricacy.

In regard to learning to speak and learning to read and write, I have suggested that, in the early stages of literacy development, learning to read and write is, in many ways, similar to learning to speak. Thus early literacy instruction can usefully be informed by what we know of how children learn their oral language. However, as literacy development continues, it becomes less and less like learning to speak. The analysis of the short section of text 2.2 shows that students in secondary school are still developing control of the written mode. This is because learning to read and write is an involved and complex activity, which continues throughout life. Even professional writers continue to work hard at getting their writing right. University students (at least those concerned with the quality of their work) draft and redraft their assignments. This paper, as a case in point, has been through several drafts before reaching its present stage. A more conscious, deliberate and analytic effort is involved in learning to read and write than in learning to speak. As students learn new fields, or new content areas, and new written genres, they face new demands in the use of language in the written mode. Becoming proficient in utilizing these genres takes time and effort. The further a child progresses through school, the more significant are the differences between spoken and written language, and the more important it is for teachers to be aware, and to provide information about these differences for their students. Being unable to control these differences will contribute to a student's failure at school. A 'fresh look' at literacy must acknowledge the differences, as well as the similarities, between learning to speak and learning to read and write.

REFERENCES

Barnes, D., Britton, J., & Rosen, H. (1971). *Language, the learner and the school.* Harmondsworth, Middlesex: Penguin.

Britton, J. (1970). *Language and learning*. Harmondsworth, Middlesex: Penguin.

Cambourne, B. (1985, August). *Rediscovering natural literacy learning: Old wine in a new bottle*. Paper presented at Early Years in Education Seminar. Perth, WA.

Cambourne, B., & Turbill, J. (1987). *Coping with chaos*. Sydney: Primary English Teaching Association.

Christie, F. (1984a). Young children's writing development: The relationship of written genres to curriculum genres. In B. Bartlett & J. Carr (Eds.), *Language in education conference: A report of proceedings*. Brisbane: Brisbane College of Advanced Education, Mt Gravatt Campus.

Christie, F. (Ed.) (1984b). *Children writing* (B.Ed. course Study Guide and Reader). Geelong, Victoria: Deakin University Press.

Christie, F. (1985a, August). *Language and context: The development of meaning*. Paper presented at the 14th New Zealand Conference on Reading. Nelson, New Zealand.

Christie, F. (1985b). *Language education*. Geelong, Victoria: Deakin University Press.

Eggins, S., Wignell, P., & Martin, J. R. (1987). The discourse of history: Distancing the recoverable past. *Working Papers No. 5*. Univeristy of Sydney: Linguistics Department.

Goodman, K. (1986). *What's whole in whole language?* Ontario: Scholastic TAB Publications.

Graves, D. (1983). *Writing: Teachers and children at work*. London: Heinemann Educational Books.

Gray, B. (1985). Teaching oral English. In M. Christie (Ed.), *Aboriginal perspectives on experience and learning: The role of language in Aboriginal education*. Geelong, Victoria: Deakin University Press.

Gray, B. (1987). How natural is natural language teaching? Employing wholistic methodology in the classroom. *Australian Journal of Early Childhood*, **12** (4), 87–104.

Halliday, M. A. K. (1975). *Learning how to mean: Explorations in the development of language*. London: Edward Arnold.

Halliday, M. A. K. (1978). *Language as a social semiotic: The social interpretation of language and meaning*. London: Edward Arnold.

Halliday, M. A. K. (1985a). *Spoken and written language*. Geelong, Victoria: Deakin University Press.

Halliday, M. A. K. (1985b). *An introduction to functional grammar*. London: Edward Arnold.

Halliday, M. A. K., & Hasan, R. (1976). *Cohesion in English*. London: Longman.

Halliday, M. A. K., & Hasan, R. (1985). *Language context and text: A social semiotic perspective*. Geelong, Victoria: Deakin University Press.

Ham, C., & Hill, M. (1984). *The policy process in the modern capitalist state*. Brighton: Harvester Press.

Hammond, J. (1986). The effect of modelling reports and narratives on the writing of the Year 2 children from non-English-speaking backgrounds. *Australian Review of Applied Linguistics*, **9** (2), 75–93.

Hammond, J. (1987a). Process or genre in teaching ESL children to write? *Proceedings of 5th ATESOL Summer School*. Sydney: ATESOL Association.

Hammond, J. (1987b). An overview of the genre-based approach to the teaching of writing in Australia. *Australian Review of Applied Linguistics*, **10** (2).

Hammond, J. (forthcoming). Oral and written language in the educational context. In M. A. K. Halliday, J. Gibbons, & H. Nicholas (Eds.). *Selected Proceedings of the 8th World Congress of Applied Linguistics*. The Netherlands: John Benjamins.

Martin, J. R. (1985). *Factual writing*. Geelong, Victoria: Deakin University Press.

Martin, J. R. (1986, July). *Genres and language learning: Writing as a social process in an infants school*. Keynote paper presented at the Twelfth Australian Reading Association Conference. Perth, WA.

Murray, D. M. (1982). *Learning by teaching: Selected articles on writing and teaching*. Montclair, New Jersey: Boynton/Cook Publishers Inc.

O'Brien, R. (1975). *Z for Zachariah*. New York: Fontana Books.

Painter, C. (1985). *Learning the mother tongue*. Geelong, Victoria: Deakin University Press.

Painter, C. (1986). The role of interaction in learning to speak and write. In C. Painter & J. R. Martin (Eds.), *Writing to mean: Teaching genres across the curriculum*. Occasional Papers No. 9. Melbourne: Applied Linguistics Association of Australia.

Rothery, J. (1986). Teaching writing in the primary school: A genre-based approach to the development of writing abilities. *Working Papers No. 4*. University of Sydney: Linguistics Department.

Rowles, L., & Hammond, J. (1988). Providing a balance. In J. Collerson (Ed.), *Writing for Life*. Sydney: Primary English Teaching Association.

Smith, F. (1979). The language arts and the learner's mind. *Language Arts*, **56** (2), 118–125.

Smith, F. (1983). Reading like a writer. *Language Arts*, **60** (5). 558–567.

Shutdown nearer as more hospital staff resign. (1988, 2 April). *Sydney Morning Herald*.

Walshe, R. D. (1981). *Every child can write*. Sydney: Primary English Teaching Association.

Wignell, P., Martin, J. R., & Eggins, S. (1987). The discourse of geography: Ordering and explaining the experiential world. *Working Papers No. 5*. University of Sydney: Linguistics Department.

3 Authorizing disadvantage: authorship and creativity in the language classroom

PAM GILBERT

Several years ago I planned and directed the production of a short video titled *We're Authors Too* (Gilbert, 1983). The video was filmed in a local primary school in Townsville, with a year 2 teacher with whom I had been working over a number of months. I had been impressed with the way in which this teacher organized her writing classroom, and was keen to capture on film some of her strategies and approaches.

The title for the video actually came from one of the students in the year 2 classroom. On one of the days when we were filming the group, the teacher read Christabel Mattingley's *Black Dog* to the class, and then followed the reading with a class discussion of Mattingley as an author. During the discussion, one of the 6-year-olds in the class raised her hand and remarked to the teacher and to the class, 'We're authors too — just like Christabel Mattingley'.

At the time, the girl's words provided just the catchy title I wanted for the video, for the theme of 'authorship' seemed a very appropriate one to focus on in a discussion of this classroom. When it was writing time, these children were described by their teacher as 'authors', not students; their written work was said to be 'published' when it was typed and put in cardboard covers; they were shown how they might treat their classmates' publications as 'real' literature by giving serious and apparently perceptive consideration to the texts produced; and their teacher acted as an editorial adviser and publicity agent.

The children wrote regularly and chose most of their own topics and writing forms; they read their work aloud to their classmates and their

Thanks to Bill Corcoran, Allan Luke, and Geoff Ward for their advice on earlier drafts of this chapter.

teacher, and were offered comments and advice about how such work might be changed; and the final draft written work — edited by student and teacher for conventional spelling and punctuation, and later typed by a parent — formed one of the main components of the classroom reading materials. Most researchers and teachers who are concerned about positive and supportive classroom environments for early learners would have been, I am sure, as impressed as I was by the way in which the acquisition of early literacy skills seemed to be facilitated by this authorship game.

For it was, in fact, a 'game' — a pretence, a 'role play' — and like other games children must play at school, it reinforced particular values, in this case those of independent student learning and responsible group work. It also offered a seriousness of purpose ('real' writing, as 'real' writers supposedly write) and some authenticity of response to children's school work — both often regarded as necessary ingredients for a successful writing programme. It meant that children's experiences could be valued and their decision making respected, and it offered the possibility that the work of text construction — the labour of authoring — could become a legitimate focus of study in the writing classroom.

However, in the wider public sphere, authorship has often not been associated with the work of writing, nor with most forms of writing. Consider how few forms of writing are currently associated with an author, for instance, the writing of legal contracts, of advertising copy, of journalistic reports, of textbooks, of instruction manuals and leaflets, of the documents of government, banking, commerce and industry. Most of the language encountered in our daily lives is *not* 'authored' language. Instead, authorship has come to be associated with a romantic concept of writing, through its identification with a particular type of reading and writing, a particular form of discourse. The term *romantic* as it is used here derives from its older meaning that developed in the late eighteenth and early nineteenth centuries. It was in particular associated with traditions of writing literature which tended to value freedom of the imagination more than attention to form. A romantic interest in literature, incidentally, emerged at about the same period as the interest in rhetoric declined, a matter dealt with in some detail by Christie in chapter 1 of this book.

Currently, it is *literary* works — creative, imaginative works — that are traditionally 'authored', and the construction of an artistic text that demands 'authorship'. Of all the many contemporary written forms, it is still only literary discourse which relies so obviously on concepts of authoring and authorship to function. And even this is relatively modern. In the Middle Ages, for example, literary works were not authored, but instead were seen to be part of a collective enterprise, the product of the culture at large. The need to have an author's name attached to a work came with the romantic shift to the individual, the human person. An author's name could then protect the property of a work by indicating if plagiarism had occurred. As a result, any concept of an author as a worker, as one who crafted and constructed language as in the Middle Ages, was obscured by the concept of an author as the individual who 'owned' a work, the individual who owned the imagination which inspired the work. Consequently, the sources of an author's inspiration, of an author's imagination, or of an author's creativity, have often been regarded as special, even unique, and hence they have become the focus of the study of literature.

Not surprisingly, the introduction of authorship concepts into literacy learning has come since the 1960s, in the wake of a strong classroom commitment to the personal, imaginative and creative nature of language. This focus has been particularly responsible for an interest in children's expressive and imaginative writing, and also, in more recent years, for the switch from basal reading schemes to literature-based early reading programmes. As a result, the aspects of authorship which mesh most closely with popular assumptions in literacy classrooms are not about work, not about texts, and not about construction. Instead they are about imagination, expression, and creation: about personal and creative growth through language.

The limitations of such a focus are not as immediately obvious in early primary years as they are later. However, the confusion and disadvantage generated by personal growth-oriented language theories compatible with authorship concepts become very apparent in the secondary school. At the same time as I was preparing the *We're Authors Too* video, I was also working with a year 12 English teacher and her class in a study of differing perceptions of school writing and reading. The shift from the year 2 'authorship' classroom to a senior English classroom at the other end of the school, in which assessment is of considerable significance, was a salutary one. So, too, was the shift from the 'authorship' discourse of the year 2 classroom to the many other discourses about writing which abound, not only in writing research studies, but in the descriptions of school writing offered by students and teachers, and also in contemporary critical theory. Some of these perceptions will be introduced in this chapter.

I now feel less confident than I initially did about the value of terms like *authorship* for literacy classrooms. Far from regarding authorship as a novel and reasonably effective way of encouraging children to write and to read, I am now concerned about the way this term, like many before it, may operate to the disadvantage of many children by perpetuating romantic notions of writing as creative and individual expression, and of reading as personal and original meaning making. I am concerned that concepts like authoring might obscure the fact that school writing is about the acquisition of *specific cultural capital*, to use Pierre Bourdieu's term (1973). The term is a useful one, for it proposes that there are certain kinds of knowledge that are culturally valued and privileged. It is in this sense that knowledge becomes 'capital' which one can use. The cultural capital that concerns me now is knowledge about the ways in which our language system works.

As a result, I would claim that the use of authoring or authorship terms — like the use of the terms 'creative writing' in the 1960s and 'personal response' in the 1970s — may operate to disenfranchise many children from any real understanding of the social, learned nature of writing and reading, and to deny them access to the obvious power of cultural literacy. I would suggest that such terms serve to authorize some children's disadvantage because they construct an image of language learning which is personal, not learned; individual, not social; innate, not environmental.

This may seem an unnecessarily strong criticism to make of pedagogical practices which have offered some useful ideas for classroom strategies in the early years of schooling, and been responsible for a significant interest and concern in children's writing and reading development. But I think a note of warning should be sounded about the authorship fervour. In the rest of this chapter, I shall offer a critical re-examination of the concept of authorship, and in so doing shall:

- consider the way in which the concept has been used in terms of schooling and literacy — particularly in relation to the development of writing ability — and of how it is compatible with a number of other popular assumptions about learning to read and write which have emphasized the 'creative' and 'original' nature of writing, and the 'personal' and 'individual' nature of reading;
- reappraise these popular assumptions about reading and writing, in terms of their inadequacies as a basis for language learning, and in terms of the confusion they have helped to generate in classrooms;
- suggest other approaches to learning to read and learning to write by considering theories about the socially constructed nature of reading and writing practices;
- read some school children's writing and consider other ways of describing authorship which rely on discussions of textuality rather than creativity.

AUTHORSHIP AND SCHOOLING

To understand how the concept of authorship has become part of the language of the classroom, it is necessary to look to some of the well-known writing textbooks to see what they have claimed of the term, and how they have used it. For instance, Donald Graves, whose work has in many ways popularized the 'writing as process' approach to the teaching of writing, has this to say about the way in which children can be regarded as authors:

> . . . *no distinctions are made* between the reading of children's writing and the writing of professionals. Both are treated as important writing with the same scrutiny given to the information in each by using the same process: receive the work, discuss what is contained in the piece, then formulate questions for the author. The mystique of authorship is removed that children may find out the beauty and depth of information contained in literature itself. It is removed that children might learn to think and experience the joys of authorship for themselves. (Graves, 1983:76)

In this passage, Graves suggests links between professional published literature and children's writing. He suggests that there should be no difference in the way each is read, no difference in the way each is regarded, and — it would seem — no difference in the way each is constructed. In later sections of this chapter, I shall challenge these claims more closely, but for the moment, consider how possible such prescriptions are for student writing in the context of the school.

Is it possible for teachers to read children's writing as professional literature? Is it likely that teachers would choose to do so? Why would such a situation be desirable?

Graves follows a long line of English education writers who have argued that children's writing should be the 'literature of the classroom' (see Dixon, 1967): that children's texts have the same qualities as professional literature and deserve the same earnestness of reading. Such exhortations — well intentioned as they obviously are — urging teachers to value children's experiences and to read children's writing with care and attention, have helped to perpetuate a number of misleading assumptions about the nature of literature and of writing. Such assumptions deny — or at least obscure — the socially constructed nature of both reading and writing. It is through participation in social practice that people learn to read and to write.

Privileging the literary experience

In the passage cited, Graves claims that if the differences between published professional literature and children's writing could be dissolved, then 'the joys of authorship' would be accessible to children: the mystique of the adult professional author would be removed. Anyone could be an author and experience the joys of authorship, although Graves is not explicit about what these 'joys' are , other than to espouse a romantic concept of literature as a form of writing which has 'beauty and depth'. There are several difficulties with such assertions.

First, and most important, the view of literature which Graves asserts — and assumes — can no longer be so confidently asserted and assumed. While the dimensions of the contemporary debate about literature cannot be explored in any depth here, it should be stressed that a very significant debate does indeed exist at the moment (see, for example, Reid, 1982 and Hollingworth, 1983 for different perspectives on this debate), and has existed for the past decade or more. This debate brings into question not only the nature of what counts as literature, but also under what conditions it is possible for material to count as literature, and whose interests are best served by the traditions of literature.

Historically, literature has served some social groups infinitely better than others, and classrooms are often telling reminders of this legacy. For instance, it may be worth considering what 'beauty and depth of information' Aboriginal children in primary classrooms or adolescent girls in secondary classrooms are likely to find in both the literature available and that selected for classroom use. Literary selections in schools are still predominantly concerned with the 'beauty and depth of information' of growing up white, male and middle class, as the NATE's *Alice In Genderland* (1985), the IRA's *Sex Stereotypes and Reading* (Sheridan, 1982), and Bob Dixon's two *Catching Them Young* volumes (1977) testify.

Literature is clearly not an ideologically neutral field, and we need to be very careful in ascribing automatic value to things literary. Two earlier studies of mine have examined the ideology implicit in children's 'authored' school texts to emphasize this point (Gilbert, 1988a, 1988b). It is obviously naïve to imagine that any constructed text — professional literature, school textbook, teenage comic, or a child's story — does not carry ideological messages, and a number of important studies have emphasized exactly this issue. Rob Gilbert's study of British social science textbooks (Gilbert, 1984) demonstrates how the ideology implicit in the texts was at odds with the stated egalitarian and participatory goals of the subjects; Allan Luke's study of Canadian basal readers (Luke, 1988) indicates how the nature of the basals' narratives contributed towards a particular concept of literacy and literacy instruction; and Linda Christian-Smith's study of commercial romance novels (Christian-Smith, 1988) examines the ways in which romantic ideology is marketed at girls and women. Such studies demonstrate how important it is to question textual neutrality, and to look at how texts have been produced. We clearly need to be careful in ascribing automatic value to any text, or to any 'creator' of text.

The author as creator of texts

An orthodox view of literature — and certainly a prevailing one in school textbooks — is that literature stems from the creative unconsciousness of the individual author. It is the author who provides the imagination, inspiration and personal vision for the work, who creates and expresses the work. It is also the author who supplies the individuality and originality of a piece of literature, its claim to be treated differently from other works. Significantly, while literary study is concerned with techniques used by authors — narrative structure, characterization devices, symbolism and motifs, points of view and so on — its predominant concern is with an alleged creative vision which guides the use of these techniques, or one which is independent of them. The *craft* of writing is thus bypassed in favour of the *creativity* of writing.

As a result, convention and technique — as artificial, contrived, mechanical — are opposed to authorial expression, regarded as individual and spontaneous. As Pierre Macherey argues in *A Theory of Literary Production*, the act of creation bypasses mechanics, and becomes instead a sort of religious experience:

> The various 'theories' of creation all ignore the process of making; they omit any account of production. One can create undiminished, so, paradoxically, creation is the release of what is already there; or, one is witness of a sudden apparition, and then creation is an irruption, an epiphany, a mystery. In both instances any possible explanation of the change has been done away with . . . All speculation over man [*sic*] the creator is intended to eliminate a real knowledge: the 'creative process' is, precisely, not a process, a labour; it is a religious formula to be found on funeral monuments. (Macherey, 1978:68)

Instead of attending to the craft of writing, theories of creation dwell on a mysterious, personal outpouring of language which cannot be explained, cannot be understood and, most importantly for this paper, cannot, presumably, be taught.

Linked with this 'creative process' is the modern assumption of the unique qualities of the author's vision, of the author's originality and individuality. Such a concept of the literary text as a natural, creative and unified expression from a gifted individual presents literature as a holistic, personal, and spontaneous interpretation of human experience, and thus obscures the process of the *production* of the literary text. The emphasis is not on the nature of the social and ideologically constructed artefact, but on its idiosyncratic interpretation of human experience.

Writing as authoring

This is very much the way in which writing is described in some of the influential school writing textbooks. Consider, for instance, this statement from James Moffett's *Active Voice*, one of the best-known and most widely cited school writing textbooks:

> Educators would do best, I submit, to conceive of writing, first of all, as full-fledged authoring, by which I mean authentic expression of an individual's own ideas, original in the sense that he or she has synthesized them for himself or herself. True authoring occurs naturally to the extent that the writer is composing with raw material, that is, source content not previously abstracted and formulated by others. Teaching aimed this way would emphasize subject matter lying easily at hand within and around the writer — firsthand content like feelings, fantasies, sensations, memories, and reflections, and secondhand content as drawn from interviews, stored information, and the writings of others to the extent that the writer truly abstracts these in his own synthesis. Insisting on maximum authorship should stave off the construing or treating of writing as only some sort of transcription or paraphrasing or verbal tailoring from ready-made cloth. (Moffett, 1981:89)

School writing, in Moffett's argument, is to be regarded as 'full-fledged authoring' — with 'authentic expression', with 'original' ideas, with the 'raw material' of personal feelings and individual synthesis of experience. Authoring is thus a 'natural' process by which the individual gives expression to content which has not previously been 'abstracted and formulated by others'.

Moffett's rejection of a concept of writing as 'transcription', 'paraphrasing', 'verbal tailoring from ready-made cloth' emphasizes the creative power he gives to *authoring*. Authoring is about adding something unique to the world by giving original expression to personal experience. Authoring creates new material. Writing which lacks this creativity, originality and uniqueness belongs to the realm of the secondhand — 'transcription', 'paraphrasing' — and Moffett's tailoring metaphor reinforces this. The material for Moffett's 'author' is 'raw' — 'content not previously abstracted and formulated by others'. But the material for the non-author — the 'tailor' — is 'ready-made cloth'; language that has been used before.

Writing as natural and personal communication

Authoring, then, is considered to be the natural and authentic expression of individual subjectivity, and discourses about school writing provide interesting evidence of how such concepts have been constructed. The terms often used to describe authorship — original and creative writing — frequently include adjectives like these: personal, individual, spontaneous, natural, truthful, involved, emotional, real (see Gilbert, 1989, for a fuller discussion of this question). Many teachers will be familiar with such adjectives and comfortable with the dichotomy they establish: writing, assumed to be a natural act, must surely be most successful when it is personal, spontaneous, real, and least successful when it is impersonal, contrived, and artificial.

This emphasis on the natural, the personal, the spontaneous, is often typified in discussions of writing by the use of the metaphor 'personal voice'. Students are advised to find their own voices in writing, teachers are advised to listen to such voices, and a clear personal voice in writing is often regarded as the mark of an effective writer, an effective author. The assumptions on which this metaphor is based are perhaps worth reconsidering.

The metaphor and its associated adjectival terms share a clear commitment to an intensely personalized, individualistic and speech-oriented theory of writing. The view of writing that such concepts support is one which sees writing as 'the guise of speech' (Graves, 1983:161): as a secondary language system that must always substitute for a missing human 'voice', presence, subject. Writing will thus always seem to be different from speech — and nobody would dispute that that is the case — but different because it has no human being or presence to 'speak'. Speech, because it is delivered by a human voice, is assumed to be more natural, personal, individual, spontaneous, truthful, involved, emotional, real . . . . Writing, then, in this argument, is at its best when it approximates the features of 'presence' that speech has.

Consider, for instance, how a professional writer and teacher of writing describes the way good writing works:

> The student, in his [*sic*] writing, is speaking. The student with his own tone of voice rises off the page, perhaps in just a phrase, a sentence, a few words, but enough to reveal his whole attitude, his point of view, his tone of voice. (Murray, 1982:153)

Or read this recommendation for student writers offered by another well-known and well-published teacher:

> In your natural way of producing words there is a sound, a texture, a rhythm — a voice — which is the main source of power in your writing. I don't know how it works, but this voice is the force that will make a reader listen to you, the energy that drives the meaning through his [*sic*] thick skull. (Elbow, 1973:6)

Donald Graves calls personal voice in writing 'the imprint of ourselves on our writing', and suggests that if the voice is missing 'there is no writing, just words following words'. To take the voice away from writing is, Graves says, like taking salt from stew, love from sex, or sun from gardening (Graves, 1983:227). And yet school textbook writers are reticent to discuss how such an obviously important writing quality might be taught, or even whether it can be taught. A pattern emerges which claims that learning to write (and to read) is natural: it is 'predominantly learnt rather than taught', argues Janet Emig (1983:140). Elbow says, 'I don't know how it works', and in fact all that textbooks often advocate is a 'process writing' classroom structure which assumes that the provision of the right environment will facilitate 'voice'.

If teachers claim that they can recognize personal voice (or 'authentic authoring', or 'originality', or 'creativity') when they 'hear' it in a text, there must be identifiable features of the text that have made such recognition possible. And if that is what teachers want to read in student writing, these features should be focused on in the classroom. To do otherwise is seriously to disadvantage many students, both those who have not yet worked out what particular teachers will 'hear', and those who genuinely believe that if they write in their own 'voices' they will become successful writers.

A few comments from 16-year-old students perhaps demonstrate this dilemma most tellingly. Some of these students had worked out what personal voice meant. Others had not.

> *Cathy:* If you're given a question to answer that's your own opinion, then I feel that no-one can mark you on your own opinion. It's your own feelings, and nobody can assess anybody I feel on their own feelings.
>
> *Suzette:* With my reading journal, I got a B. I tried really hard to make it more personalized and I rigged the whole thing to make it look really personal, whereas all the other ones I'd done, I hadn't, and I'd been given really low marks.
>
> *Susan:* I was pleased when she [the teacher] said she enjoyed reading my journal and that I understand personal voice, because that was what I was trying to achieve. I was trying to show that I understood it. I was happy that she recognized it.
>
> *Shelley:* I try to work harder . . . try to write the way the teachers want me to write — try to figure out what each teacher, what way they like you writing to give you the best mark.

While Suzette and Susan claim to have cracked the code, Cathy and Shelley have not. Cathy seems genuinely confused about how a person (here the person and the writing are entangled) can be assessed and ranked, while Shelley is convinced that there must be a 'code', a way to write what teachers want — she just doesn't know what it is.

The authorship legacy

The classroom situation these students are grappling with is one that has prevailed for some time. It is a legacy of the language theories authorized by John Dixon's report of the proceedings of the Dartmouth conference held in the United Kingdom in 1966 (Dixon, 1967) — a report which urged 'personal growth' through English and established the Growth Model as the dominant approach to language learning. Subsequent work from James Britton (1970), and his colleagues (Britton *et al.*, 1975; Martin *et al.*, 1976) reinforced such approaches, particularly in terms of the development of writing abilities. More recently, such approaches to writing development have been complemented by a flourishing of personalist and idiosyncratic approaches to reading. Take, for instance, this explanation of the reading of works of art offered by Louise Rosenblatt:

> Every time a reader experiences a work of art, it is in a sense created anew. Fundamentally, the process of understanding a work implies a recreation of it, an attempt to grasp completely the structured sensations and concepts through which the author seeks to convey the quality of his [*sic*] sense of life. (Rosenblatt, 1976:113)

Reader-response aesthetics, dominated within educational contexts by the work of Louise Rosenblatt and of Wolfgang Iser (1978), has become a dominant approach to secondary school reading, and a host of textbooks advocate the value of the personal, imaginative response to literature (Jackson, 1983; Corcoran and Evans, 1987).

But the difficulty has been that because such approaches to reading and writing cannot account for the social nature of language practices, they create considerable confusion and contradiction in social institutions like schools. A number of different and incompatible discourses mesh at the site of the classroom because schools are about — among other things — selection and sorting, discipline and punishment, knowledge and control. As a result, teachers and students need a socially critical understanding of the way language, particularly written language, works: the way in which it can be used to mystify, to exclude, to distort, to exonerate, or to delude. Such an understanding would seem to provide an infinitely better language base than one which almost implicitly endorses a false innocence and neutrality in language, and thus makes dupes of its users.

I shall now consider some of the confusion that language theories can generate in classrooms, by presenting transcripts of several 16-year-old students and their English teacher discussing 'creative writing' (and its variants) set as school tasks.

CONFUSION AND CONTRADICTION IN READING/WRITING CLASSROOMS

If writing is conceived of as natural — as personal, original creativity rather than social, textual construction — students may have considerable difficulty knowing how they can ever become 'better' writers, and teachers may have considerable difficulty deciding what can or should be taught about writing. Similarly, if reading is predominantly considered as personal discovery — both of an author's intention and of an individual reader's response to that intention — rather than as the application of a learned set of social reading practices, classroom reading is constantly hampered by a confused hunt for 'the personal' in a text, rather than the ideological or the social. The contradictions that result when writing is identified as a natural communication between writer and reader will be emphasized by drawing upon students' and teachers' perceptions of school writing.

Authentic expression for teachers

The paradoxes and inadequacies of language classrooms are often more apparent to older secondary students, who have had many years to learn how to survive and to manipulate systems. For instance, a group of 16-year-old writers whom I interviewed recently voluntarily commented on the importance of finding out what various English teachers liked: of constructing socially acceptable classroom texts.

> *Susan* . . . if you write the wrong thing, there goes your marks. You've got to write what the teacher wants . . .
>
> *Tony:* . . . it was about the first or second time I'd had her and (I was) not very sure what she's looking for . . .
>
> *Ken:* I've been in her class for two years now and I know what she looks for.
>
> *Suzette:* Before I do an essay for English, not really any other subject, I think what the teacher would like and the way they dress comes into it even. The way they'd like to see it written. Then I have to go and rewrite what I thought before into what they'd like to see . . . It's hit and miss . . . Since about grade 10 I've realized you've got to give them what they want.

But they did not always know how to construct appropriate texts, because they assumed that construction meant creativity, and creativity was a cognitive and emotional construct, not a social one.

Writing 'creatively'

Christine, a student who had repeated her final year and received an average grade for English, was rather disillusioned with English and convinced that there was no way in which she could improve her grades. When she got the results back for an 'imaginative story' she had written for assessment, she claimed that:

> I really dislike writing fantasy essays. It takes a lot of thinking and it's pretty hard to be original and to create characters. You've just got to be a bit wild in the mind to create really interesting characters. I'm terrible at writing fantasy essays. I'm just not creative.

However, another student — one who failed English that year — was far less discerning. When I talked to him before he wrote his 'imaginative essay', he told me that he was sure he would make a better job of this particular task, because in stories 'you can write anything you want':

> The story is better than other forms of writing because you can write what you want to write, type of thing. You're not set by guidelines on what you have to do . . . In a story, you can write it on anything you want, you know, anything you like type of thing.

His mate agreed with him, saying:

> A story is sort of your ideas. They're easier to develop than other people's ideas. You're using your own ideas, and you're not trying to react in some way to a certain thing. You're just using your own ideas.

Both these students were obviously convinced that writing a story was a different exercise from other forms of writing, because there were no apparent guidelines: no expectations, no rules. It was personal ('your ideas') and unstructured ('you can write what you want'). Again, a romantic concept of literature dominates in their explanations of narrative construction: stories are created out of individual subjectivity.

However, being a 'creative' individual might well incur a penalty. Another student I talked to was quite confident that she was a creative and original person ('I like art'), but assumed that this prevented her from becoming a critical and rational writer:

> Imaginative's my favourite choice of writing. I like art, I like creating. I always create at home. I paint when I feel like it, draw or write poems or anything like that so I suppose that's probably in my line I suppose. It just comes to me more easily than the other forms of writing . . . But when I deal with critical response, I really feel for the characters, so I can't really write down much about them . . . I can't criticize very well. I'm always in two minds about things.

Many of the students interviewed had convinced themselves that the reason for their lack of success in English was that they were not really 'creative' or 'original' people, and certainly the way in which 'creative writing' was treated in the classroom did nothing to alter this assumption. On the surface of things, creativity seemed to have little to do with text construction. Music was played as a stimulus for writing, students were encouraged to draw characters suitable for their stories, and the teacher urged the class to 'dredge up from your minds' descriptions and story ideas. The onus was on the students to 'use your imaginations' — not their textual repertoires — to create stories themselves.

Recognizing 'creativity'

Occasionally, a piece of work alerted the teacher to the complexities of describing and recognizing student creativity. In the following extract, she gives an honest and frank account of her response when she reread a story written by one of the less competent boys in her class:

> . . . fascinating about this. It's the way I read it. When I first read it — terrible punctuation, spelling, etc. I first read it and I was really put off. This is hopeless. I don't know why he bothered; he's got the wrong tone. I marked him down. What rubbish. Then I was starting to go through them again and I said to someone, 'Listen to this'. And then I had to read it aloud to them. When I read it aloud I suddenly — it really did have those elements of humour and surprise but because I was so put off with the lack of punctuation when I first started, I hadn't even picked them up . . . It was funny. He had that really ordinary sense of humour of someone put in an unusual situation. He didn't end it very well but the whole thing was very funny and so I had to stop and think — 'Hang on, this wasn't terrible . . .'

This description of the teacher's valiant efforts to be fair to her students and to try to give their work a serious reading — to treat her students as 'authors' — epitomizes the dilemma many teachers face. On the one hand, basic errors with the accepted conventions of written language obviously work against the placement of student texts within a literary reading frame (or of student writers within a literary frame), but, as well, experienced readers have certain reading expectations of literature which they do not have of student work.

Again, look at another remark from the teacher:

> . . . with Paul, I made a comment there, have you deliberately left out punctuation? It wasn't clear whether it was a deliberate thing in a poem or he hadn't just put it in because he never puts it in.

And then consider this complaint from one of the students who sensed the contradiction of the language classroom, but could not quite work out how it might be solved:

> Teachers just want to know what they want to hear . . . We can hardly do anything right really . . . I think by grade 12 you should be able to write how you feel. To write what you really want. There shouldn't be rights and wrongs in English. Look at some famous authors. I can't think of any offhand — but some of them will write in any type of language they want, totally free run, leave sentences totally disjointed. You know you're supposed to have a verb and a noun and all that? Well they write totally without things you're supposed to have in them. And yet who tells them — 'No, you're wrong'? Nobody.

Such confusions and contradictions noticed by teachers and students in reading/writing classrooms could be chronicled for pages, and are hardly new. Janet Emig (1971) commented on the dilemma in the first major study of student perceptions of school writing, and since then a number of Australian studies have repeatedly pointed to the different perceptions that teachers and students have of the nature of school writing (see Diamond, 1979; Bennett *et al.*, 1980; Piper, 1983; Gilbert, 1989). However, given their very different power bases in schools, different perspectives should be expected from students and teachers. Of more concern for us here is the way in which popular explanations of writing and reading may have misled teachers and students. Might other explanations of writing and reading offer a more useful base for schools?

READING AND WRITING AS CULTURAL PRACTICE

So far I have argued that the use of concepts like 'authoring' in discourses about school reading and writing serves to perpetuate particular approaches to language development. Such concepts assume — on a simplistic level — that the most desirable form of writing ('authentic authoring') involves the original expression of individuality, whereas the least desirable form of writing ('verbal tailoring') involves the mere imitation of a known language system. I shall now suggest that such a dichotomy is not only inaccurate, but it is also harmful.

Given a fixed language system, the possibilities for generating original pieces of writing are seriously limited, and nowhere is this more obvious than in the close examination of literary texts. In *Literary Theory: An Introduction*, Terry Eagleton questions the linking of authorship to original creativity, and instead argues that literary construction is more akin to Moffett's 'verbal tailoring' concept:

> All literary texts are woven out of other literary texts, not in the conventional sense that they bear the traces of 'influence' but in the more radical sense that every word, phrase or segment is a reworking of other writings which precede or surround the individual work. There is no such thing as literary 'originality', no such thing as the 'first' literary work: all literature is intertextual. (Eagleton, 1983:138)

His argument is that all texts are intertextual: all rely upon other texts and their placement in terms of other texts for any meanings they might be given. For instance, a child's reworking of the *Little Red Riding Hood* story derives its impact from its textual background — a far from innocent ideological background as Jack Zipes (1983) illustrates very well. Similarly, a child's poem derives its impact from the way in which it joins into and stands beside the vast textuality of lyrics and other verse that surround it.

Indeed this is precisely why writing can be such an enjoyable and satisfying activity for children. Once the vast world of textuality is introduced and explored (and this is clearly a role for the teacher), to write is to play with form, to juxtapose the unusual, to juggle with opposites, to parody, to imitate, to 'blend and clash' as Roland Barthes would say (1977:146). In other words, writing is about constructing from within an available signifying system — working with the known. And the more texts children know, the more possibilities there are for play and construction.

'Authentic authoring' must rely, to a considerable extent, on imitating a known language system, because if it did not, it would be unreadable: unrecognizable, unidentifiable, unclassifiable. To suggest to teachers and to children that learning to write is not learning how writing has traditionally, generically, conventionally, and playfully functioned, is to do them a major disservice. It is to perpetuate the sort of confused powerlessness that the students in the preceding section of this chapter sometimes suggested.

Now I shall first look more closely at the concept of *originality*, to display some of the assumptions on which it relies, and then turn to 'reading', particularly to consider how written texts function differently, depending on the ways in which they are read.

Originality and authorship

Two questions are initially interesting here. Why have educationists considered it important for writers to be original or creative — to have 'personal voice'? And what has become commonly recognized as original or creative writing? Both questions demand some brief discussion of orthodox views of literature and of authorship, because original and creative writers are most commonly associated with literary discourse, an 'authored' discourse. In fact, literature — unlike other discursive forms — *relies* on the personalism and subjectivity of authorship.

An author serves effectively to anchor literary texts to single meanings (those that an author 'intended'), to market literary works ('a new book by . . .'), and to validate claims that literature is a reflection of human experience ('a moving and realistic account . . .', 'a rare insight into the boy's dilemma . . .'). To distinguish literature from other forms of discourse, it is generally accepted that authors have poetic licence to fracture the existing language system (usually by breaking linguistic, generic and punctuation conventions) in order to forge new or alternative meanings. In the context of literary discourse, rule breaking is regarded as justifiable and is identified as originality and creativity.

However, this view of the relationship between authorship and originality assumes that such rule breaking will be interpreted correctly, and there are some embarrassing examples in literary history which illustrate that this has not always been the case. More significantly, for this argument, there are many examples in classrooms where rule breaking is not recognized as deliberate originality or creativity. David Bartholomae makes this point very effectively:

> When a basic writer violates our expectations . . . there is a tendency to dismiss the text as non-writing, as meaningless or imperfect writing. We have not read as we have been trained to read, with a particular interest in the way an individual style confronts and violates convention. We have read, rather, as policemen, examiners, gate-keepers. The teacher who is unable to make sense out of a seemingly bizarre piece of student writing is often the same teacher who can give an elaborate explanation of the 'meaning' of a story of David Barthelme or a poem by e.e.cummings. (Bartholomae, 1980:254–5)

However, original and creative literature may not necessarily have broken any rules of syntax, spelling or punctuation — the usual errors that teachers can readily identify. Instead, a literary text may have 'played' with — broken — accepted generic conventions; may have taken liberties with time, with character, with reader expectation. Janet and Alan Ahlberg's *The Jolly Postman*, Ted Hughes's *The Iron Man*, Aidan Chambers's *Breaktime* have achieved much of their acclaim as original and creative texts because they have 'played' with generic expectation.

But the interesting aspect of originality and creativity in this sense is that a text can only be labelled 'original' and 'creative' because certain of its features are recognizable. And if features can be *recognized*, they can be repeated. If they can't be repeated, they can't be recognized. As Jonathon Culler argues in *On Deconstruction*:

> Something can be a signifying sequence only if it is iterable, only if it can be repeated in various serious and nonserious contexts, cited, and parodied. Imitation is not an accident that befalls an original but its condition of possibility. There is such a thing as an original Hemingway style only if it

> can be cited, imitated, and parodied. For there to be such a style there must be recognizable features that characterize it and produce its distinctive effects; for features to be recognizable one must be able to isolate them as elements that could be repeated, and thus the iterability manifested in the inauthentic, the derivative, the imitative, the parodic, is what makes possible the original and the authentic. (Culler, 1983:120)

But then a further and more difficult question emerges. What is there, say, about Margaret Mahy's style or Roald Dahl's style that is exclusively literary? As it stands, literature clearly does not mark out a domain of language which is in some way different from other language domains. There are no criteria which serve objectively to mark out certain types of language as discretely belonging to literature. Literature has not always been the province of 'imaginative' writing as it is in a contemporary sense, nor does it use language in any way that is not common in daily discourse. Metaphors, alliteration, onomatopoeia, synecdoche are just as much a part of the language of advertising and of conversation as they are of literature.

While texts obviously have identifiable features, such features are not only the province of one form of writing. The Ahlbergs' *Jolly Postman* letters are good examples of that. Instead, texts are designated as works of literature, and then they can be read as works of literature. In other words, once a work is read from within a known set of discursive expectations and placed within a reading *frame*, it can be produced in a particular way. Until it is 'framed' — until it is read in a particular way from a particular reading practice — the work can be produced in a number of very different ways. Ian Reid's discussion of this issue both in *The Making of Literature* (1984) and in the introduction to *The Place of Genre in Learning* (1987) is particularly helpful. School scripts are excellent examples of precisely this problem, as the teacher's comments earlier made perfectly clear.

Reading as a cultural practice

However, while reading is obviously not always the same, it is misleading to think that reading is individualistic. Ian Hunter claims that while there are many different readings of texts, these readings are not just different subjective experiences of the text. Instead, he argues that different readings are 'the result of the application of different rules and practices of reading' (Hunter, 1982:86). Reading, then, is like writing: it is a learned cultural practice and, as such, can be unpicked and examined.

Within an educational context, there are many examples of different reading practices and of the way in which they may be culturally learned. One of the best known would be that provided by Britton *et al.*'s study *The Development of Writing Abilities (11–18)* (1975), which offered an implied set of practices for producing what is called 'expressive', 'poetic' and 'transactional' writing, and which subsequently spawned an international reading practice which emulated the rules that Britton's team had formulated. Similarly, Purves (1968) devised a set of practices for recognizing different types of student response to literature, and again the practices were imitated and used internationally.

Once reading is acknowledged as a cultural practice, the features of various readings can be examined and critiqued. The features of examiners' readings, of literary critics' readings, of book judges' readings, of children's readings, are all important for language teachers, as are, of course, the features of teachers' own different reading practices. The role that reading plays in any discussion of writing can never be ignored. If the craft of writing is to become accessible to students, reading — in its strongest sense — becomes of paramount importance.

AUTHORSHIP AND CREATIVITY IN THE CLASSROOM

I began this chapter by questioning some of the ways in which the concept of 'authoring' is used for the encouragement of reading and writing activities in classrooms, but I suggested that the introduction of the term had little to contribute to an understanding of the craft of writing. In fact, the uncritical use of terms like 'authorship', 'creativity', or 'originality' may positively work against the development of successful reading and writing classrooms — particularly as students progress through the school years — because the terms do not help teachers or students to understand the nature of reading and writing. I have focused on the ways in which much of the 'authoring' discourse assumes a particular superiority and privilege for things literary, creative or expressive, and on the ways in which it says little about how children might learn to become critical and competent participants in literate societies. 'Authorship' is but one of the newest of a long line of discursive devices which serve to entrench personalist, individualist, speech-oriented theories of writing in schools.

I shall now pose questions about some school texts in light of my arguments in this chapter. The first two pieces of writing come from students in their final year of secondary school. I have deliberately chosen this level to begin with because I want to emphasize how, for one of these students, twelve years of schooling and of writing instruction has been largely unproductive. I shall then look at two pieces from primary school students: students in the middle of their compulsory schooling experience.

Authoring in the secondary school

Texts 3.1 and 3.2 (pages 72–3) are extracts from two first pages of a 'magazine' article students in a year 12 class had been set as one of their school English assessment tasks. This is how the teacher described what they were to do:

> They were given a topic (Are creative writers always abnormal?) and they were given a set of information about those people — they were given a sheet about Shakespeare or Oscar Wilde etc. so that they did not have to research it — they just had to select the information they wanted to use to back up their argument and we previewed that by a discussion in class about what was abnormal or not . . . After they'd written the first draft we talked about tone and I also read them out some examples from newspapers

> like the *Australian* that I told them they were trying to aim for, and showed them things. For instance, sophistication of language in the newspaper article — that's what I told them they were trying to aim for. I think they found that pretty difficult. They couldn't imagine that they could write anything like that so I am not sure how successful that was . . .

As it turned out, the magazine article was not very successfully completed, and in a subsequent interview, the teacher offered her reaction to the task:

> The only one who did it well was Susan. The others didn't achieve that — well — funny blend between being personal writing and yet impersonal writing, because it's in a newspaper. They equate *personal* with 'I think', not with a style of writing. They don't seem to have that yet. But she did — but then, typical. She's a good English student and does most things well and understood what was wanted.

Both teacher transcripts illustrate some of the points made earlier in this chapter. The teacher was able to recognize a 'style of writing' when she read it, but she lacked the knowledge to deduce from her reading a set of distinguishing features of the style she wished the students to use. As a consequence, she was unable to teach it, and teacher education clearly has much to answer for in this regard. Very few pre- or in-service programmes provide teachers with an understanding of the ways in which language functions in social and cultural practice. At best, secondary English teachers receive some background in university-style literature study, but primary language arts teachers are often given little, if any, specialist language work.

As well, it is obvious from these transcripts that the 'good' English student was able to work out 'what was wanted', to do 'most things well', while less competent children were obviously disadvantaged by the lack of teaching and assistance provided by the teacher for this task. In addition, the teacher and many of the students had quite different perceptions of 'personal', the teacher regarding it as a style of writing, and the students as an indication of personal opinion.

Text 3.1 is the beginning of the first page of the assignment constructed by Susan, the student who 'did it well'. And text 3.2 is from the first page of Ken's assignment — a student who did not do well at all.

Initially, the differences in presentation are quite striking and, I would suggest, immediately help to frame the teacher's reading. More importantly, the 'authorship' of both works has influence in an interesting way: Susan's name activates particular teacher expectations, as does Ken's. The teacher expects to read Susan's work differently, expects to make meaning, expects to find something of interest. Consider these comments the teacher made to me about Susan's work:

> She immediately had that elevated literary type tone, that being personal, until in the first paragraph she used a word I had to look up in the dictionary to find out what it meant. So that sort of combination made it have an impact.

Are creative writers always abnormal ?

In many minds exists the notion of a creative writer. It may be the image of a budding poet, a ponderous youth, cramped in a dismal attic weaving webs of delight and love. Or perhaps it's the image of an erotic and demonic soul, volatile in temper, unrestrained, wild and bizzare in manner. Wherever your fantasy lies, the perception of a trouvère is that he is inspirational, sensitive or different, thus abnormal.

Yes, we the majority believe creative writers are abnormal. What is abnormality? Is it an exception to the rule, a contrary spirit, the non-conformist, or is it as the dictionary defines something not usual, a deviation from normal? Thus all masterful writers who have born the fruits of success earn themselves distinction and diverge from the essence of the human race. They become celebrities,

Text 3.1 Extract from English assignment by 'good' student (reduced size)

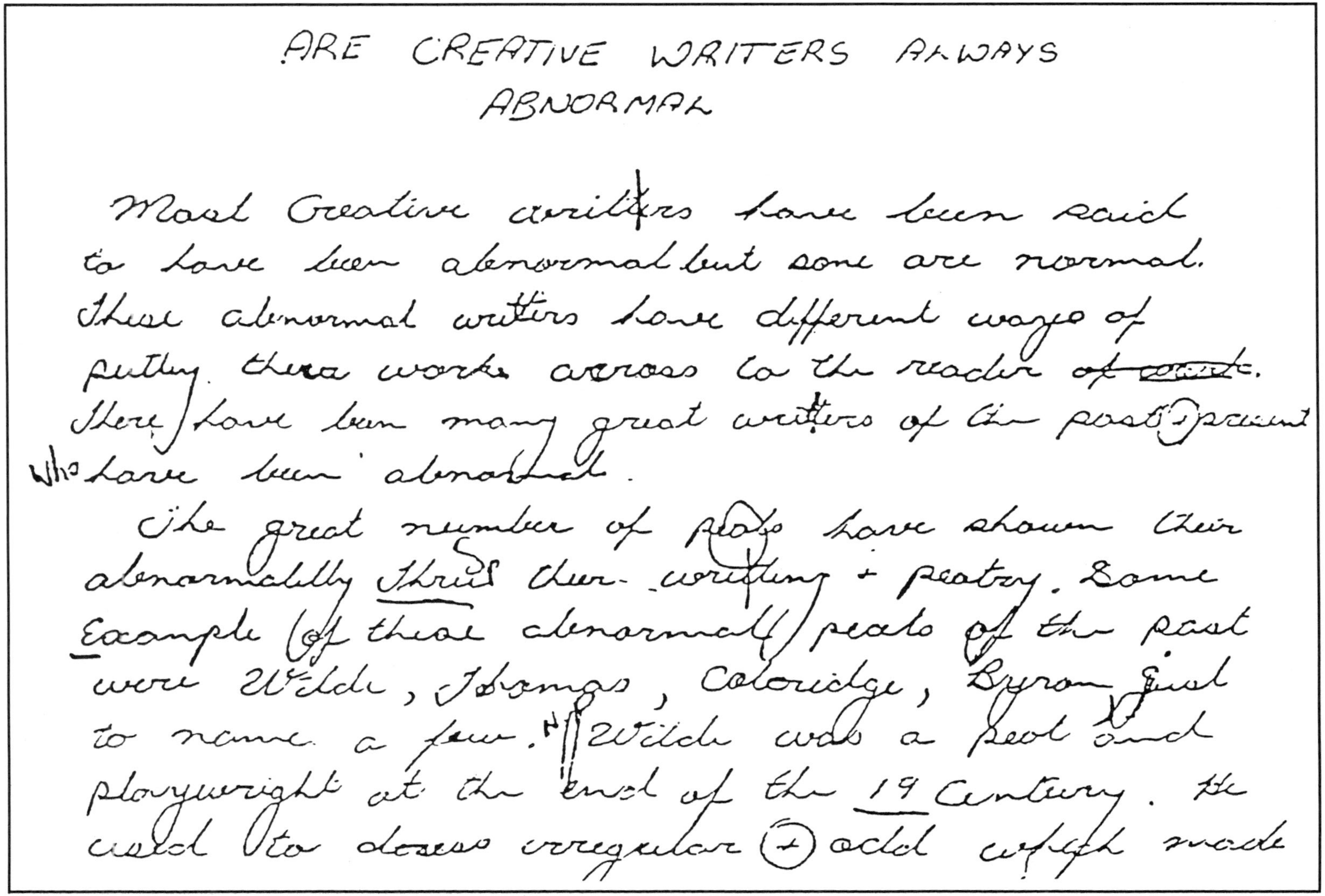
ARE CREATIVE WRITERS ALWAYS
ABNORMAL

Most Creative writers have been said to have been abnormal but some are normal. These abnormal writers have different ways of putting thera works across to the reader of work. There have been many great writers of the past + present who have been abnormal.

The great number of poets have shown their abnormalility through their writing + peatry. Some Example of these abnormall poets of the past were Wilde, Thomas, Coloridge, Byron just to name a few. Wilde was a poet and playwright at the end of the 19 Century. He used to dress irregular + odd which made

Text 3.2 Extract from English assignment by less competent student (reduced size)

Not surprisingly, the teacher could not remember a great deal about Ken's assignment when she was interviewed, but she had written on the bottom of his work:

> Ken, you must proof-read *much* more carefully. A magazine article cannot have such basic errors . . .

Even a cursory reading of Ken's assignment will suggest to you that Ken needs to do more than proof-read more effectively, but the teacher felt rather helpless about what else she could suggest and was honest enough to admit this:

> In lots of cases I can say things like 'No — this isn't quite the tone of a newspaper article', but they honestly don't know how to get that tone, and I really don't know how to tell them. And I think that's frustrating . . .

When Susan was interviewed about her work, she explained how she had worked on the magazine article:

> I tried to write really sophisticated, and tried to be really fluent — not stop and start sort of thing. I'm usually stopping and starting. I tried to be more fluent and also to put in lots of big words and things used in the magazines. I got a thesaurus out and sat down and went all the way through it to sort of get words to go with what I was doing.

Susan was able to do more than use 'big words' in her assignment. She demonstrates her awareness of a number of features common to some forms of journalism: the first person plural pronouns, the rhetorical questions, the pairs of juxtaposed sentences. Notice, too, the control she has over sentence introductions and sentence patterns, compared with those in Ken's text. It is interesting to notice that the question mark is missing from Ken's headline, and that his assignment reads like a school essay on abnormality. Ken does not pose a mock internal debate in his assignment. Instead, he has written paragraphs from the notes the teacher gave to the class.

In many ways, the teacher in this classroom tried to set up an exercise for her students which followed most of the prescriptions contemporary writing pedagogy advocates. She framed the purpose and audience of the task, she initiated discussion and some reading beforehand, and she provided the students with information to write about. But she couldn't teach the class the typical generic expectations of this style of writing: she couldn't break down the particular linguistic features of texts that are often recognized as journalistic opinion. Most of the class didn't know how to organize given pieces of information into an acceptable journalistic format, and merely being told the audience and the purpose for this task was no compensation for them. As adults we might well know by whom a legal document is to be read and what its purpose might be, but most of us would still be unable to construct an appropriate legal text — one that would be recognized as conventional and appropriate by the legal profession.

Authoring in the primary school

While it is common to see senior secondary school students trying their hands at a number of different writing forms — in fact that is usually a requirement of any writing curriculum in the secondary school — in the primary school it is unfortunately much more common to see writing classrooms almost totally preoccupied with story writing. However, despite an emphasis on writing narratives in the first years of formal schooling, many children's understanding of the literary devices of written narratives is slight.

Consider, for instance, these two stories (texts 3.3 and 3.4) about sea creatures written by 10-year-olds. The first is given to you in its entirety; the second is the first page only of a four-page narrative.

Text 3.3 Story by 10-year-old

The Sea Creature

In the town of Jughead some people saw a strange sea-creature. One day a child went swimming at the beach. He was in the water and a sea creature attacked the boy and he was gobbled up. The same day a twelve-year-old child saw the sea creature. There were four investigators, Russell, Peter, Keith and myself, Len. The four of us went to see the twelve-year-old boy. He said the sea creature looked like it had red eyes and it was green.

One day I said, 'Let's go to spy on the sea creature.' So we did. We went to the top of the hill. We pitched the tent on the hill. The first night Keith was looking out for the sea creature. When Keith fell asleep, the sea creature popped up and ate him. The next day we found Keith dead.

The next night I had a laser pistol and the sea creature came up and I shot at him but missed. At twelve o'clock that night Peter was on guard but he went to sleep and the sea creature came up to eat him. Russell woke up first and found Peter dead. I saw a hand-print and I checked it with Russell's hand-print. The sea creature came up. I saw it and I raced for the laser pistol. I shot the sea creature but it wasn't a sea creature — IT WAS A MAN!

Text 3.4 First part of story by 10-year-old

Clanie the Seamonster

Clanie was a seamonster that lived in the spooky, misty and scary swamps of Shoogolas.

Clanie had big green eyes and long black eyelashes. Great big spikes on her back made her look terribly, awfully scary. She had a long, long tail with a very sharp point at the end. Clanie was a very shy sort of monster but although she tried not to show it, Clanie could be very angry when somebody interrupted her graceful sleeping. She sleeps like a tyre in the water — she drifts.

One day I was walking on the banks of the Shoogolas swamp when I saw the strangest creature. I described it as 'the strangest thing that ever met my eye'. I froze as I saw it. I don't know what came over me but I started screaming! The animal dashed underwater with a great shock. The water turned green and back to blue again. In two minutes all this had escaped from my mind. I went home that night forgetting all about the sea creature . . .

In this class, both students were identified as 'authors' and both had constructed these stories in the class writing time scheduled daily. The teacher had suggested that the theme of 'sea monster/sea creature' might be a good writing topic, and these students had both chosen to write on that theme. Even when the stories are printed — as they are here — with due regard to conventional spelling, punctuation, and paragraphing, I think there are several differences between them which indicate something of the likely success these students will have in writing classrooms of the future.

While both students construct feasible narratives, text 3.4 draws more obviously upon literary narrative conventions. Note the title, the first sentence formatted on its own, the concern to provide a verbal picture of the narrative's central character, the use of figurative language. Consider, too, the literary conventions employed in constructing the pattern of events: an important non-human character is introduced, then set aside temporarily; a moment of high significance occurs and is effectively noted; readers gain privileged information and are invited to suspend their disbelief. When *Clanie the Seamonster* is set beside *The Sea Creature*, we can see marked textual differences: differences obviously in length and complexity of the narrative, but also differences in the level of sentence variations and range of vocabulary employed, and differences in mastery and understanding of literary convention. Being able to write an effective short story (an 'original' short story?) has much to do with all these. For those teachers familiar with the short stories that many 10–15-year-olds write, *The Sea Creature* will sound depressingly familiar. Many students never progress beyond a basic competence with subject-verb agreement and spelling and punctuation conventions; they never progress to an understanding of the conventions of literary narratives. And some of this failure to master the conventions of literary 'authorship' must lie in the mistaken belief that writing is not craft but imagination; not construction but creation. Is it creative imagination that will let the writer of *The Sea Creature* do well in secondary school? Or is it an understanding of the recognizable generic conventions that he will be expected to reproduce?

The role of the teacher

Throughout the chapter I have tried to argue for an important role for the teacher in reading/writing classrooms. While the roles of facilitator, organizer and supporter (editor?) may indeed be useful for teachers, they can merely supplement the main role, which is to make written language accessible to students — *all* students. Of course the craft of writing can be taught to students, as those fortunate few who have been taught could well testify. Many adult writers will remember with gratitude the teacher/lecturer/friend/editor who taught them aspects of how language forms are constructed, and may perhaps wish that many more such people had crossed their paths.

Learning how to write an effective short story or a modern lyric can be compared with learning how to participate in a formal debate, or learning how to chair a meeting. Interestingly enough, it seems easier for teachers to accept that the craft of speech making can be taught than that the craft of writing can. Similarly, one might wonder why the construction of visual art forms — particularly film — is so readily associated with skill and craft. Types of shots, colour, locales, motifs, musical score, actors: the tools of the film director's craft seem readily understood and accepted.

Any semiotic system has rules and conventions — arbitrary and cultural though they are — to which some people have greater access than others. A language is a semiotic system of primary importance, particularly in learning, and any attempt to provide greater equality of access to this system seems to me to be an important part of what literacy learning should be about, and to be an important role for schools. By placing such an emphasis on the personal and idiosyncratic aspects of literacy learning, as often applies in schools today, the social and constructed nature of language tends to be obscured. Concepts like authorship focus on the creation of a text, on the originality of a text, on particular emotional qualities of a text — but not on *how* a text has been made. The making of a text demands that attention be paid both to textual construction and to reading practices: to the social and cultural nature of literacy.

Rather than authorizing disadvantage by focusing on the mystique of authorship, could we not instead promote critical social literacy by focusing on the cultural construction of reading and writing practices? The way forward lies in shedding much of the unnecessary personal and romantic 1960s discourse while holding firm to its important emphases on children's needs and rights. A fresh look at the basics will start with where children are, and will value the experiences they have. But it will also endeavour to extend them through challenging new learning, and this will necessarily involve introducing them to the broadest possible range of texts, for it is in these that many new forms of experience reside.

REFERENCES

Barthes, R. (1977). *Image music text* (S. Heath, Trans.). London: Fontana.

Bartholomae, D. (1980). The study of error. *College Composition and Communication*, **31** (3), 253–269.

Bennett, B., Bowes, D., Jeffery, C., McPhail, S., Sooby, A., & Walker, A. (1980). *An investigation of the process of writing and the development of writing abilities (15–17)*. Perth: University of Western Australia.

Bourdieu, P. (1973). Cultural reproduction and social reproduction. In R. Brown (Ed.), *Knowledge, education, and cultural change: Papers in the sociology of education*. London: Tavistock Publications.

Britton, J. (1970). *Language and learning*. Harmondsworth, Middlesex: Penguin.

Britton, J., Burgess, T., Martin, N., McLeod, A., & Rosen, H. (1975). *The development of writing abilities (11–18)*. London: Schools Council Publications.

Christian-Smith, L. (1988). Power, knowledge and curriculum: Constructing femininity in adolescent romance novels. In S. DeCastell, A. Luke, & C. Luke (Eds.), *Language, authority and criticism: Readings on the school textbook*. Lewes: Falmer Press.

Corcoran, B., & Evans, E. (Eds.). (1987). *Readers, texts, teachers*. Montclair, New Jersey: Boynton/Cook Publishers Inc.

Culler, J. (1983). *On deconstruction*. London: Routledge & Kegan Paul.

Diamond, C. (1979). *The constructs, classroom practices and effectiveness of Grade*

Ten teachers of written expression. Unpublished Ph.D. thesis, University of Queensland.
Dixon, B. (1977a). *Catching them young. Vol. 1: Sex, race and class in children's fiction*. London: Pluto Press.
Dixon, B. (1977b). *Catching them young, Vol. 2: Political ideas in children's fiction*. London: Pluto Press.
Dixon, J. (1967). *Growth through English*, London: Oxford University Press.
Eagleton, T. (1983). *Literary theory: An introduction*. Oxford: Basil Blackwell Publishers.
Elbow, P. (1973). *Writing without teachers*. London: Oxford University Press.
Emig, J. (1971). *The composing approach of twelfth graders*. Urbana, Ill.: National Council of Teachers of English.
Emig, J. (1983). *The web of meaning*. Montclair, New Jersey: Boynton/Cook Publishers, Inc.
Gilbert, P. (1983). *We're authors too*. James Cook University of North Queensland: Audio Visual Unit.
Gilbert, P. (1988a). Student text as pedagogical text. In S. DeCastell, A. Luke, & C. Luke (Eds.), *Language, authority and criticism: Readings on the school textbook*. Lewes: Falmer Press.
Gilbert, P. (1988b). Stoning the romance: girls as resistant readers and writers. In F. Christie (Ed.), *Writing in schools* (B.Ed. course Reader) Geelong, Victoria: Deakin University Press.
Gilbert, P. (1989). *Writing, schooling and deconstruction: From voice to text in the classroom*. London: Routledge & Kegan Paul.
Gilbert, R. (1984). *The impotent image: Reflections of ideology in the secondary school curriculum*. Lewes: Falmer Press.
Graves, D. (1983). *Writing: Teachers and children at work*. London: Heinemann Educational Books.
Hollingworth, D. (1983). Crisis in English teaching. *The use of English*, **3**, 3–8.
Hunter, I. (1982). The concept of context and the problem of reading. *Southern Review*, **15** (1), 80–91.
Iser, W. (1978). *The act of reading*. London: Routledge & Kegan Paul.
Jackson, D. (1983). *Encounters with books: Teaching fiction 11–16*. London: Methuen Educational.
Luke, A. (1988). *Literacy textbooks and ideology*. Lewes: Falmer Press.
Macherey, P. (1978). *A theory of literary production*. (G. Wall, Trans.). London: Routledge & Kegan Paul.
Martin, N., D'Arcy, P., Newton, B., & Parker, R. (1976). *Writing and learning across the curriculum 11–16*. London: Ward Lock.
Moffett, J. (1981). *Active voice*. Montclair, New Jersey: Boynton/Cook Publishers Inc.
Murray, D. (1982). *Learning by teaching*. Montclair, New Jersey: Boynton/Cook Publishers, Inc.
National Association for the Teaching of English (NATE). (1985). *Alice in genderland*. Language and Gender Working Party.
Piper, K. (1983). *Curriculum style and English language*. Hawthorn, Victoria: ACER.
Purves, A. (with Rippere, V.) (1968). *Elements of writing about a literary work: A study of response to literature*. Urbana, Ill.: National Council of Teachers of English.
Reid, I. (1982). The crisis in English studies. *English in Australia*, **46**(3), 259–265.
Reid, I. (1984). *The making of literature*. Australian Association for the Teaching of English.
Reid, I. (Ed.). (1987). *The place of genre in learning: Current debates*. Geelong, Victoria: Centre for Studies in Literary Education, Deakin University.
Rosenblatt, L. (1976). *Literature as exploration* (3rd ed.). London: Routledge & Kegan Paul.
Sheridan, E. (Ed.). (1982). *Sex stereotypes and reading: Research and strategies*. Newark, New Jersey: International Reading Association.
Zipes, J. (1983). *The trials and tribulations of Little Red Riding Hood: Variations of the tale in sociocultural context*. London: Heinemann.

4 Literacy in science: learning to handle text as technology

J. R. MARTIN

EVALUATION

Early in 1988 Ben, aged 8, wrote the explanation of the origin of our planet (accompanied by a picture of the Earth, with certain of what appear to be continents marked) shown in text 4.1 (page 80). His teacher's comments on his text are clear:

> Where is your margin? This is not a story.

And on his illustration:

> Finish please.

Ben's parents were naturally rather upset. Small wonder. Ben has a keen interest in science and enjoys reading in this area. His text is clearly influenced by his reading, but not copied word for word. And it is a perfectly readable account of the history of our planet. As a piece of scientific writing, taking the child's age into account, it is quite appropriate. Yet like many other young writers interested in the nature of things, Ben is being given a clear message: 'Literacy in science is not the business of primary school; here we write narratives. Drawing is important; spend more time on your pictures.' Or to put this in more blatantly sexist terms: 'Why don't you write like a girl?' (see White, 1986, for a discussion of science, gender and writing; also see chapter 6 in this volume).

It is obvious what has gone wrong: the teacher's expectations have not been met. More seriously, these expectations have not been clearly explained to Ben. Instead of being evaluated on its own terms, as a perfectly valid piece of writing in science, Ben's text is rejected outright. Things could have been worse. The teacher might simply have given it a lower mark or more negative comment than a narrative, obscuring further the criteria on

Text 4.1 An 8-year-old's scientific explanation (reduced size)

OUR PLANET

Earth's core is as hotasthe (x hot as the) furthest outer layer of the sun. They are both 6000c°.
Earth started as a ball of fine. Slowly it cooled. But it was still too hot for Life. Slowly water formed and then the (firstsx) first sign of life, microscopic cells. Then came trees. About seven thousand million years later came the first man.

where is your margin? This is not a story.

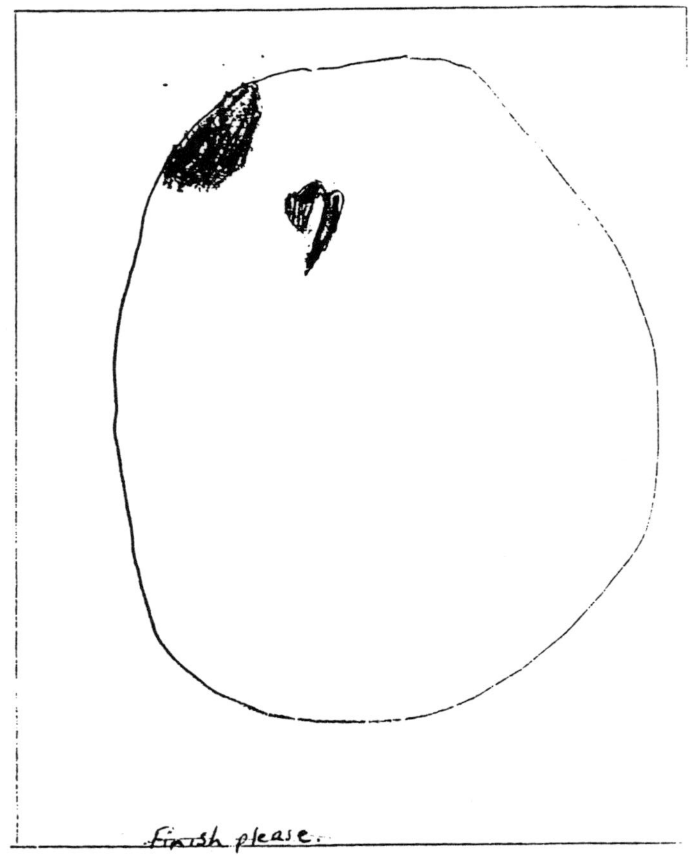

which the evaluation is based. As things stand, the message is clear, misguided though many of us might feel it to be.

The point of course is that writing in science is different from writing in other parts of the curriculum and that scientifically oriented criteria have to be used to evaluate it. Developing subject-specific criteria for evaluating writing is an urgent need in Australian schools. And this implies a much greater consciousness among teachers of the special nature of writing in different areas of the curriculum than is currently made available through pre-service training, syllabus documents and what little in-service training remains.

In order to develop scientifically oriented evaluation criteria, we have to be very clear about the kind of knowledge science is trying to construct and also about the ways in which scientists package this knowledge into text. Neither the knowledge nor the packaging can be understood without looking very closely at the language scientists work with when they talk and write. The language science uses to construct scientific understandings will be explored in this chapter, and the written genres used to document and explore this knowledge will be reviewed. Lemke (1988) provides a useful introduction to the social semiotic perspective on the role of language in science adopted in this chapter.

Adopting such a perspective is critical at this time because of the steady emergence in Australia of documents stressing the importance of using non-scientific language to explore science in primary and junior secondary schools. The recent *Writing K–12* document, for example, heads its list of recommended forms of writing in science with stories, especially science fiction, personal reports and descriptions of observations, plays, poems and cartoons (NSW Department of Education, 1987:125). The same department thrusts students into very demanding forms of scientific writing in years 11 and 12 and uses writing of this kind as the basis for evaluation in the statewide Higher School Certificate examination. Christie (1989: section 1) includes a valuable case study of one student's experiences in coping with the literacy demands of senior secondary physics and environmental science, among other subjects, in Victoria, for which he had received little preparation in the previous ten years of schooling. As more and more emphasis is placed on doing science 'in your own words' (cf. Wignell, 1987), the situation is deteriorating rapidly to the point where young science writers such as Ben are not only not encouraged but are actually being nipped in the bud. Without a clear understanding of the fundamental role of scientific language in doing science, this problem cannot be properly redressed.

Throughout this chapter I shall make use of quotations from a variety of science textbooks together with examples of student writing. The textbooks are important because they are the main source of models of written scientific language for most students; they are also focal because most extended writing in science is in fact copied more or less directly from such books (see again Wignell, 1987). The reason for this is that writing in science is not taught, and students have no better way to learn.

Whatever their demerits, the removal of traditional textbooks (e.g. Messel *et al.*, 1964) from science classrooms over the past twenty years has meant that increasing numbers of students are exposed to fewer and fewer models of scientific discourse. This is compounded by the fact that recent textbooks, such as the *Science for Living* series (Cull and Comino, 1987), provide very fragmented models of scientific text. Both developments are fundamental obstacles to learning the language of science in Australian schools.

LITERACY IN SCIENCE

One of the first images that comes to mind when thinking about science is the experimental laboratory. People in white coats are busy with various sorts of technological apparatus — scientists with the tools of their trade. Most of us are also aware that scientists can be hard to understand. It is not only their tools which are technical; their words are technical too. There are not many people in our culture who can make sense of the language of text 4.2.

Text 4.2 Scientific language in a school textbook (Heffernan and Learmonth, 1981:221)

Coniopteris frutiformis n. sp.

DIAGNOSIS.

Leaf, bi- or tri-pinnate, length unknown, portions preserved maximum length 15 cm. Pinnae, length 1 – 10 cm., attachment alternate about 1 cm. apart at angle of about 60° on rachis. Pinna shape tapering arrow tailed, apex pointed.

And it is not just the words. The grammar is special too. The text is not written in sentences, but in long nominal groups (or naming groups, such as *the text*, *sentences* and *long nominal groups* in this sentence). The point of both the technical terms and the grammar is to compress as much information as possible into a short space. The palaeontologist at work wants to document the fossil as economically as possible — there are many thousands of other fossils to record.

We can see from texts such as this that one of the most important pieces of technology used by scientists, and one that is often overlooked, is language. To be literate in science means to understand the technical language that is used. To appreciate this we have to look more closely at what scientists are trying to do.

SCIENCE AND COMMON SENSE

Scientists think about the world differently from other people, and at times they are very critical of common-sense understandings. (Many of the texts quoted in this paper contain references to figures which have not been reproduced for reasons of space; I have included the references to reinforce the point that scientific writing interacts with figures, diagrams, tables and graphs in important ways. Text 4.3 demonstrates both these characteristics.)

Text 4.3 Example of figure reference in a science textbook, and of subtle denigration of common-sense experience (Heffernan and Learmonth, 1981:34)

> ***Meteors and meteorites***
>
> **Meteors,** often wrongly called 'shooting stars' or 'falling stars', look spectacular as they flash briefly across the night sky (Figure 2.42). They, however, have nothing to do with stars. They are simply tiny pieces of rock rushing through space and being burned up by friction as they hurtle into Earth's atmosphere at speeds of about thirty kilometres per second.

In text 4.3 the astronomer is criticizing common sense for classifying meteors as a kind of star. Astronomers see the world differently, defining meteors as 'tiny pieces of rock rushing through space and being burned up by friction as they hurtle into Earth's atmosphere'. Underlying this is a picture of life, the universe and everything, in which the universe is composed of billions of galaxies, and galaxies are composed of millions of solar systems. Solar systems are organized into parts and wholes along the lines of figure 4.1.

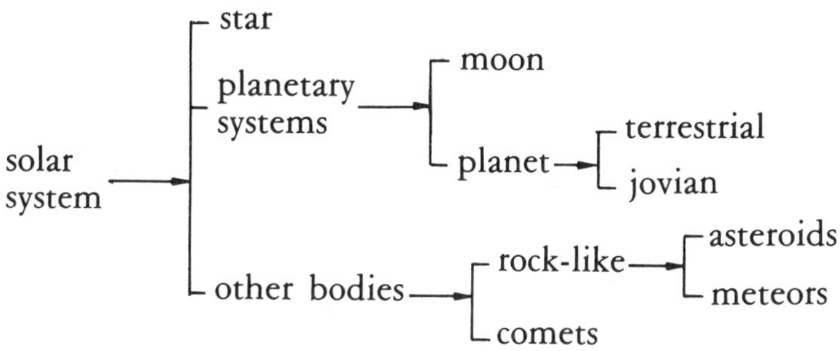

Figure 4.1 Scientific classification of astronomical bodies

In this world view, meteors are only distantly related to stars. But we should not be too quick to dismiss common-sense understandings. To the naked eye, stars, meteors and planets look very much alike; and a meteor is indeed a star that falls from the sky. The common-sense view of heavenly bodies can in fact be mapped out in a similar way to the scientist's, though the relationships are very different. In particular, one's point of departure is the planet Earth rather than the universe. Figure 4.2 shows what we see on looking up.

When we compare the common-sense and scientific maps of the universe, we can see that both organize reality. This they have in common. What differs are the criteria used as the basis of this organization. To the naked eye the Morning and Evening Stars are different objects and quite justifiably stars: small shining objects that appear in the sky at dawn and dusk. For science, they are the same planet — Venus: looked at through a telescope in an observatory it is clear why a scientist adopts this point of view.

The common-sense view depends on careful observation with the naked eye. Science augments this with observatories, radio telescopes, space ships,

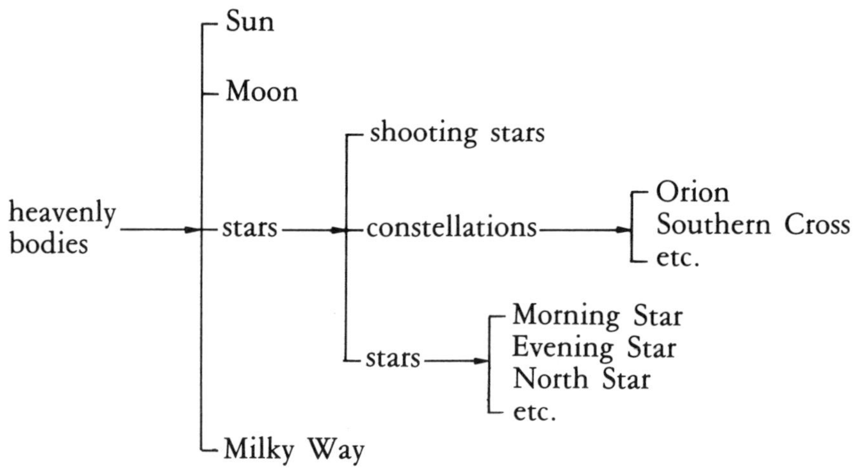

Figure 4.2 Common-sense classification of astronomical bodies

studies of meteorites (meteors which make it to the ground) and other types of information gathered in various ways, and accordingly produces a different picture. Rather than saying that science is right and common sense is wrong (or vice versa when religious beliefs are introduced as evidence), it is more important to understand common sense and science as different pictures of reality, based on different organizing criteria. The function of science, then, is to construct an alternative interpretation of our world to that provided by common sense. In our culture, this is its job.

This has important implications for teaching practice. It means that common-sense knowledge can be a very useful *starting point* for learning science, since it organizes the world in ways that can be clearly related to scientific understandings. At the same time it is clear that common-sense understandings differ from scientific ones and that schools have a crucial responsibility to induct students into the alternative scientific world views. Teachers need to be constantly aware of the dangers of beginning at the point where students are and leaving them there — in effect, stranding students in common-sense understandings. This guiding role, bridging across common sense and science, is put very clearly by Britton (1979:31):

> Surely it is the *links between* 'commonsense' and 'theoretical' concepts, the links between 'ordinary language' and 'theoretical language' that make learning possible — whether in school or out — and it is the ability to move back and forth across that continuum that characterises thinking at any mature stage.

ORGANIZING THE WORLD: THINGS

Classification

Classification is a fundamental part of every science. One important function of science textbooks is to introduce novices to this form of organization as it has been projected on to reality as a result of centuries of research. The

Text 4.4 Example of classification in a school textbook (Heffernan and Learmonth, 1981:90)

> **Mixtures** are substances that can be easily separated without making any new chemicals. We have already seen that most of the materials around us are mixtures (Chapter 3). The air, water, soil and rocks around us are all made of chemicals mixed together. Mixtures can be divided into a number of groups (Figure 5.1). **Solutions** are mixtures that have the same properties throughout. When sugar is mixed with water the solid crystals disappear. The solution formed can be seen through and looks the same throughout. If we mix sand with water, we see that the *large* grains soon settle to the bottom. Here it is easy to see solid and liquid mixed together. If soil is mixed with water, some of the fine grains, which we can just see, take a long while to settle to the bottom. A **suspension** is said to have been formed if these fine grains can also be filtered out. When some clay is mixed with water containing a little sodium hydroxide, a mixture with properties in between solutions and suspensions is formed. The very tiny grains do not settle out but do pass through filter paper. Such a mixture is called a **colloid.**

extract in text 4.4 is designed to socialize high school students into one aspect of chemistry — mixtures.

This passage is organizing mixtures into three subtypes. The relationships can be represented in a diagram like those used in figures 4.1 and 4.2, where terms to the right subclassify those immediately to their left — see figure 4.3.

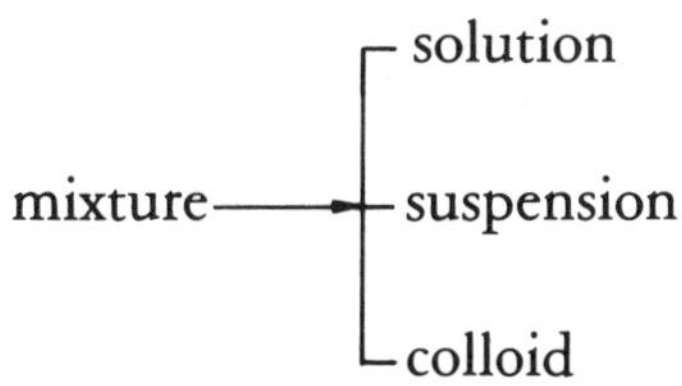

Figure 4.3

Each term in the diagram is a technical term. And in the textbook, these terms are specially highlighted in bold face. At a first glance, three of the terms are familiar everyday words: *mixture, solution* and *suspension*. One is unfamiliar: *colloid*. This term is used mainly in chemistry, and can thus be described as indexical of the field (i.e. once we hear the term, we know what field we're in). It is this kind of term that is commonly referred to as *jargon*.

We must, however, be cautious here, because the familiarity of *mixture, suspension* and *solution* is deceiving. None of these terms means the same thing in chemistry as it does in common sense. Each is just as much jargon as *colloid*. The text makes this very clear by defining each term, giving it its special meaning in chemistry:

Term	*Definition*
mixture	substance that can be easily separated without making any new chemicals
solution	mixture that has the same properties throughout
suspension	mixture in which fine grains can be filtered out
colloid	mixture in which tiny grains do not settle but do pass through filter paper

The function of definitions is to translate common-sense understandings into scientific ones. This always involves a certain amount of condensation. It is easier to refer to 'mixtures' than to 'substances that can be easily separated without making any new chemicals'. Without this condensation scientific texts would become very long, and probably unreadable, even for professionals.

The process of translating common sense into science is a long one. Most definitions use familiar technical terms to introduce new ones (e.g. *substances* and *chemicals* in the definition of *mixtures* above). So only relatively few scientific terms are ever completely defined in everyday words.

Alongside defining the technical terms, the passage also organizes these terms with respect to each other. The critical sentence is 'Mixtures can be divided into a number of groups'. This tells us that solutions, suspensions and colloids are kinds of mixtures, enabling us to build up the diagram in figure 4.3. So knowing the definitions of the terms is not enough to understand the text; it is also crucial to determine precisely how the terms are related to each other.

Perhaps the best metaphor for technical language is that of *distillation*. Technical language both *compacts* and *changes the nature* of everyday words — just as a vat of whisky is both less voluminous and different in kind from the ingredients that made it up. Marsupials, for example, are not simply Australian animals: wombats, possums and kangaroos. For the biologist they are warm-blooded mammals that give birth to live young with no placental attachment and carry the young in a pouch until they are weaned; and they contrast with the two other groups of mammals: monotremes (egg laying) and placentals.

People sometimes complain that science uses too much technical language, which they refer to pejoratively as jargon. They complain because the jargon excludes: it makes science hard to understand. This *is* a problem. Jargon is often used where it is not needed. And translating jargon into common sense is an important social responsibility of all scientists that needs to be more seriously addressed.

However, the fact is that scientists simply cannot do their jobs without technical discourse. Not only is it compact and therefore efficient but, most importantly, it codes an alternative perspective on reality to common sense, a perspective accumulated over centuries of scientific enquiry. It constructs the world in a different way. Science could not be science without deploying technical discourse as a fundamental tool.

It is thus very worrying when syllabus documents discourage teachers from using technical language with students, especially in the early years (emphasis added):

> **Developing Science Vocabulary**
> Appropriate science vocabulary will become part of the child's spoken language. This vocabulary will be introduced *only when it is needed*, or when it is desirable to communicate more effectively about something that has *already been thoroughly explored* by the child. (Department of Education, Victoria, 1981:3.41)

The idea that personal writing can be used in science is equally troubling. Given appropriate contexts for writing, children take up scientific language without difficulty at an early age (see Christie 1986; 1988). Note how patronizing the following advice for teachers would be if passed on to students like Ben, our young writer, and how misguided the unsubstantiated comment on using personal writing for abstract thinking:

> **Narrative and imaginative writing**
> 9.2 Personal writing can be especially appropriate for the earlier years and the more concrete thinking levels. However, in certain contexts, it can be *appropriate for abstract thinking* as well. (NSW Department of Education, 1987:127)

Composition

As well as classifying the world, science reorganizes it in terms of composition — the ways in which parts are related to wholes. One way a biologist does this is by using microscopes. This technology, combined with the use of various stains, has made possible accounts of cell structure like that in text 4.5 (note how the technology augments our senses in such a way that the scientist makes observations about phenomena for which there is no common-sense classification).

Text 4.5 Understanding of composition augmented by the technology of the microscope (Heffernan and Learmonth, 1981:152)

> All animal cells have a number of parts in common (Figure 9.9). They all have a **cell membrane**. This is a thin 'sack' that controls which chemicals can enter and leave a cell. The liquid contents of a cell are called the **protoplasm**. These liquid contents are divided into the nucleus and cytoplasm.
>
> The **cytoplasm** looks like a liquid that has very few other things in it. But it really is very complex. The cytoplasm is mostly water with many chemicals present. Most of the cell's chemical reactions take place in the cytoplasm. These include synthesis and respiration. **Synthesis** are the chemical reactions that make new materials for repairing the cell and for cell division. We call all the different chemical reactions that take place in a cell the **metabolism**. When a cell is stained many

more things can be seen in the cytoplasm. A number of small 'sacks' called **vacuoles** are found. These store food materials and many other chemicals. Small dark rod-shaped objects called **mitochondria** can also just be seen. These move around the cell to supply energy where it is needed.

Here we find the same pattern of highlighted technical terms and definitions as for classification. What is different is the relationships among the terms. These are now of part to whole, rather than of class to subclass. Sentences like the following control the composition (my emphases):

All animal cells *have a number of parts* in common.
They all *have* a cell membrane.
The liquid *contents of* a cell are called the protoplasm.

The relationships built up can be diagrammed as in figure 4.4.

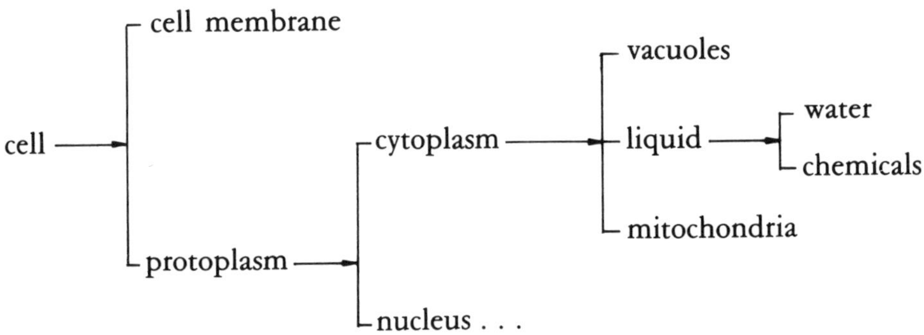

Figure 4.4 Diagrammatic representation of the relationships outlined in text 4.5.

Diagramming

In general, science uses different types of diagram for classification and composition. The diagrams (figures 4.1–4.4) we have used so far are modelled on those used by systemic linguists. When *classifying*, a scientist would normally turn these diagrams around 90°, with the largest class considered on the top, as in figure 4.5 (an abstraction from Messel *et al.*'s table, reproduced fully in text 4.8). Diagrams of this kind, model what are known as taxonomic relations and are referred to as *taxonomies*.

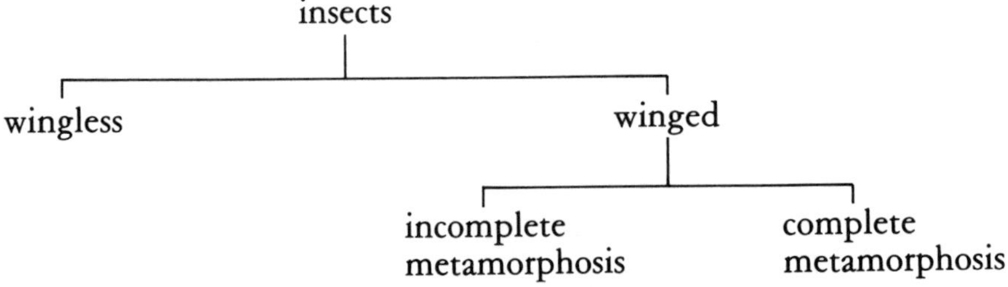

Figure 4.5 Type of diagram used in science for classifying

Composition is handled through labelled pictures or diagrams. Messel *et al.*'s labelled diagram for the structure of an insect is given in text 4.6.

Text 4.6 Example of the type of diagram used in science for composition (Messel *et al.* 1964:41-15)

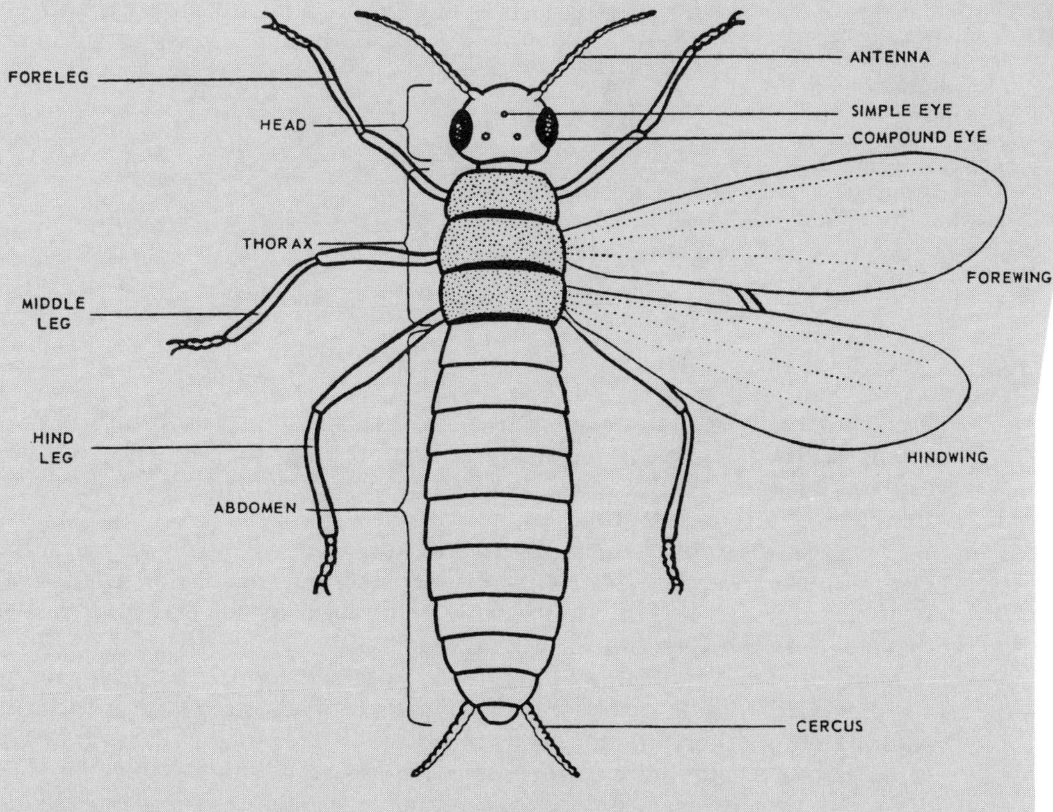

Figure 47.16 The structure of an insect. The wings on the left side have been removed. Use this diagram to ident the parts of insects collected

When the compositional relationships become complex, with parts, subparts, sub-subparts and so on, the kind of diagram used by linguists can represent the relationships involved more clearly than a labelled picture.

One of the problems with all the diagrams used so far is that although they clearly display the relationships between the terms, they do not include an account of the criteria forming the basis of the organization. These have to be recovered from passages of text. This can be overcome to a limited extent by adding extra labelling to the diagrams. Cull and Comino's classification of arthropods, reproduced in text 4.7, is a diagram of this kind.

Such diagrams quickly become overloaded with information, and the explanations given are rather cryptic. But as a summary device they are no doubt very useful. Unfortunately, Cull and Comino use diagrams of this

Text 4.7 Example of extra labelling on a classification diagram (Cull and Comino, 1987:162)

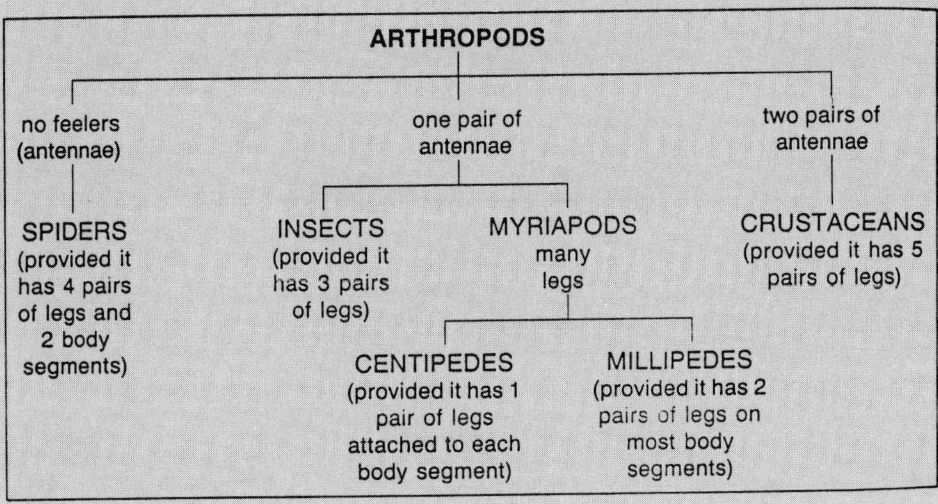

Figure 12.16

kind *in place of* text to define terms and explain the relationships between them. Textbooks like this are really little more than supplements to teacher explanations and photocopied notes; they cannot function on their own as resources of science information.

Messel *et al*. amplify their classification diagram (text 4.8) with examples of the insects in each class and pictorial representations of the criteria used. In their case, this information is fully elaborated in the text and thus the diagram functions as a kind of summary.

Morris and Stewart-Dore (1984:48–56) use the term *structured overview* to refer to diagrams displaying relationships of classification and composition (among others) in text. They recommend that such a diagram be used as an 'advance organizer to introduce readers to a topic' (1984:53). Their appendix provides sample lessons in science, describing step by step how teachers might construct these diagrams with students (1984:201–2). Being able to shunt in this way between text and diagrams is certainly a fundamental aspect of science literacy. Morris and Stewart-Dore introduce the technique with a view to effective reading in the content areas (ERICA); from the perspective of writing, translating structured overviews into text would be equally useful.

For example, in preparing students to write science, teachers can work with them to build taxonomies of relevant scientific information on the board, discussing the kinds of relationships between the phenomena being considered. Here, a great deal of teacher-guided talk, in which the students rehearse and clarify their understanding of such relationships, is an important part of preparing for writing. A subsequent step involves beginning to plot the overall pattern of the scientific genre to be written (see discussion under scientific genres, below). At this point teachers need to prepare students for some of the linguistic features of the written genre and, depending on their previous experience, take considerable care in examining

Text 4.8 Example of a classification diagram that can also act as an information summary (Messel *et al.*, 1964:47-14)

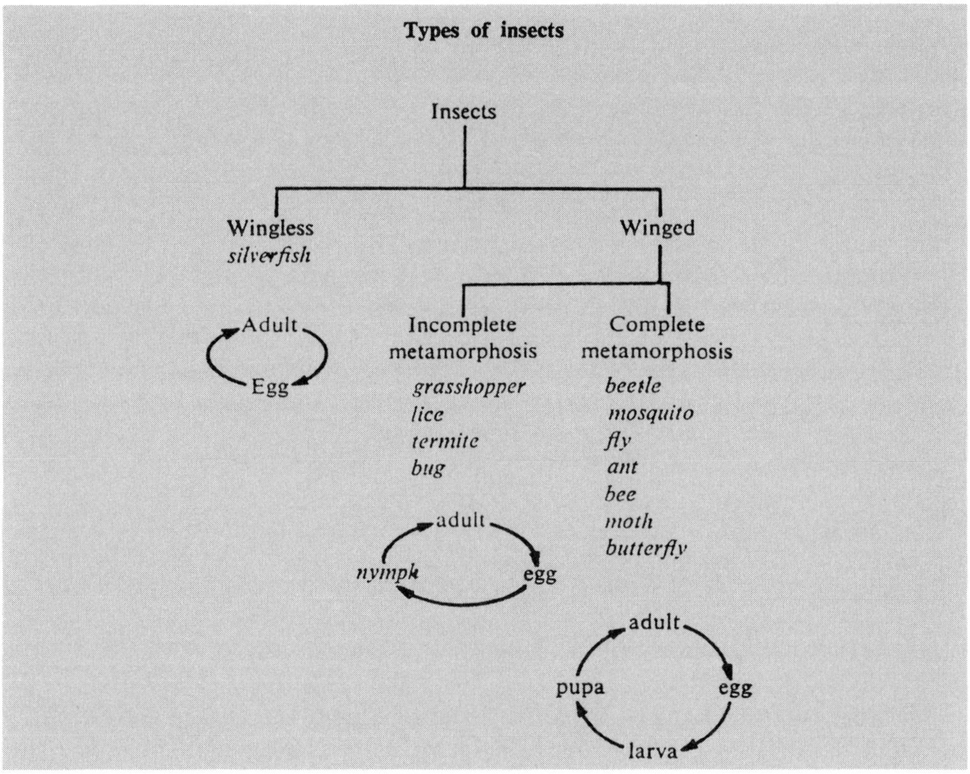

the genre to be produced. This is critical because of the differences between talking about and writing science (for differences between speech and writing, see chapter 2).

Teachers may in addition provide models of such genres on charts or in textbooks (McNamara, 1989, discusses the use of models by a secondary science teacher). Alternatively, they may write sample models on the board, and have students help with the writing. In either case, teachers and students should discuss the sequence of steps to be followed, and some of the principal linguistic features which mark the opening and the development of each phase in the text. Some possible ways to approach the teaching of writing along these lines are provided in Christie and Rothery (1989).

Once a repertoire of different scientific texts has been built up over several months of work, the nature of the discussion of the written genre for any particular science lesson will of course be considerably enriched, because students can then take all their accumulated experience of earlier writing and bring it to bear on the new task. As they develop confidence in writing science, they will be able to adapt the writing to their own purposes, even to the point of spoofing it — as current writing syllabuses are so eager to recommend. The point is, however, that playing with scientific language depends upon first controlling it. Science fiction writers like Tiptree, Asimov and Clarke were, after all, first scientists and then writers; they did not learn their science through science fiction.

ORGANIZING THE WORLD: PROCESSES

Classifying processes

Scientists do not simply organize things, as in the examples studied above. They are also concerned with *processes* — what is going on. Heading *et al.* (1967:114), for example, define geology as 'a study of the rocks and minerals of the earth's crust, and of the *changes that have occurred in the rocks since the earth first came into existence*' (my emphasis). Consequently geologists classify rocks and minerals and break down their composition; at the same time they are concerned with change. The concern with processes can be illustrated by considering two of the principal agents of change in geology — weathering and erosion (text 4.9).

Text 4.9 Two processes defined in a science textbook (Heading *et al.*, 1967:116)

> The destruction of a land surface by the combined effects of abrasion and removal of weathered material by transporting agents is called erosion.
>
> The production of rock waste by mechanical processes and chemical changes is called weathering.

The text then goes on to break weathering down into types according to the agents involved (three dots after a term in diagrams means that the textbook provides further subclassification not included in the diagram), as shown in figure 4.6.

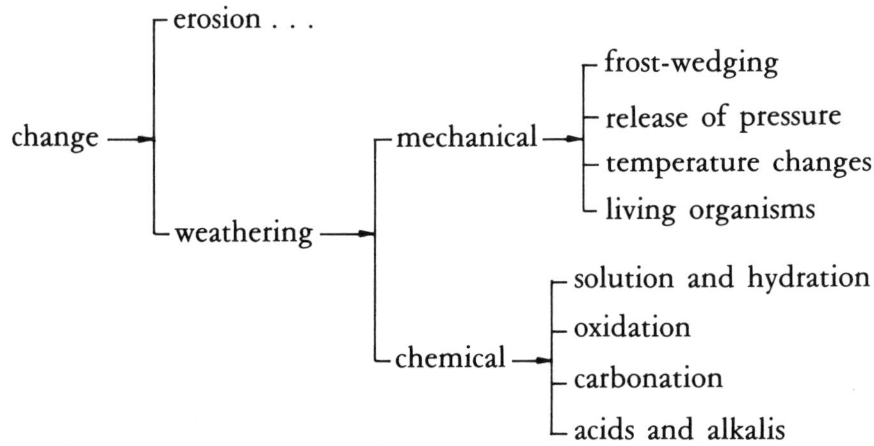

Figure 4.6

All the terms in figure 4.6 refer to processes rather than to things. *Carbonation*, for example, is the technical term for the process described in text 4.10.

Text 4.10 Example of one process as subcategory of another process (Heading *et al.*, 1967:119)

> As rain falls through the atmosphere, small amounts of carbon dioxide dissolve in it. If this water lies on swampy ground where decay is occurring, it will dissolve additional carbon dioxide.
>
> As water containing even small amounts of dissolved carbon dioxide soaks into the ground, it immediately begins reacting with carbonate minerals. One of the commonest of these is *calcium carbonate* or *limestone*. Limestone in contact with ground water for a long time slowly reacts with it to form a solution containing calcium ions and bicarbonate ions.
>
> The slow "dissolving" of limestone produces *sink-holes*, *caverns*, and *underground streams* (figure 7-F).

Commonly, during the explanation of processes, technical 'things' are introduced — such as the sink-holes, caverns and underground streams referred to in text 4.10. For a geologist, part of the meaning of the term *sink-hole* refers to the way sink-holes are formed, which relates closely to the meaning involved in classifying sink-holes and decomposing their structure. As a result, one criterion that can be used for classifying things has to do with the way in which they were formed. Geologists' classification of rocks is based on this principle — as text 4.11 (page 94) shows.

Note that the taxonomy in text 4.11 gives examples of each type of rock and provides some annotation of the processes involved. Teachers could usefully guide their students into some discussion of the value of such annotations, about where they are placed, and about the kinds of advantages to building meaning that they offer. Such discussion can be put to good use in the students' own writing, where diagrams with annotations may prove to be an essential part of some of the texts they need to write.

Decomposing processes

Because *carbonation* is a term referring to a process, its definition is much longer than is typical when things are defined. A number of essential steps are covered:

1. rain falls
2. carbon dioxide dissolves in rain
3. water soaks into ground
4. carbon dioxide reacts with carbonate minerals
5. sink-holes, caverns etc. form as limestone dissolves

These step-by-step definitions for processes are referred to as *explanations*. The steps form an implication sequence: that is to say, if step 1,

Text 4.11 Classification according to formation processes (Heading *et al.*, 1967:308)

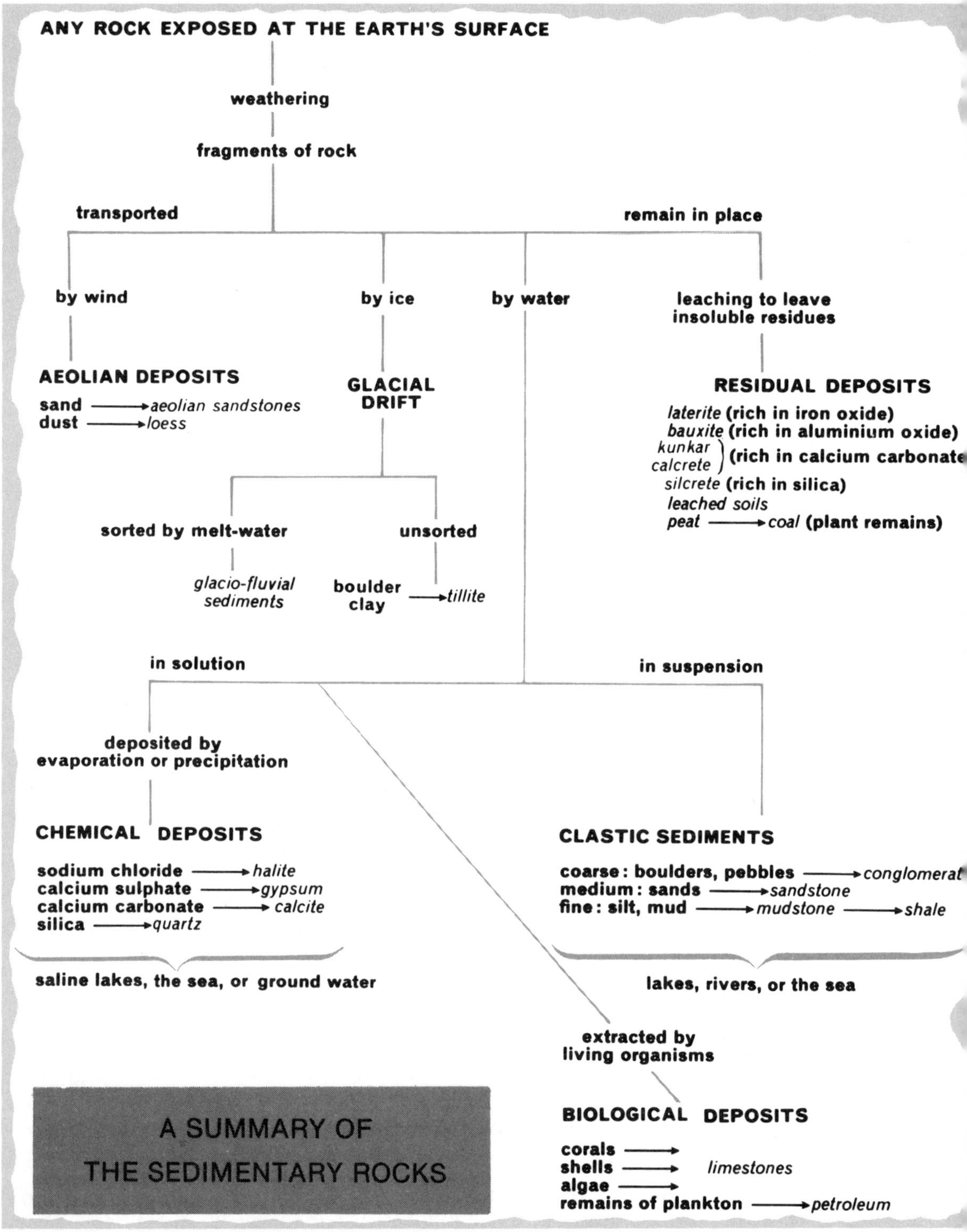

then step 2; if steps 1 and 2, then step 3; and so on. Some of the clearest examples of explanations occur in meteorology. Text 4.12 breaks down the process leading to sea breezes.

Diagrams are commonly used to represent processes such as these. Text 4.13 is the diagram used in the textbook to accompany text 4.12.

Text 4.12 An explanation in science (Messel *et al.*, 1964:7-2)

Sea breezes. Sea breezes begin during the afternoons of hot days when the air over the ground becomes heated. Radiant energy from the sun is absorbed by the ground and this energy is converted into heat energy which raises the temperature of the rocks and soil. Thus the air in contact with the ground is heated, and tends to rise. At the same time, the radiant energy from the sun which is received by the sea is partly used up in converting the water into water vapour. The temperature of the sea surface does not rise as much as that of the land, because water requires more heat than other substances to produce the same rise in temperature. Thus the air above the sea is cooler than the air over the land. The result is that the heated air above the land rises, as the cooler air from the sea flows in to take its place. See Figure 7.2.

Text 4.13 Diagram representing the process explained in text 4.12 (Messel *et al.*, 1964:7-2)

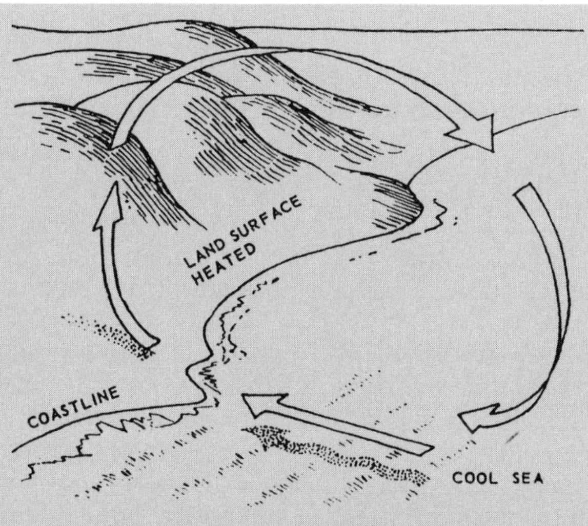

HEATED AIR OVER HOT LAND RISES. COOL AIR FLOWS IN TO TAKE IT'S PLACE

Figure 7.2 A sea breeze

EXPERIMENTS

Scientific method

So far we have considered the results of scientific enquiry — the kind of information involved in a scientific reconstruction of the world. Another important consideration is the way in which this enquiry proceeds. Australian science syllabus documents all stress the value of teaching scientific method to students, involving the ability to 'recognize patterns, generalize, formulate hypotheses, observe, experiment and establish controlled situations where possible' (NSW Department of Education, 1984:5). Messel *et al.* describe the 'scientific method', rather controversially (see Kuhn, 1962) as in text 4.14.

Text 4.14 The scientific method as described in one science textbook (Messel *et al.*, 1964:1-13)

> It is then, however, that the second important part of the scientific method is used. Scientists look at the results of all their observations and try to develop a theory or a model of how whatever it is they are investigating might work. A theory or model which is successful at the time is one which fits all the observed results and makes them seem quite natural. This model or theory can then be used to predict the results of new observations; if these turn out to be correct the model is further substantiated. If, on the other hand, new observations give results contrary to the model, then it must be either discarded in favour of a new model or improved.

Experiments in school

Experiments in science classrooms are designed to illustrate the way scientists work. They can, however, be used in two ways. One way, which we might call inductive, would be to use experiments to make observations for which a theory needs to be constructed by way of explanation. The second, which might be called deductive, is to illustrate (or perhaps 'test') existing theories.

Messel *et al.* (1964:5-9) use the experiment in text 4.15 to exemplify osmosis, asking students to carry it out themselves rather than simply reporting on what happens (as do for example Heffernan and Learmonth, 1981:156).

The text then points out that the water in the funnel should rise and that tasting it will show that the sugar is still in the funnel, not in the beaker. The explanation for this can only be that water particles have diffused through the cellophane into the funnel (osmosis) but that sugar particles have not diffused into the beaker.

The sheer volume of information prescribed for students to digest in

Text 4.15 Classroom experiment exemplifying a process (Messel *et al.*, 1964:5-9)

Osmosis occurs when a solution is separated from some of the pure solvent by a special kind of partition called a **semi-permeable membrane.**

Experiment 5.20. Tie a piece of cellophone over the mouth of a thistle funnel, invert the funnel and partly fill it with a concentrated sugar solution. Make sure the string around the funnel and cellophane is tied tightly so that no leaks occur. Now place the funnel with its mouth in a beaker of water and clamp it to a stand. Set the apparatus aside and notice the level of the sugar solution in the stem of a thistle funnel from time to time during the day and also next day. See Figure 5.10 for details.

Text 4.16 Diagram illustrating text 4.15 (Messel *et al.*, 1964:5-11)

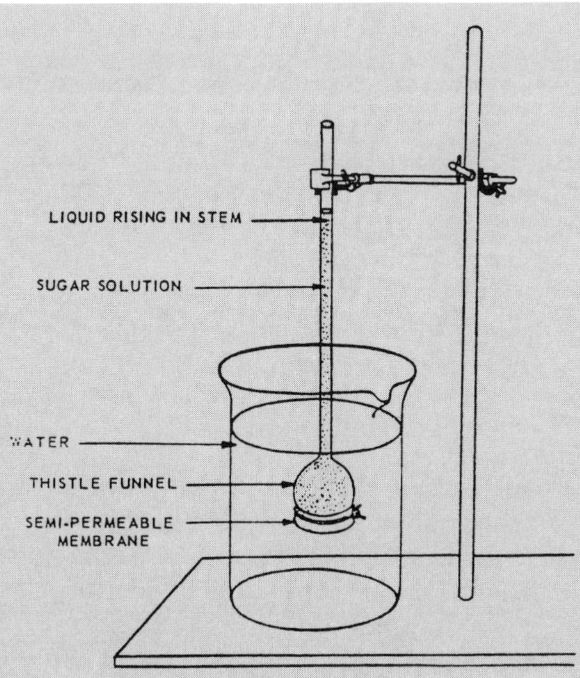

Figure 5.10 Osmosis

secondary school and the high cost of much of the relevant technology means that experiments are mainly used to exemplify scientific understandings. Teachers have to be selective about which areas they choose to approach inductively, because using experiments to build up observations as the basis for constructing a theory can take a long time. The strong emphasis on processes in current Australian science syllabuses puts teachers in a difficult position. The NSW *Science 7–10 syllabus* advises as follows:

> The proportion of time spent on practical activities will vary with the content area. However, practical work including classroom, field and laboratory activities, should form the basis for the majority of the science experiences of students. (NSW Department of Education, 1984:6)

The implication of this kind of advice is that individual students recapitulate the history of scientific discovery in their learning, something no professional scientist would ever attempt. What seems to be happening here is a kind of denial of the use of scientific language to accumulate and document the results of previous research in such a way that it can be taken as the starting point for new investigations. Learning scientific method is obviously important; but it is not necessary for every student to rediscover every wheel.

Cull and Comino's progressive *Science for Living 1* (1987) challenges the use of experiments as exemplification by setting out activities which can only be approached inductively. Consider the experiment in text 4.17, designed to provide observations which explain why granite crystals are larger than basalt ones.

Text 4.17 Classroom experiment using inductive method (Cull and Comino, 1987:121–2)

Activity 9.1. Why are the crystals in granite larger than the crystals in basalt?

In order to suggest an answer to this question we shall experiment with bluestone crystals.

Procedure

★ Add about a teaspoon of powdered copper sulphate to a 20 mm test tube.

★ Three-quarters fill the test tube with hot water. Fit a stopper and shake to dissolve as much powder as possible.

★ Allow any undissolved powder to settle and decant the clear solution into a petri dish.

★ Watch the solution closely. Use a hand lens if necessary.

Two pictures follow, one of the solution after a few minutes, the other after a few hours. Then there are the questions in text 4.18.

Answers to these questions are not provided. Some indirect help is given in the text preceding the experiment: see text 4.19.

Text 4.18 Questions which extend the observations provided by text 4.17 (Cull and Comino, 1987:122)

Questions

1. **How long was it before crystals started to appear? Were they large or small?**
2. **Did you notice anything about the shapes of the crystals?**
3. **Did any larger crystals appear? When?**
4. **Explain why granite has larger crystals than basalt.**

Text 4.19 Textual information related to text 4.18 (Cull and Comino, 1987:118)

Rocks formed beneath the surface

Sometimes the magma pushes up into the crust but doesn't quite make the surface (see figure 9.8).

Because it is now close to the surface it cools fairly quickly and turns into rock. This rock becomes part of the Earth's surface when the material above it is worn away.

For the same reason, cores of extinct volcanoes are sometimes exposed, as in figure 9.10.

Figure 9.11 shows the whole crust pushed up without cracking. There is still a thick crust above the magma. Under these conditions the magma takes a long while to cool, and it could take a million years for it to solidify into rock. Granite is one of the rocks formed in this way.

But nowhere does that text explicitly explain that basalt has smaller crystals because it cooled more quickly than granite. The point is that it is much quicker to write a sentence or two to explain the difference in crystals than to work through an experiment and surrounding text implying this explanation (some dozens of sentences and several hours of experimenting).

What worries science teachers is that if they just tell their students the information, they won't learn it — involvement in a process is felt to lead to 'real understanding'. On the other hand, the price that must be paid for working inductively is that much less science can be taught.

Some kind of balance must be struck. The present trend is to emphasize inductive processes in primary and junior secondary schools, which puts tremendous pressure on the upper secondary level to shift radically away from process and experimentation to make up the lost ground. In sorting this out we need to remember that scientific language has evolved in order to accumulate information in a way that makes it unnecessary to repeat the same research from one generation to the next. Students can be taught to access these genres, beginning in infants' school (see Rothery, 1986, on report writing in year 2). The nature of these genres will now be explored.

SCIENTIFIC GENRES

Storing facts

So far we have looked at writing in science from the point of view of field (or, less technically, its content or subject matter) — the way in which scientific knowledge is constructed. This information, as we have seen, can be formulated in various ways: in diagrams or in text; and, if in text, then in different genres. The genres are adapted to the particular aspects of science being written about.

A necessary part of becoming a proficient science student is learning to read and write the various genres particular to science fields, and for that reason teachers need to think carefully about the genres they want their students to learn. As noted earlier, much contemporary advice to teachers does not do justice to the actual genres of science, and often recommends that genres more appropriate to fields other than science be taught. This leaves many students uncertain about what is expected, which has serious ramifications for individuals during public examinations — and for a country badly in need of upgrading its skills in science and technology.

Reports

The major genre in science textbooks is what is technically called a *report*. The textbooks themselves are in fact large reports, broken down by headings and subheadings into sections. The main function of these reports is to organize information about things, typically by classifying them or decomposing them.

A number of examples were given above. Here are further examples of reports concerned with classification (text 4.20) and composition (text 4.21). The report in text 4.20 defines and classifies algae, fungi and lichens, exemplifies each and gives brief descriptions of their size and habitats. The report in text 4.21 functions similarly, except that the terms defined are organized into parts and wholes rather than classes and subclasses.

Text 4.20 A report that classifies information (Heffernan and Learmonth, 1981:169)

> Plants are divided into a number of groups (Figure 10.2). The algae, fungi and lichens are similar in that they have no real stems, roots or leaves. The **algae** are simple plants that contain chlorophyll and live in water. They vary in size from the green 'scum' growing on the walls of fishtanks to the very large brown seaweeds called kelp. The **fungi** are different from algae in that they contain no chlorophyll. They are able to feed on other plants and animals. Fungi vary in size from the tiny yeasts used in brewing and baking, to large mushrooms and toadstools found in fields and forests. Mould on bread and the disease 'tinea' or athlete's foot are due to fungi. The **lichens** are some of the hardiest of plants. They are a partnership of fungus and algae living together to help each other. Lichens can be found clinging to rocks and posts in most parts of the world.

Text 4.21 A report that decomposes information (Heffernan and Learmonth, 1981:241–2)

> All ecosystems have certain features. Figure 14.4 shows that they all have five parts.
> 1 The Sun gives light energy to the system. No ecosystem can exist without a supply of the Sun's energy.
> 2 The green plants use this light energy, with other chemicals (water, carbon dioxide and soil minerals) to make compounds needed by each plant to live and grow. (See Chapter 10.) Since they produce their own needs (except energy), green plants are called **producers**.
> 3 Animals eat these plants directly (or other animals which may have eaten plants) and are called **consumers**. They are called consumers, because they do not make their own food.
> 4 There are also **decomposers** present in all ecosystems. As they feed, they break down dead plant leaves, animal remains and wastes. They break them down into minerals, as well as getting their own needs.
> 5 These breakdown products are thus put back in the soil and can be reused. These minerals, as well as water and some of the gases in air, are called **nutrients**.

Reports typically begin with some kind of general organizing statement:

> Plants are divided into a number of groups (Figure 10.2).

> All ecosystems have certain features. Figure 14.1 shows that they all have five parts.

Where these are oriented to classification and composition, the rest of the report is organized around the relevant subclasses and parts. Reports have a number of distinctive linguistic features, principally:

- generic participants (e.g. *plants, ecosystems, animals*)
- timeless verbs in simple present tense (e.g. *shows, have, are divided*)
- a large percentage of *being* and *having* clauses (e.g. *have, are, are called*)

In primary and junior secondary schools most students write reports which focus on specific subclasses, rarely on taxonomies as a whole. These reports begin by placing the subclass in the relevant taxonomy (e.g. 'Dolphins are sea mammals') and go on to describe appearance and, in the case of living things, behaviour. In text 4.22, an example from a year 6 student in a class using a genre-based approach to literacy development (see Rothery, 1986), the second paragraph focuses on composition.

Text 4.22 Year 6 student's report

Dolphins are sea mammals. They have to breathe air or they will die. They are members of the Delphinidae family.

Dolphins have a smooth bare skin. Only baby dolphins are born with a few bristly hairs on their snouts. These hairs soon fall out. They have a long tail and the fin on the top of their backs keeps the dolphins from rolling over. The female dolphins have a thick layer of fat under their skins to keep them warm when they dive very deep. The dolphins' front fins are called flippers. They use them to turn left and right. Dolphins grow from 2 to 3 metres long and weigh up to 75 kilograms.

Dolphins hunt together in a group. A group of dolphins is called a pod. They eat fish, shrimp and small squid. They live in salt water oceans. Dolphins can hold their breath for six minutes.

When dolphins hear or see a ship close by, they go near it and follow it for many kilometres. Dolphins can leap out of the water and do somersaults. Sometimes they invent their own tricks and stunts after watching other dolphins perform.

Dolphins are very friendly to people and they have never harmed anyone. They are very playful animals.

In a major project developed by the Victorian Catholic Education Office, McNamara and her colleagues worked with a number of secondary teachers in several subjects, including science. McNamara (1989) discusses the importance of models and structured questions when introducing students to report writing. She describes the work of one science teacher who wrote a sample genre showing the kind of writing he wanted and then provided his students with the following list of questions to help them structure their text.

Text 4.23 Teacher-provided questions to guide report writing

1. How does the dung beetle use animal waste?
2. Is the dung beetle a consumer, producer or decomposer? Explain.
3. What are the limitations of the Australian dung beetle?
4. What problems developed as a result of the introduction of hooved animals?

5. Why do you think so many species were originally brought out from Africa?
6. Why were experiments carried out before releasing the beetles?
7. Explain the success of the project.

The students used the model and questions as a guide, as well as drawing on information in a video they had seen. With modelling of this kind, the writing was as a whole the best the class had produced. Questions are only one kind of scaffolding and unless carefully used may lead some students to write incomplete sentences and disjointed text. For example, MacLean (1984:161) cites a teacher question: 'Are all rabbits wild?' as part of the scaffolding for a rabbit report. The most appropriate answer to this question in spoken English is *No*. If answered in this way, the question will not prove very helpful to a young report writer.

In addition, it is important to separate questions such as these designed to scaffold a report from those most commonly used in science teaching, where short answers are required to test knowledge. The philosophy behind short-answer testing appears to be that science is about learning technical terms. As we have seen, science does indeed make use of technical language; but there is far more to science than that. The relationships between terms and the criteria forming the basis of the classification and composition are essential understandings. Short answers do not provide students with opportunities to explore or display relationships of this kind. The fact that most students make very little use of report writing to integrate their understanding of classification and composition in a holistic way, critically debases their socialization into scientific understandings of our world.

The following page from a year 8 geography student's workbook illustrates the fragmented nature of much short-answer writing. Each entry has been graded separately by the teacher (it would be impossible to evaluate a non-text of this kind as a whole). The only thing that unifies the text is its focus on technical terms associated with deserts.

Text 4.24 Year 8 student short answers

Definitions

ERG — A unit of energy, amount of work done by a force of one dyne acting for a distance of one centimetre.
EXFOLIATION — Process of scaling or peeling. The bark, skin or bone that is coming off in scales or peeling in layers.
NOCTURNAL — Referring to animals who sleep during the day and come out at night to hunt or find food etc.
EPHEMERAL — Short lifed, non woody. Fleeting, transitory, of short duration, soon passing away.
ARTESIAN — 'Artesian well' — one which is bored into a water-bearing stratum, from which a constant supply of water rises through a narrow pipe.
BOLSON — These are desert basins into which desert streams drain.
SUCCULENT — Juicy, full of juice or sap.
XEROPHYTE — A type of plant which has adapted to dry hot conditions.
DROUGHT — Exclusive dryness; spell of dry weather lasting enough for the land to become parched.

Explanations

As noted above, textbooks are basically large reports made up of a series of smaller ones. When the smaller reports focus on processes, either to classify them or to use them as criteria for classifying things, another genre, the explanation, is used. Text 4.25 is an example. This genre differs from reports in two main ways:

- it has a higher percentage of action verbs
- the actions are organized in a logical sequence

Like reports, explanations have generic (e.g. *boulders, pebbles, rivers*) rather than specific participants, and make use of timeless verbs (e.g. *become, rounds, smooths*).

For many students, explanations are the main source of extended writing. Text 4.26 is a — largely copied — text from a year 7 student's geography workbook.

Text 4.25 An explanation genre from a school science textbook (Heading *et al.*, 1967:291-2)

As boulders and pebbles are tumbled along the beds of rivers, they become rounded and smooth. Wave action along coastlines also rounds and smooths large rock fragments eroded from the cliffs. Thus we find accumulations of water-worn stones close to the shores of rocky coastlines, or in the beds of fast-flowing streams.

In time, finer sediment may fill the spaces between the pebbles, and become hardened by loss of water and cementation. A rock in which are embedded water-worn pebbles and boulders is called a *conglomerate* (figure 17-B). The water-worn stones may themselves be pieces of sedimentary rock, or pieces of granite, or possibly a mixture of rocks of more than one kind.

Text 4.26 Explanation from a year 7 geography student

Convectional rainfall

Air in contact with a warm surface will become heated and expand causing it to rise. As it rises it cools. When it reaches DEW POINT (the temperature where the air is 100% saturated with water) the (conden) CONDENSES and convectional clouds form. Thunder storms will often result.

Exemplifying and testing facts

Besides learning facts, science students as we have seen are expected to participate in experiments, which for the most part are designed to exemplify selected facts. Accordingly, science textbooks include large numbers of procedural texts which function as recipes for these activities (text 4.27).

Text 4.27 Experiment — procedural — from textbook (Heading *et al.*, 1967:190–1)

The following experiment shows that leaves have an important function in the loss of water from the plant.

Experiment 11.3

Cut a leafy shoot of a plant under water[2] and put the stem in water contained in a test-tube. Cover the water with oil to prevent evaporation from the surface. Support the test-tube with a thread of cotton and cover the shoot with a bell-jar (figure 11-D). The ground base of the bell-jar should be coated with petroleum jelly to ensure a proper seal. Set up, as a control, another apparatus similar in all respects, except that the leaves are removed from the shoot used.

[2]Cutting the stem under water prevents air bubbles from blocking the cut ends of the conducting vessels.

After several hours, note the levels of water in the test-tubes and examine the insides of the bell-jars for droplets of condensed water.

The results of the experiment suggest that water is lost from the plant by evaporation from the leaves.

One of the most distinctive features about this genre is the use of imperatives to direct the student activity (e.g. *note the levels of water, examine the insides of the bell-jars*).

Unlike some reports and explanations, experiments have a very clear staging structure: Aim, Method, Results, Conclusion. Like all generic structures, this structure is functional. The Aim shows the relation of the experiment to the scientific knowledge being constructed. The Method section provides explicit instructions so that the experiment can be replicated. The Results stage provides for comparability across replications. And the Conclusion relates the results to the purpose of doing the experiment. The structure of the experiment genre symbolizes the scientific method discussed above and has evolved to enable scientists to document their research. Halliday (forthcoming) quotes a text from Newton which provides a useful example of an earlier stage in this genre.

The experiment in text 4.27 clearly realizes this structure:

- Aim — paragraph 1 (*The following experiment* . . .)
- Method — paragraph 2 (*Cut a leafy shoot* . . .)
- Results — paragraph 3 (*After several hours* . . .)
- Conclusion — paragraph 4 (*The results* . . .)

Less commonly an account is given of an experiment, in place of the recipe style just considered. Text 4.28 (page 106) is an example.

Text 4.28 Experiment — recount — from school textbook (Heading *et al.*, 1967:192–3)

Scientists have devised the following experiment (see figure 11-F) to test a *theory* on how water can move upward in plants.

The stem of a leafy shoot was cut under water and the end inserted into a short piece of rubber tubing. The other end of the rubber tubing was connected to a 40-foot length of fine-bore glass tubing filled with water. The glass tubing was carefully lowered from the roof of a tall building and the open end of the tubing inserted into a bucket of boiled water[4] which had been brightly coloured with dye. Care was taken to ensure that there were no leaks in the apparatus.

[4] Boiling the water removed dissolved air which might have formed bubbles in the glass tubing.

The coloured water slowly began to rise up the bore of the glass tubing from the bucket. Finally, the water reached the tip of the stem, having travelled a distance of almost 40 feet.

What provided the force necessary to raise the water to this height? It is clear that atmospheric pressure is not sufficient to provide this force; you have learnt (Book 1, chapter 24) that even at sea-level, atmospheric pressure cannot force water to heights greater than about 34 feet.

As atmospheric pressure is the only force acting from below which could push water up the tubing, it appears that water is *pulled* up the tubing from above. In being pulled up the tubing, it replaces the water lost from the leaves by transpiration. This pull is known as *transpiration pull.*

The main difference here is that the imperatives in the Method stage are replaced by past tense verbs recounting what happened. Note that the participants, as well as the events, become specific in both the Method and the Results stages. In the Aim and Conclusion sections they are generic, as in reports and explanations. The text also makes frequent use of the passive in its Method section, in order to establish the following pattern of Themes:

- *The stem of a leafy shoot*
- *the end* (of the shoot)
- *The other end of the rubber tubing*
- *The glass tubing*
- *the open end of the tubing*
- *which* (boiled water)
- *Care*

Had these sentences been written in the active voice, then the scientists conducting the experiment would have been topical Theme in every clause. But the text is not about scientists; it is about leafy shoots in a rubber tube. So passives were selected to get the point of departure for each clause oriented to the organization of the Method stage.

Patterns such as these are crucial to effective write-ups of experiments. Yet, as has already been suggested, much curriculum advice to teachers, and consequently much teaching practice, tends not only to play down the significance of such patterns, but even to encourage children to write inappropriate ones. It is, for example, troubling to read the following advice to teachers:

> 8.2 Initially personal and informal forms of reporting are more appropriate than the classic report style. As students gain skills and confidence, the formal report format and the use of third person and passive voice can be developed. (NSW Department of Education, 1987:126)

Advice such as this is based on two unsubstantiated assumptions. The first, taken from the work of Britton *et al.* (1975), is that transactional writing grows out of the expressive. Collerson (1984) and Newkirk (1984), however, have independently documented evidence showing that preschool children quite commonly write a variety of transactional texts. There is now no doubt that factual genres do not grow out of narrative, but have their own roots in spoken and written language, the function of which is to explore the world (see Halliday, 1975 and Painter, 1984, 1985 for explorations of this kind).

The second assumption relates to a set of rather patronizing and romantic attitudes to children, which are discussed in Martin (1989) under the heading *childism*. These involve among other things the idea that science is too hard for children (especially girls, who are better suited to narrative) and that the language of science (and thus the science itself) has to be watered down and made personal, expressive or imaginative for children to understand it. There are now several research studies (Rothery, 1986; Christie, 1986, 1987, 1988) which have demonstrated that children can be introduced to factual writing from the beginning of school and that the main factor which has made it appear difficult in the past is simply that effective contexts for teaching writing have never been properly developed.

McNamara (1989) has also worked with science teachers on writing up experiments. One teacher produced the scaffolding for writing up science experiments reproduced in text 4.29 (page 108). Scaffolding such as this, which includes a description of the function of each stage in the genre along with some consideration of the grammar used to realize each stage, is an extremely useful and powerful adjunct to the use of model texts and questions (described for report writing above). In practice, every genre that science teachers expect their students to write needs to be deconstructed in this way and taught explicitly, if the students are really to write science.

Morris and Stewart-Dore refer to scaffolding of this kind as a *graphic outline* (1985:57–84), and describe its use in science lessons again in their

Text 4.29 Teacher-provided scaffolding for writing up science experiments (McNamara, 1989)

Heading	*What to write*	*How to write it*
Aim	What do you think we were trying to find out in this experiment?	Write a short, single sentence statement beginning with the word 'To' . . .
Method	Describe in your own words exactly what you did.	1. Write numbered statements. 2. Use the word 'we' instead of 'I'. 3. Use past tense — 'was' and 'were', etc.
Results	Include a table of results.	
Conclusion	What did you discover in this experiment?	Write a few short sentences explaining what you found.

appendix. They point out that, from the point of view of reading, these outlines allow students to 'survey a text efficiently' and are very useful in summarizing, an important study skill (1985:83–4).

McNamara (1989) discusses the following year 10 text, which recounts an experiment that 'tests the ability of liquids to pass through a substance which is acting as a "stand-in" for the wall of a cell' (text 4.30). Note that the writing follows closely the staging of experiments as they are modelled

Text 4.30 Year 10 student's written report of an experiment (McNamara, 1989)

Science
Passing Through Walls Experiment

Aim. To observe how a cell membrane works. (in a similar way).
Method. In this experiment we placed two thin plastic tubes (which were acting as cell membranes) in two (separate) beakers. In these tubes were two chemicals acting as the cell's nucleus (the other insides of the cell). These two chemicals were Conga Red and Potassium Permanganate. We then filled the beakers with water and placed the tubes containing chemicals in the observations. After a couple of days we observed the changes. The potassium permanganate was starting to leak but no other changes had occurred in the beaker with the tube containing Conga Red.

[diagrams omitted]

Conclusion. Our results showed that the Potassium Permanganate leaked through the tube but the Conga Red did not.

This means that the molecules of the Potassium Permanganate are small, so they are able to fit or leak through the tube (cell membrane). Then of course this means that the molecules of Conga Red are large and cannot fit or leak through the cell membrane (tube).

Conga Red can act as a cell nucleus unlike Potassium Permanganate.

for students in science textbooks: the passive is not used to reorganize Themes in the Method stage.

OTHER GENRES

Reports, explanations and experiments are the most common genres used to introduce students to scientific facts and research methodology. Two other less common but significant genres are biography and exposition. Biography is used to review the history of science. It may focus on the work of one individual; or it may cover the work of several scientists building on each other's work in a particular line of enquiry.

Exposition

Exposition is a genre used to present arguments to justify a given position. This genre is quite rare in science textbooks, probably because textbooks present scientific knowledge as certainty. Contentious interpretations are either dressed up as though uncontentious, or omitted. Exposition is used in text 4.31, however, to review the arguments in favour of reinterpreting dinosaurs as warm-blooded animals.

Text 4.31 Example of exposition in a science textbook (Heffernan and Learmonth, 1981:232)

> Reptiles are cold-blooded animals. This term (see Book One) means that their body temperature depends on their surroundings. 'Warm-blooded' animals use a lot of their food to keep their bodies at a certain temperature. Until recently, dinosaurs were assumed to be cold-blooded too, like other reptiles. Recent studies have put some doubt into this belief. The bone structure of dinosaurs is close to the structure of warm-blooded animals. Fossils of dinosaurs in areas which would have been very cold when they were alive have been found. Warm-blooded animals survive much better in colder areas, because their warm bodies are able to move more quickly in the cold climate. Thirdly, warm-blooded predators need to eat more than cold-blooded predators, because they need food to keep their bodies warm. The number of fossils of other animals which some dinosaurs would have eaten, found with their bones, is larger than you would expect for cold-blooded animals.

The Thesis of this exposition is that dinosaurs were in fact warm blooded. Three arguments are used to support this proposition:

- bone structure like warm-blooded animals
- fossils found in very cold areas
- large numbers of bones of other devoured animals found with fossils

Narrative (imagination)

Narrative writing is not found in science textbooks; but the recent NSW *Writing K–12* syllabus contains the following list of recommended forms of writing in science, putting narrative at the top of the list:

- Stories in science and agriculture, especially science fiction
- Personal reports and descriptions of observations
- Plays, poems and cartoons
- Formal reports on laboratory work and excursions
- Definitions
- Essays and extended answers
- Explanation of own understanding
- Designing science puzzles and board games
- Analysis of data
- Notemaking and lecture record keeping
- Keeping a diary or learning journal
- Graphic presentation
- Constructing an interview questionnaire
- Designing advertisements or captions for cartoons or photographs

(NSW Department of Education, 1987:125)

The syllabus further recommends that students use 'imaginative writing: for example, I am Joe's heart, or the biography of a molecule of carbohydrate through the digestive tract' (1987:125). As an example of personal imaginative writing of this kind, the syllabus includes the narrative in text 4.32, which appears to be an excerpt from a longer text (note, in passing, the highly gendered nature of this example).

Text 4.32 Example of narrative writing in science as recommended by the NSW Department of Education syllabus

Journey to the Brain
OK boys, on the count of three. One, two, three . . . Oh no, the ear flaps have caught my vibrations. NOT AGAIN. I shoot through the auditory canal at very high speeds, going along bumps and ridges, through every nook and cranny. Then SMASH. I hit the ear drum, jarring my whole body and making my head spin like a merry-go-round. Then without any rest, I collide with three other bones, all pushing into one another. On again off again and here I go. This time to a roundabout which I must add has some greenish-grey, gooey fluid. Oh gross. (NSW Department of Education, 1987:127)

It is instructive to compare text 4.32 with a report and explanation from Cull and Comino, reproduced in text 4.33; these are accompanied in the textbook by a cross-sectional diagram of the ear with the outer ear, eardrum, middle ear, Eustachian tube, small bones, inner ear, cochlea (which is mislabelled) and auditory nerve labelled.

By comparing these two texts, we can determine just how much science is included in the narrative passage. First, it contains four technical terms referring to parts of the ear: *ear flaps* (or more technically *pinna*), *auditory canal*, *eardrum* (more technically *tympanum*) and *three bones* (technically the *ear ossicles*; more particularly the *hammer, anvil* and *stirrup*). None of these terms is defined, although their relative positions in the ear can be

Text 4.33 Report and explanation in a science textbook (Cull and Comino, 1987:98–9)

How does the ear work?

The outer ear

This is the part we can see. It is shaped to guide the sound into the ear and along the *auditory canal*. This canal is lined with hairs and produces wax to keep out insects and protect the ear from infections.

The middle ear

This is a tiny, air-filled chamber about the size of an aspirin tablet. It is separated from the outer ear by the *eardrum*, a thin membrane.

An air passage from the throat, the *Eustachian tube*, allows the air to enter the middle ear to equalise the pressure on both sides of the eardrum.

In the chamber are three tiny bones that conduct the sound across the middle ear.

The inner ear

Unlike the air-filled middle ear, the inner ear is filled with fluid.

The *semicircular canals* control the body's balance.

The *cochlea* contains the nerve that sends the impulse to the brain.

How is sound heard?

Sound waves pass along the outer ear to the eardrum. The waves strike the eardrum, causing it to vibrate. These vibrations start the first bone of the middle ear vibrating. The first bone sets off the second, which in turn sets off the third.

The bones are connected like levers.

The third bone triggers vibrations in the liquid of the inner ear. These vibrations set up electrical pulses in the cochlea. The electrical pulses travel along the auditory nerve to the brain, which interprets them as sound.

Text 4.34 Explanatory diagram from science textbook (Messel *et al.*, 1964:29-13)

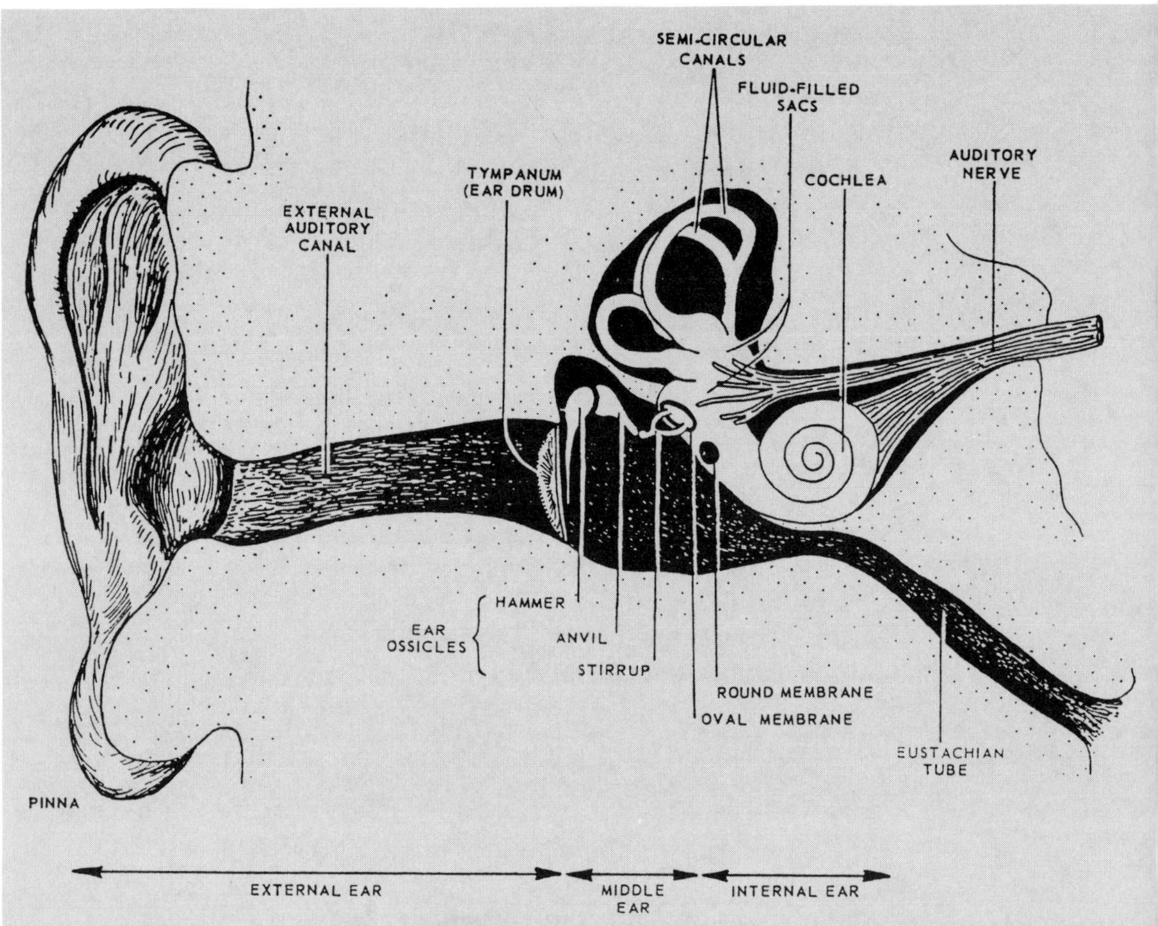

Figure 29.14 The ear of man

deduced from the time-line of the story. The function of the ear flaps (catching my vibrations) and possibly of the small bones (pushing into one another) is mentioned, and the fluid contents of the inner ear (the roundabout) described.

The real test of this content would be to see how much of Messel *et al.*'s ear diagram (text 4.34) could be reconstructed from the narrative, and how much from the Cull and Comino text. A further test would be to ask how much of Cull and Comino's explanation of how sound is heard can be reconstructed from the narrative.

White and Welford (1987:15) make the further point that a strong personal response, empathizing with the subject matter, actually leads writers to make inaccurate observations in a task requiring students to compare and contrast two insects:

> The point to be stressed is that once committed to the narrating of impressions and personal fantasies, the possibility of introducing anything

> so bald as figures or measurements recedes even further. In this respect the narrative is a restrictive mode for a task in which precise descriptions are required.

It is only through careful comparisons of narrative and scientific discourse that the real value of using imaginative narrative to learn science can be determined. It is already clear that narrative itself is a very inefficient way of exploring the ways in which science interprets the world, and that it positively distracts students from building up scientific understandings. It is not the function of narrative to classify, decompose, measure and explain. For this, the genres that science has itself evolved are naturally far more appropriate.

As a final note of caution, it is very damaging to assume that all students are effective writers of narrative, in spite of the fact that recent syllabus documents take as given that personal, expressive, imaginative writing comes naturally to all students. Many writers, and in our culture this is partly conditioned by gender, are much more comfortable with factual than with expressive genres. Syllabus documents emphasizing the role of personal writing in leading children into science are doing a great disservice to students like Ben who are more interested in the nature than the nurture of things.

SCIENCE LITERACY

In this chapter, I have pointed out that language is a fundamental tool in science. It is used to classify, decompose and explain, and to recount the investigations that form the basis of a scientific world view. It follows that to be illiterate in science is to be denied access to a crucial aspect of its technology. Most significantly, it follows that science cannot be understood 'in your own words'. It has evolved a special use of language (Halliday, forthcoming) in order to interpret the world in its own, not in common-sense terms.

I have also pointed out that literacy in science has to be considered from the point of view of both field (the knowledge being constructed) and genre (the global patterns of text organization that package this knowledge). This distinction corresponds to Morris and Stewart-Dore's (1985) development of the structured overview to focus on field and the graphic outline to deal with genre. Most science teachers focus mainly on field rather than genre, although many do explicitly teach the structure of writing up experiments.

In spite of the focus on field, very little writing is used to extend or consolidate knowledge in this area. For the most part, field is explored orally; what writing occurs is restricted to definitions, short-answer questions, fill-in-the-blank exercises and the like. The main function of this writing appears to be that of testing students' understanding of relatively isolated technical terms. When students are asked to write at length it is in projects or research reports they work on at home in the evenings and on weekends, and for the most part they end up copying, with minor editorial adjustments, passages of text from research materials they have found

(Wignell, 1987). Nationally (McNamara, 1989; Christie and Rothery, 1989) and internationally (Spencer, 1983; White and Welford, 1987) the picture appears to be much the same.

Recent syllabus documents reflect an increasing emphasis on *doing* as opposed to *learning* science. The Victorian primary science syllabus describes science as a 'practical process':

> The role of science in the primary school is to provide children with opportunities to investigate their world in an ordered way. Investigating and manipulating everyday things allows children to collect information about their environment. When this information is collated and tabulated conclusions can be drawn. Conclusions based on ordered information can be readily tested by others duplicating the same activity. (Department of Education, Victoria, 1981:2.0)

Here we have the model of the child as miniscientist, participating in activities analogous to those undertaken by scientists centuries ago as they began to formulate their picture of the world. The effect of the advice given is to foreground doing (observing and experimenting) and to background language, especially written language (reports and explanations). This means that children are not taught to access the genres science has evolved to store information, and leads to a tremendous inefficiency in the science curriculum.

The NSW 7–10 syllabus takes a more balanced view, placing equal emphasis on learning scientific method and on scientific knowledge:

> Science can be defined as a body of collected knowledge comprising the interconnected sets of principles, laws and theories that explain the Universe. People who take this view refer only to science content — the facts, principles and laws used to describe the world around them.
>
> Science can also be defined as a set of processes that can be used to systematically acquire and refine information. People who take this view consider the scientific enterprise to be a set of processes for obtaining information.
>
> For the purposes of this document the definition of Science encompasses both points of view because one point of view cannot be learned or understood without the other. (NSW Department of Education, 1984:2)

With the appearance of textbooks such as Cull and Comino's *Science for Living* series, however, it would appear that an emphasis on science as activity is gaining momentum, particularly in primary and junior secondary schools. Compared with Messel *et al.* (1964), the text emphasizes activities, inductive questioning sequences, diagrams and photographs. Writing in report and explanation genres is very fragmented. This kind of textbook may be a useful adjunct to current teaching practice, but it does not provide satisfactory models of extended writing in science; nor does it provide useful reference material since every topic is dealt with in such a partial way.

What seems to have gone wrong in the development of science textbooks over the years is that an attempt has been made to make science more accessible by downplaying science literacy. But diluting scientific discourse necessarily involves diluting the science that is taught. As we have seen, science is unthinkable without the technical language it has developed to construct its alternative world view.

To rehabilitate literacy in science, teachers and students will have to work towards a much clearer grasp of the function of language as technology in building up a scientific picture of the world. Technical language has evolved in order to classify, decompose and explain. The major scientific genres — report, explanation and experiment — have evolved to structure texts which document a scientist's world view. The functionality of these genres and the technicality they contain cannot be avoided; they have to be dealt with. To deal with them, teachers need to understand the structure of the genres and the grammar of technicality. With this knowledge they can begin to tackle the problem of science literacy along the lines of the work of Christie and Rothery, McNamara, Morris and Stewart-Dore, reviewed above. Without it, they will continue to focus on content without taking language into account, probably with an increasing emphasis on science activities rather than science texts.

The linguistic technology is the key — not just to science literacy but to understanding and practising science itself. Ways must be devised to provide access to this technology. And the answer must not involve watering the technology down.

REFERENCES

Britton, J. (with Barrs, M., & Burgess, T.) (1979). No, No, Jeanette! *Language in Education* **1**, 23–41. University of Exeter.

Britton, J., Burgess, T., Martin, N., McLeod, A., & Rosen, H. (1975). *The development of writing abilities*. London: Macmillan.

Christie, F. (1986, July). *Learning to write: Where do written texts come from?* Paper presented at the Twelfth Annual Conference of the Australian Reading Association on Text and Context, Perth.

Christie, F. (1987, July). *Language and literacy: Making explicit what's involved*. Paper presented at the Thirteenth Annual Conference of the Australian Reading Association on Language and Learning, Sydney.

Christie, F. (1988). The construction of knowledge in the primary school. In L. Gerot, J. Oldenburg, & T. Van Leeuwen (Eds.), *Language and socialisation: Home and school*. Proceedings of the Macquarie Conference on Language in Education, Macquarie University, 17–21 November 1986. Sydney: School of English and Linguistics, Macquarie University.

Christie, F., & Rothery, J. (1989). Writing genres: Exploring the written mode and the range of factual genres. In F. Christie (Ed.), *Writing in schools* (B.Ed. course Study Guide). Geelong, Victoria: Deakin University Press.

Collerson, J. (1984). Discovering what writing is for. In F. Christie (Ed.), *Children writing* (B.Ed. course Reader). Geelong, Victoria: Deakin University Press.

Cull, R., & Comino, G. (1987). *Science for living 1*. Milton, Queensland: Jacaranda.

Department of Education, Victoria. (1981). *Science in the primary school. Vol. 1: Providing for enquiry*. Melbourne: Department of Education.

Halliday, M. A. K. (1975). *Learning how to mean: Explorations in the development of language*. London: Edward Arnold.

Halliday, M. A. K. (1985). *An introduction to functional grammar*. London: Edward Arnold.

Halliday, M. A. K. (forthcoming). On the language of physical science. In M. Ghadessy (Ed.), *Registers of written English: Situational factors and linguistic features*. London: Pinter.

Heading, K. E. G., Provis, D. F., Scott, T. D., Smith, J. E., & Smith, R. T. (1967). *Science for secondary schools 2*. Adelaide: Rigby.

Heffernan, D. A., & Learmonth, M. S. (1981). *The world of science: Book two*. Melbourne: Longman Cheshire.

Kuhn, T. S. (1962). *The structure of scientific revolutions*. Chicago: University of Chicago Press.

Lemke, J. L. (1982). Talking physics. *Physics Education,* **17**, 262–267.

Lemke, J. L. (1983). *Classroom communication of science*. Final report to the US National Science Foundation. Arlington, Va: ERIC Documents Service (ED 222 346).

Lemke, J. L. (1988). Genres, semantics and classroom education. *Linguistics and education*, **1**(1). New Jersey: Ablex Publishing Corporation.

Lemke, J. L. (1989). *Using language in the classroom*. Language education series. Oxford: Oxford University Press. (Originally published 1985 by Deakin University Press.)

MacLean, R. (1984). Expository writing. In F. Christie (Ed.), *Children writing* (B.Ed. course Study Guide). Geelong, Victoria: Deakin University Press.

Martin, J. R. (1989). Technicality and abstraction: Language for the creation of specialised knowledge. In F. Christie (Ed.), *Writing in schools* (B.Ed. course Reader). Geelong, Victoria: Deakin University Press.

Martin, J. R. (1989). *Factual writing: Exploring and challenging social reality*. Oxford: Oxford University Press. (Originally published 1985 by Deakin University Press.)

McNamara, J. (1989). The writing in science and history project: The research questions and implications for teachers. In F. Christie (Ed.), *Writing in schools* (B.Ed. course Reader). Geelong, Victoria: Deakin University Press.

Messel, H., Crocker, R. L., & Barker, E. N. (Eds.). (1964). *Science for high school students*. Sydney: Nuclear Research Foundation, University of Sydney.

Morris, A., & Stewart-Dore, N. (1984). *Learning to read from text: Effective reading in the content areas*. Sydney: Addison-Wesley.

Newkirk, T. (1984). Archimedes dream. *Language Arts* **61**(4), 341–350.

NSW Department of Education. (1984). *Science 7–10 syllabus*. Sydney: NSW Dept of Education, Secondary Schools Board.

NSW Department of Education. (1987). *Writing K–12*. Sydney: NSW Dept of Education.

Painter, C. (1984). *Into the mother tongue: A case study in early language development*. London: Pinter.

Painter, C. (1989). *Learning the mother tongue*. Oxford: Oxford University Press. (Originally published 1985 by Deakin University Press.)

Painter, C., & Martin, J. R. (Eds.) (1986). *Writing to mean: Teaching genres across the curriculum*. Occasional Papers No. 9. Applied Linguistics Association of Australia.

Rothery, J. (1986). Teaching writing in the primary school: A genre-based approach to the development of writing abilities. *Working papers in linguistics No. 4: Writing project report*. Department of Linguistics, University of Sydney.

Spencer, E. (1983). Written work in Scottish secondary schools. Edinburgh: Scottish Council for Research in Education.

White, J. (1986). The writing on the wall: Beginning or end of a girl's career? *Women's Studies International Forum* 9.5. 561–574.

White, J., & Welford, G. (1987). *The language of science: Making and interpreting observations*. London: Assessment of Performance Unit, Department of Education and Science.

Wignell, P. (1987). In your own words. *Writing project — Report 1987*. Department of Linguistics, University of Sydney. (Working Papers in Linguistics 5.)

Wignell, P., Martin, J. R., & Eggins, S. (1987). The discourse of geography: Ordering and explaining the experiential world. *Writing project — Report 1987*. Department of Linguistics, University of Sydney. (Working Papers in Linguistics 5.) (To be republished in *Linguistics and Education*.)

5 Literacy in the social sciences

BILL COPE & MARY KALANTZIS

The teaching of literacy and the teaching of social science have changed dramatically in the past few decades. Or, at least, one would think so from a glance at the syllabuses and curriculum guidelines that have come out since the Second World War. In the case of teaching literacy, for example, there has been a move from spelling lists, traditional grammar, cloze activities, and so on, to 'process' writing in which simply writing for a purpose precedes or even supersedes teaching language conventions. These conventions are now supposed to be best learnt 'naturally', through use.

In the case of the social sciences, primary school social studies has moved from learning social facts and contents to 'enquiry' learning in which students are active makers of their own social knowledge, relevant to themselves and their particular sociocultural circumstances. In secondary school history, there has been a move from students having to imbibe 'facts' of various kinds, and from a view of history itself as singular, uncontroversial and universalistic. Instead, new emphases are placed on students learning to be historians, by engaging in the 'processes' of behaving like historians — working with documentary evidence which raises problems, investigating local history, and so on. The parallels between teaching literacy and teaching the social sciences are striking indeed. The changes must be explained as aspects of a changed view of the curriculum that has developed especially since the 1960s. As a shorthand, this chapter calls the old content-laden and authoritative curriculum 'traditional' and the new 'process' child-centred curriculum 'progressivist' (Cope, 1986).

We argue that the rise of the progressivist curriculum was founded on a very perceptive critique of inherent weaknesses in the traditional curriculum, and that this critique did point the way to some desirable changes. However, we also argue that progressivism is itself seriously flawed. This is the more unfortunate because some of the contemporary problems of the progressivist curriculum only encourage those of the 'back to basics' persuasion, who want to argue that we must have a return to the 'good old days' of the traditional curriculum. We want to see neither a return to the traditional curriculum with all its significant limitations, nor the continuance of the excesses of progressivism. Where the traditional curriculum stressed 'content' as something to be passed on and accepted in an unproblematic way, the progressivist curriculum stresses 'process', with no appropriate attention to what is to be learned.

The particular problems in teaching literacy and the social sciences can be understood through debating fundamental educational paradigms which often appear to the ordinary person to be mere fashions. We shall therefore begin with the debates that are the root of a number of serious dilemmas in the teaching of both literacy and the social sciences. Reviewing the paradigms of traditional and progressivist curriculum is a basis for working through the issues and helps us to understand the various ways language is deployed and learnt in the social sciences in different pedagogical models.

In chapter 1 of this volume, Christie discusses in detail both the old paradigms for teaching literacy, and the problems of the more recent with their preoccupation with 'process'. Consequently, we shall not discuss contemporary approaches to teaching literacy, merely noting that we argue, as indicated above, that the paradigms for language and social science are often very similar. Just as Christie argues for the adoption of approaches to teaching literacy which do justice to the manner in which knowledge is structured in the discourse patterns of various disciplines, so we would argue that in teaching the social sciences, an appropriate sense of the structure of the disciplines should be taught.

We shall then discuss the Social Literacy Project (Kalantzis and Cope, 1989) as an example of the kind of curriculum we have in mind. This is a curriculum materials development project for the upper primary and lower secondary school which has attempted to resolve in a practical way the theoretical impasse between traditional and progressivist curriculum in teaching social science. We feel that some findings of this project provide lessons of general pedagogical import, of relevance to the development of new approaches to the teaching of literacy.

The pedagogy used by the Social Literacy Project is directly parallel and complementary to the genre-based approaches to developing literacy now emerging from the systemic-functional linguistics school (see chapter 4). The basic pedagogical principle behind Social Literacy is that the various forms of knowledge and information known as the social sciences, like all other forms of knowledge, are socially constructed. These forms may be those of sociology, history, geography, anthropology or commerce, to mention the better known examples. Each form of knowledge or 'discipline' has its own concepts, and its own ways of dealing with experience in order to construct views of reality. These ways of dealing with experience constitute methodologies — the structured ways of exploring aspects of human experience. Being explicit about the methodologies or frameworks of the various forms of knowledge is as important as 'doing the subject'. In fact, strictly speaking one can never 'do' a subject at all unless one knows the structured methods of working associated with that subject. In this sense, our pedagogical principles are very like those proposed by others in this volume, with their commitment to a genre-based approach to literacy: language is structured in various ways according to social function and purpose, and this structure can be explained using functional-grammatical concepts. Being explicit about the relationship of language conventions to the social purpose of language is as important as being an active, confident and purposeful writer. In their respective interests and emphases, the Social Literacy Project and genre-based approaches to literacy share a concern about the one-sidedness of progressivism: its proper involvement with students' motivation, but its neglect of structure and explicit teaching.

The Social Literacy Project has thus attempted to be explicit about the language of social science. We initially developed social studies materials for years 4–12 of schooling and, to supplement them, also developed experimental language support materials for the year 5 level. These analyse the language functions of each of the year 5 Social Literacy units and present students with activities which give them a variety of experiences in reproducing these functions. More recently, we have drafted supplementary materials for the year 8 Social Literacy series which take a genre-based approach to literacy. They examine the various text types presented to students as models of different genres and the writing then expected from students. On this basis, explicit information is given on how these genres are structured to function and how to meet the writing requirements of the social science activities.

In this chapter we argue that there is no going back to the supposedly 'good old days', and that experiments such as the Social Literacy Project show that there can be a way forward which builds on the strengths of progressivism while bringing structure and intellectual rigour back into learning literacy and learning social science. Central to this move forward is the presupposition that learning a 'discipline' such as social science is essentially no more than one element in the larger educational process of developing literacy.

TRADITIONAL VERSUS PROGRESSIVIST PARADIGMS

Traditional social science

Texts 5.1–5.3 are examples of social science materials drawn from the older traditional model of curriculum to which we have alluded. They reveal a lot both of the assumptions about knowledge made in that model, and of the pedagogical assumptions regarding the ways students should learn. Text 5.1 is an extract from the official NSW social studies syllabus of the 1950s to the 1960s, while texts 5.2 and 5.3 (page 122) have been reproduced because they show the kind of textbook material provided and used in the light of that syllabus statement.

From the perspective of the progressivist period, one of the remarkable things about the social sciences curricula of the 1940s, 1950s and 1960s was just how little they were concerned with processes of learning, with methodology or pedagogy. Their purpose almost exclusively was to impart social content. Textbooks religiously followed the syllabus, chapter by chapter, and both were lists of content areas to be covered sequentially.

Text 5.1 Extract from 1959 NSW Department of Education social studies syllabus for primary schools

OTHER LANDS AND PEOPLES

This section should aim at broad basic presentations, linked with group and individual assignments, to give an appreciation of our British heritage and some understanding of the growing interdependence of nations.

A. The Commonwealth of Nations

An introductory talk on the Commonwealth of Nations leading to the identification on the map of the United Kingdom, Canada, New Zealand, South Africa, India, Pakistan, Ceylon, Malaya, Ghana and other nations that have become members of the Commonwealth.

(1) Our Mother Country.

(a) Basic geography.

A knowledge of the map; the general build, climate, principal industries and cities of the United Kingdom. (Contrasts and comparisions with Australia will clarify and reinforce the teaching.)

(b) Cultural features

A description of *two or three* of the following interesting places and historic buildings: Universities of Oxford, Cambridge and Edinburgh: Stratford-on-Avon; Buckingham Palace, Westminister Abbey, Tower of London, St. Paul's Cathedral, the House of Parliament; Edinburgh Castle, Carnarvon Castle.

Text 5.2 Activity material from a 1959 textbook: *Effective social studies* by J. B. Gregory and J. M. Wicks

ASSIGNMENT

1. Where were the first English colonies made ? ……………
2. Who is often called the "Father of British Colonization" ? ……………
3. What did all of the British colonies form throughout the world at one time ? ……………
4. In those reign did these colonies reach their greatest height ? ……………
5. What right has since been given to many of these colonies ? ……………
6. Into what have all of the British countries formed themselves now ? ……………
7. What do the British countries celebrate each year ? ……………
8. When is it celebrated ? ……………
9. What person is looked upon as head of this big family of nations ? ……………
10. Which nation is the mother nation ? ……………

Text 5.3 Page from a 1960 textbook: *Social studies for sixth grade* by G. T. Spaull

SECTION IV.
OTHER LANDS AND PEOPLES.

PART I.
THE MOTHER COUNTRY.

Study 1.
A Talk on the British Commonwealth of Nations.

The British Commonwealth consists of a collection of countries, peopled by men and women differing in language, colour, religion and in their way of life. Yet, although scattered about the world and divided by the oceans, they are held together by the same ideals — a love of freedom and justice, a willingness to help one another in time of need and a desire to live together in harmony and peace.

How, one might ask, has this peace been preserved in a world that has been so often torn by armed conflict. The answer is that Great Britain has, step by step, in the past, granted to the various peoples that were under her control, when the claim was made, the right to manage their own affairs—that is, the right to govern themselves.

The various nations belonging to the British Commonwealth are shown in the map on page 114. Some of them have already been mentioned, others will be dealt with more fully in later studies. Nearly all of them owe their present prosperity to the energy and enterprise of the British in the past. For example, under British control in *Malaya,* the rich tin-mining and rubber industries were founded; *Singapore* was changed from a swampy area, peopled by a few Chinese and Malay fishermen, into a wealthy and populous trading centre; and *Ghana,* once known as the Gold Coast, has become the greatest cocoa-producing country in the world.

But this content-ladenness and the syllabus–textbook relation embodied an unconscious or semiconscious pedagogy of social prescription. The nature and purpose of history and society were centrally defined truths, to be accepted and learnt by all. In this centralized model of curriculum, the teacher was locked, by the inspection and external examination systems, into working to the same content and the same implicit pedagogy as the syllabus and the textbook. At the bottom of this pedagogy was a profound sense that the story of history and society could be told through a singular, universalistic narrative and that 'facts', to be learnt and regurgitated by students, gave this story a universal truthfulness. There was no concession to students' diversity; to culture, gender or ethnicity. It was the one story for all. (For detailed evidence to support the generalizations about curriculum in the social sciences that follow, see Cope, 1987; Cope and Kalantzis, 1988.)

There are many features of the progressivist critique which we endorse. As the progressivists have pointed out, students might well be able to learn facts and social values by rote, but this is hardly a potent form of pedagogy. In fact, getting to the bottom of this whole problem, the entire emphasis on transmitting content through the curriculum has been at the expense of learning how to learn, or the process of learning. There is, moreover, an inarticulate and ill-considered pedagogy at work in traditional curriculum: to teach students to be passive recipients of other people's knowledge, socially constructed in the form of facts and universal moral truths. This hidden curriculum works against autonomous, critical or creative thought, producing people unable to make their own knowledge, unable to innovate and to adapt to a society in rapid and constant change.

At the same time, traditional curriculum dictates a singular social narrative to students whose needs, cultures and interests are diverse. Most frequently measured in the terms of the dominant culture, the old, centralized curriculum marginalised large numbers of students according to their class, gender or ethnicity, through irrelevance or sheer boredom. Finally, formal examinations of fixed social truths do not measure learning the 'facts' so much as they measure a student's mastery of examination technique and mastery of school as a system of rewards and credentials. This is very much a class- and culture-bound skill, and does not necessarily reflect learning in any lasting or effective sense.

To summarize, we return to the texts with which we opened this section. Much as did the traditional curriculum generally, these texts offer a view of the social science syllabus as a kind of 'shopping list' of desirable contents, arranged sequentially and structured around the topic. To understand the Commonwealth of Nations, you begin by setting the overall scene, then start detailed study by introducing the geographical and cultural features of the 'mother' country, as the core of the Commonwealth (text 5.1). The textbook followed the syllabus, content area by content area, chapter by chapter. The storyline is singular and uncontroversial, not allowing the possibility that some might dispute the virtues of the British legacy. This legacy could be factually supported by reference to the map of the world, or it might be measured in productive achievements of various kinds (text 5.3). Then, 'knowledge' could be tested, as in the assignment from Gregory and Wicks (1959), there being only one 'factual' answer possible for each question (text 5.2).

But what use is this curriculum for Aborigines or students of non-English-speaking background? (They will surely get some of the answers 'wrong'.)

What use would it be to score well in the test if, by adulthood, these seemingly 'fixed' social contents were to prove to be anachronisms?

Progressivist social science

Now we turn to an examination of a progressivist position on social science curriculum. Once again, in text 5.4, we start by introducing an extract from a recent social science curriculum document from NSW, and in texts 5.5 and 5.6 (page 126) we examine curriculum materials intended to support such a document.

Text 5.4 Extract from 1983 NSW Department of Education syllabus: *Investigating social studies K–6*

ROLES AND RESPONSIBILITIES — TEACHERS AND CHILDREN

PLANNING

A unit structure offers an effective way of planning learning experiences in Social Studies. A unit should flow from the framework of the school Social Studies plan and be expanded to include:

focus;

objectives;

questions;

content samples;

resources;

evaluation strategies;

teaching and learning activities

from which inquiry will emerge. Teachers will select an approach to suit the needs of the group.

Focus questions used to explore the content samples from the Personal,

Each focus question:

- sets a problem judged to be of concern and meaning to the child;
- is capable of stimulating curiosity and a process of inquiry;
- promotes concept development and the formulation of generalisations;
- is chosen within the context of the whole school plan.

In selecting and formulating focus questions consideration should be given to the interests and abilities of the children, the expertise and experience of the teacher, the relevance of the content for the children, and the resources available.

A focus question will need to be reduced to more specific contributing questions asked by either the children

Social and Environmental areas encourage inquiry. Children are assisted to participate in framing the inquiry by co-operative planning of some contributing questions with the teacher.

or the teacher. These contributing questions have a bridging function between the high level focus questions and the content samples selected.

The contributing questions reflect the thinking, feeling, valuing and acting objectives in manageable inquiry segments.

Text 5.5 Extract from 1978 textbook: *Australia's two centuries* by W. H. Blackmore *et al.*

Has this chapter ('An Australian Identity') been a complete waste of time? In showing that people are different aren't we making our world harder to live in? If different people throughout the world feel proud of being different, doesn't this make world peace hard to achieve? It is often said that we can learn from our mistakes. You might agree that history is full of mistakes!

Armed with some very impressive educational arguments, the progressivists have spent the last couple of decades righting the wrongs of the traditional curriculum. The overwhelming methodological emphasis emerging in the 1970s and 1980s has been on curriculum as open process. Take the NSW primary social studies syllabus, of which text 5.4 is a sample. No longer are there the lists of social contents as in the past: the early settlement in year 4, the Australian states in year 5 and the British Commonwealth in year 6 (for example, 1952, 1959 and 1963 syllabuses; see text 5.1). Since its radical 1975 revision, the syllabus has simply advocated child-centred 'enquiry' processes of learning and the content is left open to the needs and interests of teachers, students and the school community. The old, singular storyline can no longer be imposed.

With students as active investigators of their social world, it becomes obvious that there is no single, true answer to any problem, but rather that knowledge is a matter of one's perspective, particular circumstances, subjective starting point and practical needs. At this stage, the concept of relevance supersedes the old telling of universalistic historical and social narratives. Not that the old curriculum set out to be irrelevant. Relevance for progressivism, as distinct from the one old universal relevance, really means lots of different relevances; according to particular local community or cultural 'needs' and circumstances, for example.

And the only way to realize these necessarily diverse relevances is school-based curriculum. To be relevant, the social sciences have to begin with the student's and the school's particular experiences. With this move was supposed to come a whole new institutional structure and set of work practices

Text 5.6 Extract from 1984 social science curriculum document from Riverside Girls' High School, Sydney

YEAR 7 SOCIAL SCIENCE

UNIT 1. **WHAT IS OUR HERITAGE?** SUB-UNIT (iii) **HOW HAS ETHNIC DIVERSITY CONTRIBUTED TO OUR HERITAGE?**

OBJECTIVES

TIME ALLOWED: 4 WEEKS

KNOWLEDGE	ATTITUDES/VALUES	RELATED CONCEPTS	TEACHING STRATEGIES
Impact of different families/groups on: • food • architecture/housing • products • handicrafts • clothing/costumes • music • language • family traditions • festivals • famous people.	Appreciation that Australia's heritage is partly an outcome of ethnic diversity.	tradition diversity conserving culture	• Case studies — group work, lecturettes. • Carnivale Riverside — full form activity including music, food, clothing, customs, and other cultural activities. • Involvement of the school community.
SKILLS		**GLOSSARY**	**RESOURCES**
Group assignment — case study		tradition diversity culture conservation taboo	*Multicultural education materials* kit (South Australia) C.D.C. *The Australians: living in a multicultural society* — kit.

for teachers: 'in-service' training, time for writing 'programmes', curriculum 'consultancy', 'release days' for curriculum development and co-ordination, 'seeding grants' for innovative school-based curriculum development, curriculum 'resource' centres, and so on.

These structures were intended to support teachers in learning to teach the new social sciences, though as often happens in curriculum activity, the support for teachers has frequently been quite minimal. At the same time as the certitudes of the older curriculum were disappearing, the support to teachers in interpreting the new social science curriculum has lessened rather than increased.

For example, gone are the 'facts' of the social sciences. In history, students study source documents representing conflicting perspectives on social events. Students, playing historians, are posed problems which can be resolved in a number of ways, in the last analysis explicable in terms of the individual student-historian's own point of view. Curriculum is thus a process of open enquiry in which students make their own knowledge through active investigation. Learning how to learn is seen as more important than what you learn.

Naturally, the move to progressivism has not been so clear-cut as this quick sketch of curriculum paradigms can allow. In everyday curriculum practice, in what teachers actually do in class and with the materials they use, for example, many traditional teaching practices remain alongside progressivist innovations. And, of course, practices with only process and no content are impossible. But there is still a basic truth to the caricature we have just sketched of movements in curriculum in the social sciences during the past few decades; certainly if one looks at how teachers are trained, at official syllabuses, modern curriculum materials, and at much of what happens in schools.

Yet, as we all know, education is in a state of extraordinary flux and crisis at the moment. At least part of this is because progressivism, despite its idealism, has failed almost as dramatically as it alleged the traditional curriculum to have failed. Curriculum has become eclectic and fragmented. In history, for example, we see the demise of the old, unilinear, singly authored and singularly authoritative texts. This move is evident at every level, from the historically and socially conditional manner of speaking to the replacement of the continuous and universal narrative of society and history with various 'themes' (women, or ethnic groups, or Aborigines, or local history, or ordinary working people). History is a matter of problems to be solved from the perspectives of individual student-historians working with contradictory, conflicting, provocative primary source documents. But as much as one might object to the form of traditional curriculum (authoritarian and based on poor learning theory) and its now dated contents, its virtue at least was to present theory: an intellectual edifice in which every now and then, at least, all the bits actually ended up fitting together. Process curriculum, in its very nature, need only be fragmented or eclectic, because being an historian (the process) rather than learning a coherent historical world view (the old content of history) is the aim of learning.

Progressivism, moreover, is naïve about the relation of process to content. It is quite meaningless to imagine that you can become an historian (the process) unless you can actually deal with a content and learn a methodology for handling it. The obsession with process is at the expense of disciplined approaches to handling contents.

The progressivist claim that diversified curriculum meets particular needs and interests is also seriously flawed, even though it has the disarming quality of appearing to be the truism that curriculum should be relevant. It is true, of course, that authoritarian, centralized curriculum, in its profound irrelevance to the immediate needs of many students, was simply an institutionalized exercise in passing and failing particular social groups and rationalizing this as evidence of individual 'ability'. But, equally, creating more and more diverse curriculum from school to school produces inequities. Very often the curriculum is in fact adjusted, in the name of 'relevance', to the particular community of students in a school, frequently in a very patronizing manner, for it is argued that this way no-one should fail. Thus, some schools get into a multiculturalism of food and dance on the grounds that these are appropriate for the 'less able' or 'more disadvantaged' students, rather than choose the harder options involving mastery of significant skills and capacity to handle new information in testing ways. One justification sometimes offered is that the development of such 'relevant' programmes in the social sciences will ensure that the students do not fail. The truth is that many of these programmes offer no satisfactory introduction to the intellectual skills that the social sciences are intended to develop. But in other schools, usually those found in the more affluent communities where parental pressure creates a demand for another kind of 'relevance', such traditional studies as geography and history are still taught. In these schools, despite the limitations of the programmes pursued, the students typically emerge better skilled than those from poorer communities: thus does the school system often perpetuate, not overcome, inequality.

Apart from these problems of principle, the school-based curriculum necessary to sustain diversified, differentially relevant curriculum becomes practically unworkable. The move to progressivist ideals has been particularly strong in the social sciences. But, especially with cut-backs to the support structures, school-based curriculum really means curriculum on the cheap, and shifting curriculum responsibility on to teachers and students. There is no need now even for a significant textbook allowance. Teachers are curriculum developers as well as teachers. The social sciences have particularly suffered in this move, especially in the primary school. (For more detailed argument on the failure of progressivism, see Cope, 1986; Cope and Kalantzis, 1988.)

To sum up on a progressivist social science, we can link our arguments to the texts at the beginning of this subsection. Text 5.4, from the current NSW primary social studies syllabus, spells out no necessary content. It simply outlines processes of school-based curriculum planning and development, left open and general to meet the needs and interests relevant to a particular school and particular students. History is now conceived as a series of problems, as in text 5.5. Students-as-historians will draw their own conclusions according to their own perspectives. Finally, the individual teacher has no more than a school programme (e.g. text 5.6) which is spelt out in such general and vague terms that full curriculum responsibility, effectively, is in his or her hands. Social content is arbitrary and circumstantial.

THE LANGUAGE OF THE SOCIAL SCIENCES

According to whether their curriculum works through traditional or progressivist paradigms, students receive the social sciences through different types of language and are also expected to generate different types of text. We begin this section by summarizing the work of Martin, Wignell and Eggins on the language of the social sciences. (See chapter 4 for a discussion of the language of science.)

The language of geography

Through an analysis of traditional geography texts, Wignell, Martin and Eggins uncover the ways in which the discourse of geography orders and explains the experiential world. In geography:

> First, language is used to 'observe' the experiential world, through the creation of a technical vocabulary — a process of dividing up and naming those parts of the world which are significant to geographers. Second, language is used to 'order' the experiential world through the setting up of field-specific taxonomies. And third, language is used to 'explain' the experiential world, through the positing of implicational relations between natural or man-made states. (Wignell, Martin and Eggins, 1987:26)

Geography involves using a linguistic 'technology of technicality' (1987:57). Geographers' language is not a variation of everyday language purely at the level of theme or subject matter. It involves a new technical vocabulary in which things are classified as distinct from each other in ways different from everyday classifications. Names become technical terms when they are given field-specific meanings (1987:35). Taxonomy is a crucial tool in doing this. Climate that is sticky, balmy or miserably cold in the vernacular becomes tropical, humid, subtropical, temperate, cold (boral, polar or highland as possible subclassifications of cold), or dry. Then, unlike the vernacular in which we talk about things ('It's miserably cold outside'), geographical language relates its technical terms by talking about processes ('Climate *is* the relationship between temperature, air pressure systems and atmospheric pressure') (1987:26).

It is often argued in a common-sense way that 'language levels' in textbooks are too high for particular groups of students and thus that they are badly written. For example, it might be said that some geography texts use unnecessary jargon and difficult language to get across the substantive message about the natural and human worlds that is geography. Lower-achieving students do not get a 'fair go' in geography as a result of the inappropriate language levels of textbooks. These students need better written, less pretentious, jargon-free texts. Attempts to provide these are sometimes one element in the progressivist package of 'diversified' curriculum. As Wignell, Martin and Eggins put it (1987:58):

> The jargon notion of *technicality* holds that technicality functions to obscure communication and restrict access to a field. This notion is based on the belief that for any technical term there exists already a perfectly adequate 'common or garden' word which could be used in its place, so that technicality is just a process of substituting names for things and that the use of a jargon word is designed to impress listeners or to create feelings of inadequacy in them.

In fact, the discourse of geography describes the world in technical terms which are not simply translatable into everyday language. It is this that constitutes geography as a peculiar discipline and as a discourse. Moreover, technicality is a shorthand enabling concise communication between specialists (Wignell, Martin and Eggins, 1987:59). Watering down the language of geography does not in itself give more students access to the power of the discipline's discourse.

The language of history

Eggins, Wignell, and Martin, analysing some traditional history textbooks, show how language is used in a number of ways to remove people and to create themes and trends in history, building these up in sequences of events or in settings. Consider how people are removed in the following:

> The new society developed first in central and northern Italy.

Or consider how actions become things in:

> The new learning was a rediscovery of the culture of the past.

Finally, note how a sequence becomes a setting such as an era or an age:

> During the Renaissance men abandoned medieval ways of looking at life.

Prestigious writing in history:

> is abstract rather than concrete, is concerned with organizing an argument through exemplification, and focuses on what classes of people or actions dressed up as things do or have done to them . . . This is the technology of history: the process of turning a story into history. (Eggins, Wignell and Martin, 1987:80,82)

History is sometimes condemned as obscure, even elitist, by progressivists, who want children to learn to tell history 'in their own words'. But this is confusing. To be an historian is to learn to behave as one, and that means adopting the patterns of discourse in which the methods and knowledge of history are expressed. In this sense, studying history is an initiation into a method of working that is valued and valuable in the culture.

Progressivist attempts at 'real' history, making history 'come alive', are often aimed at the dryness (read 'abstraction'), irrelevance (read 'generalizing distance') and difficulty of historical language which exclude lower-achieving students from prestigious or elitist versions of its discourse. And it is indeed true that a large number of students sit for traditional history, face an impenetrable discourse, and fail. But bringing history 'alive' to make it more relevant to lower-achieving students does not mean that these students are learning the same history. It means that the diversified curriculum does not attempt to teach those forms of history considered most prestigious and which, by the examination for the final school credentials, are the only ones that will secure accreditation for higher education. Nor is this prestige simply a prejudice — it is a reflection of those types of historical reasoning, as embodied in the discourse of academic history, which have the greatest interpretative power in our society.

Writing in the traditional social science curricula

How do students learn the discourse of history or the discourse of geography? Very few texts indicate consciousness of their own roles as models of discourse, and certainly not to the point of evolving an explicit language development pedagogy. In an ethnographic study of year 7 social science classes in a Sydney selective school, Peter Wignell analysed the way students learn to write history and geography. Being a selective school, the place prided itself on its traditional academic curriculum (Wignell, 1987).

The students reported that when they came to high school, they were expected to deal with unfamiliar 'styles' of writing. Much of their primary school writing had been 'creative' or 'stories'. This the students consequently considered easier than the sort of factual writing now required in history and geography. And what they did in the classroom, copying notes and writing one- or two-sentence answers (from the textbook) did little to teach writing in these new factual discourses. Writing of any length, by and large, was set to be done outside class time. These 'projects' or 'assignments' came to be called 'essays' by upper secondary school (Wignell, 1987:5–7).

'Where', asks Wignell (1987:12), 'do kids learn how to do different kinds of writing', such as factual writing in history or geography?

> I suggest that apart from some instruction on 'essays' [introduction/guts/conclusion], not at school. At school they learn what they did wrong. It's more or less up to them to get it right. There are a few ways they can learn: i) either from parents; ii) from older members of their own generation, for example a sister or brother at university, or iii) they can work it out for themselves using their sources of 'information' as models.

Let us concentrate on the third of these alternatives. Without explicit instruction, students learn by copying the textbook or 'information' source, and trying to put this 'in their own words'. The students face this challenge as a sort of logistical double bind:

> I don't think I've met a teacher yet who'd rather you just copied it out of a book.

> They try and watch for it. They see what you're saying and if your sentences are too fancy.

But:

> If you change it around and put it in your own words and all the grammar's wrong and stuff then you lose marks for that. (Wignell, 1987:9)

The solution is a shrewd compromise in which copying is still the essential means of learning to write in the discourse of the discipline:

> If the textbook's got a long word I put it in a few short ones so it looks like my writing . . . I know what they [the long ones] mean but I don't write like that and the teacher can tell cause kids of our age don't write like that . . . (Wignell, 1987:10)

Wignell (1987:18) concluded that children:

> are taught a lot of 'what', but they aren't taught a great deal of 'how'. They tend to be explicitly given the 'facts' but left to their own devices as to how to organise those 'facts' into an acceptable text, which is a large part of what they are assessed on and it is this invisible curriculum which they learn by their own resources that can mean the difference between success and failure.

The work of Wignell, Martin and Eggins attempts to demystify the discourses of traditional academic social science subjects. These subjects do not represent simple, wanton elitism and exclusion, as progressivist critics of traditional curriculum have often suggested. They cannot be watered down without compromising the peculiar interpretative power of the disciplines. Yet the real practices of the traditional academic curriculum, as described in the way students learn factual writing, are clearly discriminatory. Working-class parents, parents of non-English-speaking immigrant background, Aboriginal parents, and so on, will not be able to help their children do 'assignments' so easily. Not all students typically have older peers moving on successfully to higher levels of education who might be able to help them. And even assignment copying or the compromise of partial translation 'into your own words' is easier with some family assistance or in print-immersed environments with a variety of 'information' sources to copy and in which the power of and importance of factual text is self-evident.

This discriminatory pedagogy, which allows social context powerfully to determine educational outcomes, needs to be replaced by one that makes discipline genres, such as generic models in textbooks, explicit and to teach them directly within the school. The teaching of social science, in other words, would ideally be a self-conscious exercise in teaching language, as much as it is a matter of imparting discipline content. Students disadvantaged educationally because of social background especially need this sort of explicit skill teaching for the sake of social equity. And explicit teaching in the school setting is a more efficient process for all students than picking up the language through repeated copying while pretending not to be copying.

The progressivist critique of traditional curriculum is very perceptive about its exclusionary effects. However, the proffered solution of diversifying curriculum according to 'needs' and 'relevance', as we argued above and argue again below in the case of writing in progressivist versions of the social sciences, does not necessarily improve educational equity. Yet there are other elements in the progressivist critique of traditional curriculum with a challenge more fundamental than how effectively it is distributed among all social groups. It is not enough to develop an educational technology which more efficiently and equitably enables all students to operate in the discourses of the academic disciplines. This is because the traditional discipline discourses are not without their own inherent limitations. For example, the emphasis on content and copying as pedagogy assumes that knowledge is a matter of passive reception and learning another person's storyline. Active enquiry, in contrast, makes for more potent and useful pedagogy in a world in which today's technical or social truth is tomorrow's anachronism. Furthermore, discourses embody social content. Late twentieth-century historiography, to take one example, has largely abandoned its earlier, metahistorical pretences, the language of which is described by Eggins, Wignell and Martin (1987). History less and less is constructed as ordered ages arranged to add up to 'progress' or the 'development' of 'civilization'. The old-master narrative of history, so the new historiography argues, relegated Aborigines, women, immigrants and ordinary working people to the margins of a narrative dominated by abstract progress exemplified by great men (Cope, 1987). The move to progressivist process curriculum, in other words, also involved a shift in the social contents of the story of history. Opening the traditional academic curriculum to disadvantaged groups of students by explication of the hidden curriculum of its discipline discourse will not necessarily solve the problem of its content. The progressivist critique of this curriculum is very important. New discourses of history need to be developed which, for example, meet the now inescapable scrutiny of groups historically on the margins. Progressivism, to its credit, attempts to reconstruct traditional discipline discourses in the interest of social equity. But it fails. Why?

Writing in progressivist social science curricula

Progressivist social science is not only profoundly different from traditional social science at the level of pedagogy. Much of the time it also presents texts and expects students to write in very different discourses from traditional social science. For example, bringing history 'alive' to avoid the abstract dryness of the old history, students are asked to write along the lines 'Imagine if you were . . . [a Roman centurion/an Aboriginal person seeing white people for the first time/a soldier at Gallipoli].' History is regrounded as story, as empirical human experience. This is often called 'social history'. Then, there is a new fashion for family and local history, to highlight the closeness of history to students' individual experience and to emphasize the fact that history is made up of 'real people'. There are fewer of the grand old chapter-by-chapter world histories. Instead, there are more thematic accounts of particular group experiences, of women, working people, ethnic groups, and so on, relying heavily on biographical recounts rather than abstracted interpretative contextualization. As well, there are collections of historical 'documents', mostly in the form of personalized accounts.

The new progressivist history is not without its virtues, throwing light into the dark ideological corners of the old historical discourse. Yet it fails seriously. For a start, it takes from process writing and progressivism in general a child-centred focus on personalizing writing into simple recount or personal narrative. These are, in fact, the principal (almost sole) writing genres of the primary school and the least challenging and relevant to students working their way through a social science. They get the students writing, but do little to expand their linguistic or discipline horizons. Furthermore, in practice, progressivist curriculum is frequently a way out for lower achievers ('they can do it'): a seemingly legitimate way of lowering linguistic standards and expectations, yet still doing the subject as characterized by its 'common-sense' contents. Surely a curriculum which fills time with the immediately doable is inefficient and inequitable. Low-achieving students often don't even get the chance to fail in prestigious and well-credentialled forms of history. Meanwhile, other schools go on doing another history, 'real' in their case because quintessentially 'academic'. However, this discourse is inadequate also, as it is dated and blind to critical social and historical issues such as those raised by progressivism. No-one benefits from this polarization of progressivist and traditional curriculum.

THE SOCIAL LITERACY PROJECT

The Social Literacy Project began in 1979 as an attempt to develop social education materials which addressed sensitive social issues newly considered to be crucial in education (such as multiculturalism, sexism and Aboriginal studies), and to come up with a working solution to the impasse between traditional and progressivist pedagogies. Our aim was to bring together the content in the new areas of social concern and the ideals of enquiry learning without losing intellectual rigour, educational validity, and traditional academic skills. Social relevance did not have to mean Mickey Mouse curriculum just for the disadvantaged. Our concerns were for all students, equally.

How did we proceed? For a start, traditional textbooks, while being readily available and relatively easy to use, were not always relevant to the needs of all students. But school-based curriculum development tended to be fragmentary and often involved a slippage in educational goals. We wanted to bridge this gap between traditional and progressivist curriculum by producing materials which were cheap, accessible, easy to use, included concrete learning strategies, and emphasized academic skills (as traditional curriculum) but which at the same time incorporated the new social issues, enquiry pedagogy and openness to locally relevant study (as progressivist curriculum).

Then, in terms of curriculum methodology and framework, we set out to focus on social concepts. This means that, as our materials are concept oriented (for example, 'What is community?') rather than content oriented (for example, 'Who are the members of our community?'), teachers can refill the units with locally relevant content. The core of the materials is the framework of concepts and the focus questions through which they are developed. The content to be found in each unit is presented only as a general example of teaching strategy. New teaching methods and ways of addressing sensitive social issues in schools are best introduced by example. This is in order to give tangible substance to the otherwise daunting idealism of the new syllabuses and social policy statements.

Not only were the Social Literacy curriculum materials innovative in their approach, but the methods used in their creation attempted to break new ground, too. Instead of commercially produced textbooks and school-based curriculum, the Social Literacy materials were developed through an extended process of consultation with a group of teachers, curriculum consultants and academics, followed by research and drafting, trials in a variety of schools, and redrafting in the light of the trial results using the feedback of students as well as teachers. Thus the initiative has been decentralized, but with systems support for substantial teacher release for drafting and trial coordination.

All along, one of the main focuses has been on making curriculum change practical. We have attempted to educate the educators to new social issues and pedagogical techniques through responding to their immediate needs in the classroom. This is an important complement to the policy-syllabus/consultation model which, alone, is inadequate, inefficient and often counterproductive because it tends to spell out abstract principles rather than provide 'hands-on' materials like the old textbooks.

Beside principles of openness to local or particular cultural experience and enquiry learning, the Social Literacy Project has also attempted to take a structured and explicit approach to learning. This operates at two main levels: a microlevel (the teaching/learning strategy within a lesson or over several lessons) and a macrolevel (the learning of social concepts structured over a year or years).

As a link to the following description of these pedagogical processes, we shall first reiterate our argument so far. It is one thing to unpack the hidden linguistic curriculum of the traditional discourses of the disciplines such as history or geography or, for that matter, the discourses of progressivist versions of the social sciences. But it is quite another thing to attempt to formulate a new pedagogy. Demystifying and explicitly teaching traditional discipline discourses are certainly ways of making more efficient and effective those areas of teaching and learning which are the key to achieving formal educational credentials, linguistic/cognitive development and social power. But there are also serious problems with the social content and the pedagogical forms of traditional curriculum. So, for example, the traditional discipline of history is founded on telling a single, dogmatic historical storyline. This not only frequently excludes many social groups from its narrative (now included in recent, innovative historiography), but is based on poor and inefficient learning strategies.

Success in traditional history is a numbers game of earning credentials, which involves learning facts and copying texts as a primary way of finding out how to operate in the discourse. How useful is the content of traditional history and how useful are its lessons about how to learn for a world that increasingly demands creativity, adaptability and responsibility from those in power? Traditional curriculum is inefficient, discriminatory, boring and irrelevant to late industrial society. The project of school reform is not simply to open traditional curriculum to a broader base. This would not only be very difficult, but a waste of resources.

Yet, ironically, it would probably be more useful than progressivism. Progressivism simply ducks the issue. It reproduces educational inequity through deceptive, supposedly democratic, arguments. 'Needs', 'interests' and 'relevance' really mean lowering expectations and not attempting to initiate students into the discourses of 'success', instead of performing the invidious duty of failing students. It is centred on the self-expression of the individual child, which in practice restricts the genres of writing that students produce. And in its own particular ways it is probably much more inefficient than traditional curriculum ever was: teachers everywhere reinventing the same wheel in order to go through the pseudodemocratic ritual of school-based curriculum making; developing an unstructured, *ad hoc* and eclectic curriculum, and so on.

The lesson strategy

So, having said all this, what can be done? First, at a microlevel, the Social Literacy Project has developed the following teaching/learning sequence:

1. Focus — question
2. Consider — input
3. Analysis — critical activities relating to the input
4. Main ideas — concept naming
5. Investigation — social enquiry applying concept(s) to broader social context
6. Reflection — evaluation

We will move through our six points explaining what each involves, and contrasting it with the methods of both traditional and progressivist approaches.

1 Focus question

At the first stage in the teaching/learning sequence, students are introduced to the point of the section of concern in the form of a focus question. This can only be answered through abstraction and concept generalization and will be addressed through subsequent steps in the sequence; for example, 'What is community?'.

Traditional curriculum, in contrast, begins characteristically with a statement, in the form perhaps of a chapter heading such as 'Life in Australia', or the teacher's introduction: 'Today we are going to learn about . . .'.

Progressivist curriculum begins with an empirical question answerable in relation to personal experience and through the medium of recount or personalized narrative, for example, 'What makes up my community?'.

2 Consider input

The next step is the 'consider' input. This is not presented as a factual answer to the focus question (in the fashion of an inverted 'comprehension') but as a problem for the students to work with. This input varies considerably according to its medium (visual/textual) and linguistic genre. It could be: a problem situation, a moral dilemma, conflicting points of view, factual information, an historical document, photos or drawings, or a combination of different text types. Moreover, as the exercise is concept rather than content oriented, the inputs can either be used as they stand, or serve as examples of the sort of material that might lead students to the concept generalization. In other words, the input could be drawn from students and local community experience. Traditional textbooks, on the other hand, simply present the author's monologue, with a closed, singular and opinionated content. In progressivist curriculum, teachers use whatever they can that will tell the students about the local community: maps, visuals, talks by community members, or perhaps an excursion. They may photocopy some bits of text and hand them out.

3 Analysis

At the third point in the Social Literacy sequence, students work critically with the input they have received, analysing the problems it raises and making concept generalizations to solve those problems:

> Communities satisfy basic human needs. One need they satisfy is the need for food. In our community we buy food in shops . . .

Meanwhile, in traditional curriculum students regurgitate the facts as presented, in the authorial monologue:

> The Australian community is fed successfully because we have mechanized agriculture and because modern transport ensures quick distribution to shops.

Students of progressivist curriculum recount the details of what they found in their community.

> When we visited our local shopping centre we saw a Lebanese shop selling Lebanese bread, a Vietnamese shop . . .

4 Main ideas

Then comes the main ideas step in the sequence. This fourth step gives the concept being developed a technical name for the purposes of the unfolding macrosequence:

> Humans live in groups and share the task of satisfying their basic human needs together. These groups are called *communities*.

Often the students have already been using this name in their analysis (step 3) of the input (step 2) in its common-sense vernacular form. There is no equivalent explicit step (the point of the whole exercise, though not an answer that can simply be learnt off by heart) in either traditional or progressivist pedagogies.

5 Investigation

The investigation step involves active social research (being an historian, a sociologist, an anthropologist or a geographer) and applying the key concepts as much as possible to the students' immediate social environment. Part of this entails reconstructing the text types modelled in the inputs through application to the students' own social context. Students might construct a questionnaire to elicit information, or write up a report, for example. At this point in the traditional academic curriculum, knowledge is left abstract and distant; it often involves reproducing — by copying while trying not to appear to be copying — the textbook writer's singular narrative in any assignments or essays, and also copying the author's linguistic technology of abstraction and distancing. At this same point in progressivist curriculum, knowledge is left empirical and diverse. Students produce common-sense recounts of the complexity and multiplicity of everyday life. There appear to be no overall ordering principles with which to comprehend society as a whole either at the level of social content analysis or the lexical and grammatical resources for generalization.

6 Reflection

Finally, there are assessment and evaluation. In the Social Literacy reflection step, students assess themselves and teachers evaluate whether students can use the concept that was the point of the original focus question. The answer to this is not 53 per cent or 78 per cent. Essentially, for any individual student it is simply whether or not the student can use the concept ably. This ultimately reflects the success of the teaching strategy in reaching the student. The reflection step involves two main questions. The first is: Can the concept be reapplied? When the students see a community other than the empirical, exemplary communities they have been studying, will they be able to generalize that this, too, is a community? And the second question is: Can the students define the concept?

A community is . . .

Except if an answer is learnt by rote, the latter question — of whether a concept, especially an abstract social concept, can be defined — is particularly difficult. The former question — whether a concept can be reapplied — is more critical. An ability to define the term adequately might evolve further down the road of concept development. Meanwhile, students of the traditional social science curriculum regurgitate facts in essays and do indeed get 53 per cent or 78 per cent, and for reasons that more often relate to the hidden curriculum of grammatical resources than to the number of facts they manage to remember. And in so far as the assessment is on facts, it measures exam technique more than it does useful substantive knowledge because, as the saying goes, things learnt off by heart one day are forgotten the next. The knowledge tested in such exams, in other words, is unlikely to be useful for the constant reworking of technical and social knowledge we have to go through during a lifetime in late industrial society, nor for actively 'reading' society and participating in it. Progressivist curriculum, in contrast, is reticent about grading students and passing judgement on them.

At best, it evaluates differential, relative success. But 90 per cent in 'communication skills' is not usefully comparable to 90 per cent in traditional English literature. Students of progressivist social science can moreover be marked subjectively — on 'presentation', for example, or on 'performance' in relation to 'ability'. Much of this is patronizing to children who would on the whole prefer the dignity of having their work taken seriously and having it carefully critiqued.

Developing concepts

This description has, of course, involved simplifying the lines of paradigmatic division for the purpose of clear argument. We shall now extend this mode of argument to look at the macrostructure, or course structure over a year or number of years.

Each year's programme in the Social Literacy materials is structured around the development of a framework of concepts, and that overall structure is ordered around principles of moving from the concrete to the abstract, from mechanical analogies to social reality, from the simple to the complex, from minor subconcepts to major complex and abstract concepts. So a *community* is a *group* of *groups* of people. *Groups* have *parts* or *members* who *share* something in *common* and who are *related* or *connected*.

The concept of *group* can be introduced concretely by set work: classifying things according to *common* characteristics. Students work out what a *group* is and does. The concept of *connections* can also be understood through concrete analogy. Take something apart. How does it work? What does it need to work? It needs all its *parts* and these need to be *connected* properly.

Then we move on to the social/abstract. Take a sports team or a family or a school class: Who are the *parts/members*? What do they *share* in *common*? How do they need to *connect/relate* for the *group* to work? *Roles, rules* and *relationships* are key ways of describing *group connections*. Then how do individuals and small *groups* form *communities*? The language for this last general, abstract social concept has by now been systematically developed.

In any Social Literacy unit, a quick reading of only the main ideas step in the sequence, each time it comes up, tells you exactly what the unit is about. For each whole year or series of units this ranges from a total of a few hundred words of text and six or ten concepts at year 4 level, to several thousand words and a broader range of concepts by the mid-secondary school.

In form, therefore, the Social Literacy materials are explicit and highly structured. Yet they are deliberately packaged in such a way that they can be reprogrammed. In each year they consist of a series of between five and eight separate small books or units. Each series of units is self-contained. However, a mix-and-match approach to the materials, within or across different series, does require very careful programming by the teacher to ensure that there is systematic concept development and not bewildering jumps to concepts for which no groundwork has been laid. The materials are also open to modification in another, more important sense mentioned earlier: to fill the concept structure with whatever content seems locally relevant or inherently interesting to students and teachers.

At this same overall level, traditional curriculum is organized quite differently. Traditional history, for example, is arranged by chronology and narrative structure, telling of abstract social processes as they move through time. Traditional history textbooks are structured around these principles, which are represented as principles of content (the abstract truth or point of the history itself) and through the medium of the hidden abstracting language described by Eggins, Wignell, and Martin (1985).

Progressivist social science curriculum, on the other hand, is eclectic and fragmented. Teachers are expected to 'programme' the school-based curriculum of teaching/learning activities. But on top of having the job of teaching, it is hardly possible even to achieve the systematic chronological and hidden linguistic coherence of, for example, history taught through traditional textbooks. So, progressivist 'programming' often really means a collage of themes (the ancient Egyptians, the Australian Aborigines, the local community), without any deeper conceptual and linguistic ordering principle. Perhaps the photocopier might provide students with something from a traditional textbook every now and then, but this does not add up to a sustained text model from which students could learn, albeit slowly and inefficiently, by repeated copying.

It should be clear from this description of the way the Social Literacy Project attempts to tackle the problems of traditional and progressivist pedagogy that the social science disciplines are not just subjects or disciplines in their common-sense definition of contents. (History is about the past, geography about humans and the environment, and social studies about human interaction.) They are simultaneously specific discourses or technologies for reading and acting upon the world. In the Social Literacy Project, we have tried to be explicit about this.

As well as this general, explicit emphasis on language-as-knowledge, Social Literacy has attempted two forays into 'language-across-the-curriculum' in a more conventional and immediately recognizable sense: language support materials emphasizing functional communicative competence supplementing the year 5 social studies units; and, more recently, genre-based language-across-the-curriculum procedures supplementing the year 8 materials.

At the year 8 level, the Project has attempted to develop a genre-based approach to the challenge of adding a more explicit language-learning component. This began with a detailed linguistic analysis of the materials by Peter Wignell. A point we have not discussed so far is that although units in each series form a coherent, developing conceptual-linguistic whole, and the text inputs to this end use a wide variety of genres, different units nevertheless develop the linguistic and disciplinary skills of the traditional social science subjects. Thus, in the year 8 series, unit H1, *Needs, Labour and Technology*, has a commerce emphasis; unit H2, *Ecosystems*, has a geography emphasis and unit H3, *Culture Contact*, has a history emphasis. In his analysis, Wignell describes both lexical and taxonomic links in the concept development and the relationships between the variety of discipline discourses and genres employed (Wignell, 1989). Then, together with Social Literacy team member Mary Kalantzis, draft genre-based language support materials were developed, taking the genres of the input texts as models, demonstrating their structure in the context of communicative purpose, and suggesting explicit strategies for teaching these genres so that students could use them in their own active social research. The Social Literacy materials already had the diversity of genres in the input models, carefully chosen for their power in relation to communicative purpose, and the requirement that students reproduce them in their own writing. The aim of these supplementary materials was to explain the 'how to' of the latter requirement in an explicit way (Kalantzis and Wignell, forthcoming).

During 1987, Peter Wignell also conducted ethnographic observation of teaching/learning writing in schools using the Social Literacy materials. He noted a range of genres in use, but not as broad a range as might have been hoped: e.g. short classifying exercises, listing, narrative, explanation, report, argument, diary writing. Nor was there much explicit teaching of how to write. Copying was still the main way in which extended stretches of writing were generated, but Wignell comments that this, itself, seemed to be working as a method of learning (Wignell, 1989). Whatever the achievements of the Social Literacy Project to this point, the new supplementary genre-based materials are an attempt to make writing strategies more explicit, and copying a less haphazard and passive learning process.

CONCLUSION

Clearly then, there is no going back to a supposed golden age when 'basics', in the form of traditional academic social science subject areas, reigned supreme. Traditional curriculum was inefficient, inequitable and involved select students in copying discipline discourses which were not necessarily relevant to the social world of the late twentieth century. Yet, in an intuitive but poorly articulated, unimaginative and regressive way, the 'back-to-basics' advocates are correct about the failure of progressivism. What has happened to 'standards'? Do they measure up to expectations? Are some groups of students still unduly disadvantaged? What are the consequences of progressivism's eclectic and *ad hoc* mode of operation? We have tried to answer some of these questions and to point to some practical ways in which we can build on the strengths of progressivism, whilst bringing structure and intellectual rigour back into the task of becoming literate in the social sciences.

REFERENCES

Blackmore, W. H., Cotter, R. E., & Elliot, M. J. (1978). *Australia's two centuries: A survey of Australian history*. Melbourne: Eureka.

Cope, B. (1986). Traditional Versus Progressivist Pedagogy. *Social Literacy Monograph 11*. Sydney: Common Ground.

Cope, B. (1987). *Losing the Australian way. The rise of multiculturalism and the crisis of national identity. A study of changing popular conceptions of Australian history and the construction of new cultural identities through schooling*. Unpublished Ph.D. thesis, Macquarie University, Sydney.

Cope, B., & Kalantzis, M. (1988). Facing the challenge of 'back to basics': An historical perspective. *Social Literacy Monograph 28*. Sydney: Common Ground.

Eggins, S., Wignell, P., & Martin, J. R. (1987). The discourse of history: Distancing the recoverable past. *Working Papers in Linguistics No. 5*. Linguistics Department, University of Sydney.

Gregory, J. B., & Wicks, J. M. (1959). *Effective Social Studies*. Sydney: Horwitz Martin.

Kalantzis, M., & Cope, B. (1989). *Social literacy: An overview*. Sydney: Common Ground.

Kalantzis, M., & Wignell, P. (forthcoming). Genre-based language support materials for the Social Literacy Project. Sydney: Common Ground.

Literacy and Education Research Network. (1985). The fundamentals of literacy: Where will *Writing K–12* take us? Mimeo.

NSW Department of Education. (1959). *Social studies syllabus for primary schools*. Sydney: NSW Dept of Education.

NSW Department of Education. (1983). *Investigating social studies, K–6*. Sydney.

Riverside Girls High School. (1984). *Social science curriculum*. Mimeo. Sydney: Riverside Girls High School.

Spaul, G. T. (1960). *Studies for sixth grade*. Sydney: Martin Educational.

Wignell, P. (1987). In your own words. *Working Papers in Linguistics No. 5*. Linguistics Department, University of Sydney.

Wignell, P. (1989). Report on the Social Literacy Project. *Social Literacy Monograph 41*. Sydney: Common Ground.

Wignell, P., Martin, J. R., & Eggins, S. (1987). The discourse of geography: Ordering and explaining the experiential world. *Working Papers in Linguistics No. 5*. Linguistics Department, University of Sydney.

6 On literacy and gender

JANET WHITE

'Boys are more to do with practical work and experiments and girls are more to learn and listen and enjoy writing.'

15-year-old boy

Learning language, learning gender

What connections are there between the ways children learn language in school and questions of gender identity? As soon as we start to ask questions about language and gender, we come across certain anomalies in the way in which 'literacy' is acquired in school. Despite an apparent equality of provision, boys and girls learn to be literate in different ways (Martin and Rothery, 1984; Gilbert, 1989) and with different degrees of proficiency (Gorman *et al.*, 1988). Furthermore, the experience of language in contemporary schooling does much to polarize spoken and written modes of communication for girls and boys alike (Kaplan, 1983), with boys typically able to trade off their poorer performance in literacy by means of their sheer volume of talk (Spender, 1980; Buswell, 1984; Swann and Graddol, 1988). Literacy likewise becomes something that can be detached from 'practical work' (as we can see in the comment of the teenage boy quoted above), and even from intellectual effort (Stanworth, 1983; Whyld, 1983; McRobbie and McCabe, 1982), although language is just as systematically concerned in the making of meaning in mathematics and science as it is in the study of literature.

One of the abiding ironies in the present schooling ethos is that, for all the public and professional promotion of 'literacy' as the touchstone of educational success, in the day-to-day encounters of the classroom it is the

The views expressed in this chapter are those of the author, and are not necessarily shared by the National Foundation for Education Research or the Assessment of Performance Unit.

quiet girl reading and writing with untroubled competence who is thought to be merely passive and probably dull, while the boy who can barely write his own name is excused on the basis of having 'flair', of being 'bored . . . not because he is not clever, but because he just cannot sit still, he has got no concentration . . . very disruptive . . . but quite bright' (ESRC, 1988).

Disparities in language learning

It has been argued elsewhere in this book that literacy is not a neutral serviceable tool but a socially mediated resource intimately bound up with the creation of meaning and structure in everyday life. The complex demands on all forms of language in the late twentieth century make the prescriptions regarding reading and writing of an earlier age seem quaint, but even after the old practices of copybook writing and rote learning have been superseded, the far-reaching subtle conditioning effects of language curricula remain (Martin, 1985). While many educators point to significant changes in their practice with respect to a diversified curriculum, a greater amount of pupil involvement in learning, and a wider range of purposes for all modes of language use, it is still the case that one nineteenth-century ideal persistently re-emerges in the outcomes of schooling for girls: that of the genteel educated female, 'literate, with a smattering of foreign languages, a future in an office, and the holder of the religious conscience' (Marland, 1983).

In this chapter I argue that, for teachers to counter the gendered outcomes of schooling, they need to be prepared to intervene in the literacy development of pupils with a clear, explicit knowledge of the way language works at all levels of meaning creation. The generic structures of speech and writing shape and create the knowledge of school subjects, but they simultaneously shape the identities of speakers and writers. Without a knowledge of how meanings are made through language, teachers are liable to unconscious collusion in the repetition of sex-stereotyped educational practices, often carried out in the name of more enlightened pedagogies, in which great stress is laid on 'starting from the experience of the child' or 'the process of learning' as being in some way distinctly more valuable than the 'product'.

Approaches which espouse such views tend to overlook disparities in the actual language experience of children, with respect to variables of race and class as well as gender (Heath, 1983; McNamara, 1989). Diminished scrutiny of the products or outcomes of learning, however dynamic the processes which lead up to these may have been, is in my view an abrogation of responsibility on the part of anyone who seeks to redress such imbalances. As Blanchard points out, 'often what is not dynamic, in this view, is the content of the curriculum' (1988:32). I will develop this criticism later on with reference to the narrative writing of children involved in process-oriented classrooms.

GENDER DIFFERENCES IN LITERACY DEVELOPMENT

Literacy in relation to other functions of language

There is by now an accumulation of research findings concerning differences in the educational experiences of girls and boys. Many of these relate directly to uses of language. Differences in the language practices of each sex group, even before literacy becomes an issue, have been documented. An observational study of a mixed-sex playgroup of 4–5-year-olds noted the following typical features:

> The girls would . . . choose to draw and write sentences alone or quietly in small groups, occasionally a boy would join them but the subjects they were drawing would be very different. The girls would draw things related to the home . . . boys would draw spaceships, cars and motorbikes.
>
> Girls could be seen reading quietly in the library corner, reading stories to themselves or to each other . . . The boys much preferred to be constructing or role playing an adventure . . . When the boys were [involved in activities that they obviously enjoyed] their language ability was far superior to that of the girls . . . When questioned about their models the boys would use intricate detail to describe their construction. The boys with spaceships then flew them around the room with excellent sound effects . . . One morning a girl joined the group of boys making guns, but when the role playing began she was rebuked by the teacher for making 'too much noise'. (Hough, 1984:6–7)

From the same playgroup also comes evidence of the extent to which girls and boys both enforce role definitions, amounting at times to intolerance of 'deviance': 'Will you please take off that dress, boys don't wear dresses' (girl's impatient comment); 'A mummy would hit her thumb with a hammer, she couldn't go for a walk on her own' (boy's pronouncement on the limits of a mother's role). A short *but nonetheless significant* lifetime of differential practice with the functions of language used to interact with the world of people and phenomena lies behind the 'choices' which girls and boys typically make in selecting and composing written texts from the stage of initial literacy onwards.

Links between reading and writing

Writing depends on reading, and what is often overlooked, as the emphasis in literacy development turns to children's 'own writing', is that children can write only those texts which they know how to read. Over the past decade numerous campaigns have been mounted through subject associations to counter sex bias in reading materials, but these initiatives are slight when weighed against the mass of print and televisual media encountered by children. Occasional light pruning of the school's bookshelves and conscientious revisions of worksheets do little to address the question of what it is that children read *for pleasure* and hence what they are most likely to turn to for inspiration when they start to write.

In this context, it is worth emphasizing the coincidence of findings from classrooms in the UK and Australia concerning patterns in children's reading and writing. In Australia, the research of Martin (1985), Poynton (1985) and Gilbert (1989) has established that in the primary school girls are much more likely than boys to write narratives in preference to reports or accounts of how things work. In the UK, a series of Assessment of Performance Unit (APU) language surveys conducted between 1979 and 1983 (Gorman *et al.*, 1981 *et seq.*) has provided a similar picture of the literacy orientations of pupils aged 11 and 15, specifically connecting reading and writing habits. This research has noted that both boys and girls enjoy reading various kinds of fiction in the primary school (with preferences differing along gender lines), but that boys rather than girls have clearly developed interests in a range of 'hobbyist' magazines (for example, fishing, cycling, model making, stamp collecting, etc.). Girls are in general more avid readers, whereas boys prefer to watch television, and both have positive cases to put for their preferred medium, as texts 6.1 and 6.2 clearly show.

Text 6.1 11-year-old boy's preference for television (reduced size)

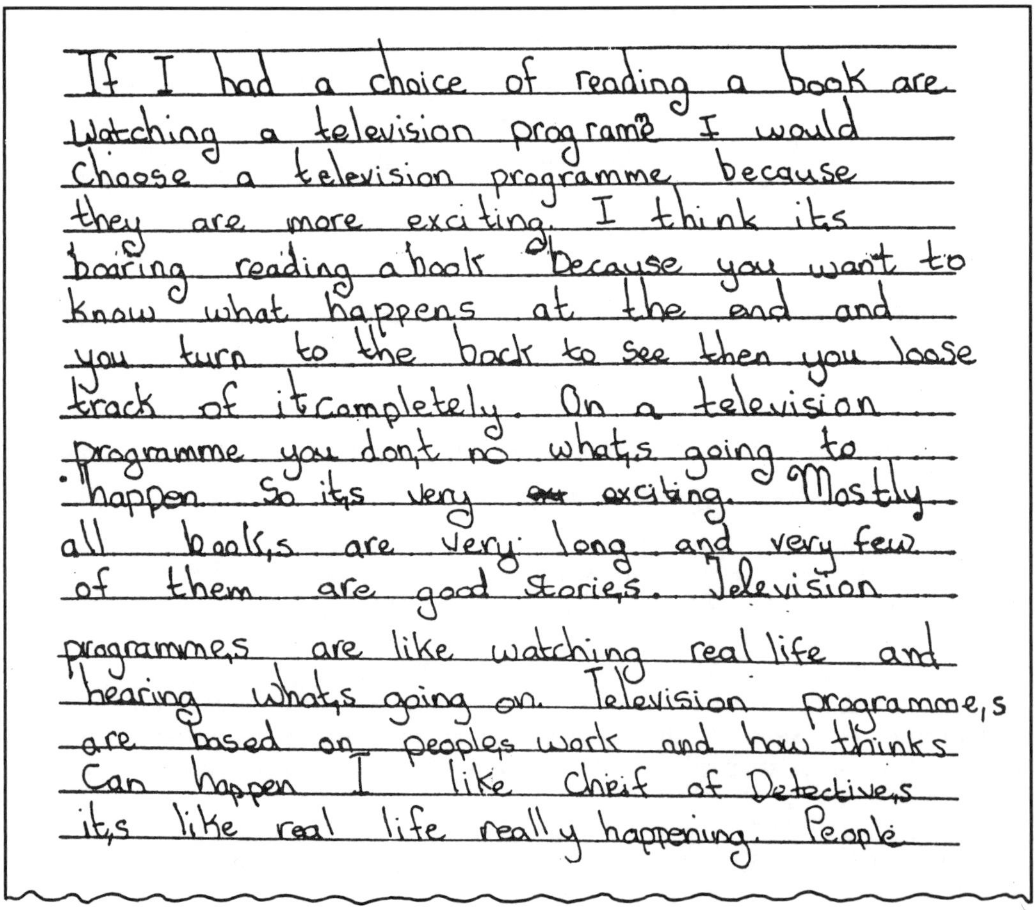

If I had a choice of reading a book are
Watching a television programe I would
Choose a television programme because
they are more exciting. I think it,s
boaring reading a book because you want to
Know what happens at the end and
you turn to the back to see then you loose
track of it completely. On a television
programme you don,t no what,s going to
happen. So it,s very exciting. Mostly
all book,s are very long and very few
of them are good Stories. Television
programme,s are like watching real life and
hearing what,s going on. Television programme,s
are based on people,s work and how thinks
Can happen I like Chief of Detective,s
it,s like real life really happening. People

have to do work like that really.
Thats why I like television programme,s
the best. When your reading a books
you cant really take it all in because
there not ~~so~~ exciting.

Text 6.2 11-year-old girl's preference for reading (reduced size)

I like reading when I have a few
minutes. I like reading in my mind it
helps me consentrate. Reading takes me into
Lands I never knew existed. It also helps
me to get ideas when write stories
in school. I like fairy stories best. The
authors I like best are Enid Blyton and
Ruth-manning-sanders, I like thick books to
read because it takes longer to read.
Mystery stories are good aswell. I read
for two-three hours every day. Reading
helps you find things out. There are
lots of things you can find out.
There are different books for people who
like different books. You can never get
bored of reading because there are
different kinds of books.

By age 15, these differences are accentuated, with many more boys than girls stating a preference for books and magazines 'which give accurate facts about hobbies or how things work'. It is clear that boys and girls are looking to reading material to provide different forms of knowledge, with girls stating that they read to 'help understand their own and other people's problems' such as those to do with sex, love and marriage. While a great deal of this reading material (love stories, comics, specialist magazines) is not the subject of official study at school, there is more coincidence between the themes of girls' preferred reading and courses in English literature. There are similarly direct links between the technical reading consumed by boys and scientific/mathematical areas of the curriculum. (See also national survey data from both the UK and the USA which relate pupils' leisure interests to their takeup of science subjects [Johnson and Murphy, 1986].)

The reading predilections of each sex group are equally evident in their writing. The voluntary writing of girls in primary school comprises often quite voluminous correspondence with pen friends, contrasted with boys who write the 'odd letter' or, in about one in three cases, never put pen to paper outside school (White, 1987).

Boys who do write fiction for their own enjoyment choose themes such as plane crashes, murders, thrillers or war exploits — poles apart from girls' interests in 'things I would like to happen to me', fairy stories or stories about horses. At age 15, girls continue to give preference to writing which is self-reflective or empathetic in character, in contrast to the practical, informative bias of boys' writing. Increasingly, boys' self-directed literacy is associated with the microcomputer, further extending earlier interests in graphics, tables and symbolic displays (EOC, 1985).

CONSEQUENCES OF STEREOTYPICAL READING/WRITING HABITS

Who is disadvantaged?

There seems to be a general consensus that the narrowing of girls' interests to genres of writing which are easily marginalized puts them at a disadvantage educationally:

> Telling fairy stories, even telling good fairy stories very well, for all that has been said about the importance of fantasy in psychological development, simply doesn't count. The real positions of power and influence in our society necessitate command of genres for which boys' educational experience provides an appropriate preparation and girls' does not. (Poynton, 1985:36)

The other genres which Poynton has in mind are not just the written ones concerned with exposition and argument, but their counterparts in talk. Many a feminist critic would be in agreement with that position, and take up the challenge: '. . . speaking up, at home, at school, on the stage, always seemed to involve a sense of danger and challenge, which I fed on' (Kaplan, 1983:52). Individual solutions aside, the advantage/disadvantage lines are not so easily drawn. Firstly, there is the question of what girls are in fact doing with the narrative forms they know so well. Secondly, there is the abiding tension between schools' official criteria for excellence in literacy, and the dispensability of these practices for all but a few rewarding occupations in the world outside (White, 1986). Thirdly, there are many questions surrounding the nature of the 'power' boys learn to wield so early on — is it an equivocal advantage?

Resistance from within

In a penetrating study of the writing of 10-year-old girls, Gilbert has shown how a conventional narrative form of romance can be, if not subverted entirely, then at least pulled and pushed by the force of the female writer's underlying resistance to depicting a passive heroine, waiting for a princely solution to her fate (Gilbert, 1989). It is undoubtedly the case that closer reading of the written outputs of other classrooms would alert us to similar writings of resistance, not only from girls. Boys too are positioned in conventional roles by much of the fiction they consume: he-man, daredevil, invincible hulk; constantly challenged to reconfirm their supremacy. Neither the all-conquering hero nor the stay-at-home princess fit the lived realities of childhood or adolescence.

Irrespective of the extent to which we may find girls and boys alike reworking conventional text types, it is important to place on record the fact that, when required to do so, girls are able to read and write a wider range of written genres than Poynton and Martin, at least, seem to give them credit for. From the data we now have in the UK, both from the repeated APU language surveys (Gorman *et al.*, 1981, 1982a, 1982b, 1983) and the International Association for the Evaluation of Educational Achievement (IEA) Study of Written Composition (reported in Gubb *et al.*, 1987), it is clear that girls' performance in writing at all the ages investigated (11, 14, 15, 16+) is in advance of boys'. Overall, the differences are statistically significant. When we review literacy achievements of each sex as a group in this way, two very different patterns of performance are evident, always with more boys than girls in the low-scoring groups, and girls forming a greater proportion of high-scoring groups.

In view of the Australian perspective on the specialization of literacy skills along gendered lines, it is interesting to note our findings that some genres of writing used in the UK surveys show a larger advantage for girls than for boys. These include varieties of autobiographical and fictional narrative, although boys as well find such types of writing relatively easy. Girls prove to be competent writers of argument, procedural plans, letters of request, and forms of writing which entail evaluation and synthesis of printed source material (reviewing data or literary criticism). Genres which seem to provide greater opportunities for boys to close the gap are typically those which allow for the use of semitechnical registers in order to explain how to carry out a skilled activity, describe how something works, or compose an argument based on a strongly held personal opinion.

The high/low performance curves disguise one important factor in the written work of girls and boys which has obvious ramifications for schooling and orientation to work in general: namely, that the subject matter or 'field' of much of what is written corresponds to conventional spheres of interest. Thus, a girl writing a procedural description will tend to choose a dressmaking/cooking operation, a boy a mechanical/'hard-tooled' one; a girl's strong opinion is quite likely to relate to questions of social welfare, a boy's to current political debates; observational reports written by girls tend to give prominence to aesthetic characteristics rather than those which can be measured or calculated, and so on.

My reading of these data suggests to me that literacy is indeed a pervasive skill, and that girls have far more flexibility in written language than is generally assumed; the question remains, though, to what extent could they do better if their abilities as writers were recognized and developed across a full range of subject areas? And how would the technocratic subjects have to change in order to accommodate the humanistic and socially responsive interests of girls, assuming girls ever became a pressure group to be reckoned with? By contrast, the performance of boys measured in relation to that of girls indicates underachievement on a scale that would be utterly disabling were it not for two factors in their language development experience: promotion of competence in oral language and the nature of their out-of-school reading. I have already mentioned the trade-off between oral and written language modes, which serves not merely to excuse boys' indifference to school standards of literacy, but actually operates to ensure a different kind of success and power in the dynamics of the classroom (Swann and Graddol, 1988; Mahony, 1988). Space does not permit further elaboration of this point here, but I wish to say something more about the voluntary interests boys have in reading.

Getting a taste for the strong stuff: boys' voluntary reading

It has been claimed by Martin (1985) that primary teachers practise discrimination against boys in refusing space for their typical interests — the reading and writing of texts with violent, sensational and media-influenced themes. Faced with a narrative incorporating the following scenario, any adult might well adopt the role of censor:

> My story started off about a dragon and this bloke going to kill it, but now it's him killing other people . . . he's turned into a psychopath. He's a tall bloke and he's lost his head. When I say he's lost his head, he hasn't personally lost his head — cut it off — *he's* cutting people's heads off. He's lost his brain. (Boy aged 12, who claims 'I like writing gory stuff')

It is true, however, that teachers of children in every age group show resistance to the notion of 'media literacy' and forms of popular culture to which their pupils are often more attuned than they are. By banishing these media from the classroom, or at best allowing them occasional space on sufferance, an important aspect of literacy is neglected. Even the most cursory glance at the range of comics and magazines which are consumed by children reveals fundamental differences in the uses of language favoured by the writers of girl- and boy-directed material.

Far from the watchful eye of the language teacher, boys of primary school age and beyond are practising reading on texts which are distinguished not simply by their themes of violence and terror, but also by their complex visual formats in which explosive actions interrupt the linearity of narrative sequence, and stylized representations of sound effects engage a more sensory, if less reflective, reading than is the case with 'classical' descriptive narration. Figure 6.1 is an example.

The fantastic world of science fiction with its attendant tales of mythical

Figure 6.1 Page from a *Masters of the Universe* comic (reduced from original)

quests introduces a distinctive and at times untranslatable vocabulary: Blusteroids, Chelnov, Excisus, Shinobo, Gryznov, The Monad, etc. Such vocabulary, however ludicrous to the adult eye, has a pedigree of scientism about it, and arguably plays its part in familiarizing the young reader with a whole range of textbooks in which the vocabulary is similarly opaque but just as authoritative. Even when there is resistance to reading such textbooks, we might assume they will be more tolerable to readers accustomed to depersonalized uses of language than to those who have been led to anticipate meaning and relevance from the printed page. Very helpfully, the writers of boys' comics print in bold their 'technical terms': 'My **mystic explosion** has trapped the fool on that plant world. The plants have no machines so he-man will not be able to **rebuild a teleportation machine**.' Conventions of capitalization are used in standard expository texts to highlight key words and concepts: on this level too, reading comics may be a useful preparation for learning some of the conventions of school textbooks.

A variety of reading positions is available within a comic which might comprise an adventure story, a detachable subtext of mechanisms of conquest, a riot of graphic elaboration, and a form of dialogue — or speechifying — which is archaic, formal and coded in a way the vernacular of interpersonal relations is not, this latter offering another possibility of distance from the narrative. These are not modes of reading which are emphasized in initial literacy schemes, nor indeed in traditional English literature classes (Barnes, 1987; Belsey, 1980). They are important though in coping with a mass of texts, literary or not, in subjects other than English and in the world beyond school. Indubitably, these modes of reading are hard to acquire, and rarely taught explicitly, but they are some of the 'advantages' which boys may derive from their out-of-school reading — in the long term. In the short term, boys swell the ranks of remedial readers, unable to cope with such texts as schools insist they do read, and presumably struggling with portions of unsupervised reading as well.

The *disadvantages* of such a diet of reading material lie in its power to generate and validate a view of experience which gives short shrift to matters of personal reflection, humane responsibilities, or the exigencies of living in a social context — areas of experience which are borne in upon girls through their 'chosen' leisure reading as much as by their school work. I shall now turn to a discussion of the ways in which these contrary world views surface in the extended writing produced by boys and girls under the auspices of the new pedagogy of the process classroom.

GENDER STEREOTYPING AND SKEWING IN CHILDREN'S WRITING

Pedagogic assumptions underlying story writing for younger readers

For many teachers and pupils, a project in which an older class writes stories for a younger one on the basis of outline plots dictated by the younger children is the most appealing way to realize numerous ideals for enhancing the experience of composition. Pupils can work in collaboration at many stages of the project; there is a real audience in prospect; the commitment to a specific reader is thought likely to sustain an extended process of drafting and revision; while the production of a finished book gives more insights into the technicalities of publication and 'real authorship'. (For some of the confusions created by too much unthinking commitment to notions of authorship, see chapter 3.) Other teachers, parents, and the wider community tend readily to support these initiatives because of their spin-off in terms of better liaison between schools, whose pupils get to visit one another's classrooms two or three times; the potential for enhancement of spoken and written language alike seems considerable under these circumstances. In so far as the genre of writing is deliberately chosen, there seems to be an assumption that story form is sufficiently familiar to provide security yet likely to be further illuminated by several weeks' work (though I shall argue that the choice of 'story' is among the most problematic and least analysed factors in the scheme).

This type of work has been one of the most popular options generated by the National Writing Project in the UK, and one project coordinator puts the case for story writing in the following strong terms:

> Here [the older children] were on an equal footing with adults. The fact that their audience was even younger must also have boosted their confidence and helped them to develop a sense of control over the writing, the courage to claim authorship, to learn the lesson that writing is about power . . . One can only speculate on the possible effects of this experience on their future development as writers and learners. (Wallen, 1986)

A closer look at assumed ideals

It is indeed appropriate that we speculate on the long-term effects of what are undoubtedly progressive elements in our current writing programmes; not in a spirit of carping, but in order to radicalize these ventures further; and in particular to analyse what they reveal about gender stereotyping and its converse — something which I shall call *gender skewing*.

In the following section, I look in detail at some of the writing produced in two classrooms in supportive conditions. One class contained about thirty-five pupils aged 9–10, who wrote for readers aged 7–8, and another contained twenty-three pupils aged 12 who also wrote for readers aged 7–8.

While it seems to be generally true that children involved in extended writing projects grow in confidence as writers — at least for the duration of the project — partly because they turn out work of a high technical standard (groaning at times about the sheer length of time it all takes), it is far from clear what they are learning about power. What is clear when we read their work closely and attend to what they have to say about their audience, is how disturbed most pupils are by the requirements to write stories according to the specifications of children of the opposite sex, and to what lengths they will go to pull these schemata back into the confines of their own gendering. This simple fact evidenced in multiple instances seems to me to have far-reaching implications. At worst, it is yet another testimony to the depth and pervasiveness of cultural and sexual stereotyping which no single classroom innovation can undo; at best, a study of children's extended written texts provides an invaluable source of information on 'where the child is' as both reader and writer. For any teacher wanting to analyse the requirements of her literacy programme, information of this kind is crucial in the attempt to loosen some of the manacles of gender stereotyping.

The child-writers' perspective

In some cases, the children chose their reader on the basis of an introductory letter; in other cases, the readers were randomly paired with writers. After the event, the children were asked whether it was, or would have been, easier to write for someone of the same sex as themselves. With few exceptions they stated that they would prefer to write for a reader of the same sex, because 'you can remember what you were like at that age'. Writers who did not feel they had to adjust to sex-specific genres, even though writing for a member of the opposite sex, were those who had drawn a reader whom they defined as atypical. For example, one boy with a girl reader commented, 'my story is more of a boy's story — perhaps she's a tomboy'. These comments were made despite the fact that the writers were proud of the work they had done, 'I didn't know I was capable of writing a story so well'; 'It is the best thing I have ever done'; 'I'm glad that I've achieved writing a book and that it looks quite nice' (comments from children aged 12 whose finished stories were often over 1000 words in length).

The children's remarks reveal a very strong awareness of sex stereotyping in reading materials, and an equally strong expectation that their role as writers is to continue in the same tradition. In this respect, they are imbibing a lesson in conformity: far from learning that writers — sometimes — have power because they are able to challenge the way linguistic artefacts structure the world, they are instead doing their best to replicate those structures. The conformism is, to my mind, exacerbated by the very fact that these children are commissioned to write for readers younger than themselves. In this situation, the triumphant claim that the children are on 'an equal footing with adults' reveals a further layer of problems for the young writer: What is an 'adult' role in relation to readers still younger than oneself? For the majority of girls, the parental/maternal role is most likely to be evoked, whereas for boys, unencumbered with caretaker responsibilities, to write stories for girls presents openings for a different order of power play, as we shall see in the examples which follow. Overall, my contention is that, by inviting children to adopt their implicit conception of an adult role as they compose stories, we are simply redoubling the opportunity for them to produce material gendered along stereotypical lines. The experiences of the preschool playgroup are glimpsed again in extended written texts.

Gender stereotyping in children's writing: 9–10-year-olds writing for 7–8-year-old readers

One class project began with a less common feature: subject matter for the stories was prescribed in advance by the teachers. The students were aged 9–10 years, writing for readers aged 7–8. All stories were to be about animals. Unfortunately, the ready availability of scenarios filled with

Text 6.3 Draft for a girl's story (reduced size)

> I am a cat my name is Rog. I am quite fluffy I am all black with blue eyes. I am a wild cat and I live in the woods all on my own. I catch mice every day. One day I was walking in the woods and I caught some mice. I saw a big fat mouse and went to chase it. I was chasing it for a long time and I went to far. and I got lost. I felt very very frightend, and lonely. The fat mouse had gone. I felt sad. I felt as if I had done it all for nothing. I thought about it for a minute I decided to follow my footsteps back. ~~I felt ever so happy. I had found my way home a last.~~ I didn't know they were some one elses foot prints. they were fairys foot print I started to follow the foot prints. they led me to a little hut. I knocked on the door.

anthropomorphized animals provides a quick and easy route into some of the most traditional sex-stereotype images encountered by young children, whether as readers or television viewers. Sadly, the animal theme suggested itself to the teacher as a potential help to 'getting the children started' without any thought as to what the topic might bring in its wake. In itself, this is graphic testimony to the low level of consciousness which matters of gender have in the minds of even the better language teachers.

How far did the children work within or beyond the conventions at their disposal? We can look at two of the finished stories written in a girl/girl pairing and a boy/boy pairing, respectively; in both cases we have the initial (dictated) draft from the younger child and the final word-processed version.

Common to many stories was the theme of animals stolen, lost or out adventuring on their own, illustrated in the two drafts in texts 6.3 and 6.4.

At this draft stage, there are several points of similarity between the two outlines, although certain features already mark the story of the dog as a boy's genre (the tendency towards serialized adventures, gratuitously

Text 6.4 Draft for a boy's story (reduced size)

I am a dog and one day I vos walking in a wood
when I saw a Squrel. it was a red Sqrel. I tried to climp
the tree to catch it when the branch brook. and I fell into a
pond. I trid to swim to the other side but there was a fire on
the other side. So I was scard. the fire was started by two
cars and they going to blow up. so you swam back to the
other side and climped out and went to get help. I bumbed
into my master and I barked at him a made him follow me
When he got near the woods he saw the fire burning in the trees.
so he ran to the nearest phone box and dailed 999 and aske
for the fire bregaid. They got to the wood in just five mins.
and put the fire out. My gave me a new caller and Kennel for
being a brave dog.
The next day somone came to me and asked me to track
down a thief. because he stole her money. in five mins Time
he set of north. the thief was heading for a cave on a hill. back
home the women was waiting for me

exploding cars, cops and robbers), while the adventures of Rog are less obviously gendered, apart from the emphasis on the emotions of loss and loneliness (we might question whether 'Rog' is short for Roger . . .). Both outlines are given as first-person narratives told by the humanized animal, and each recounts a series of adventures which start from a solitary walk in the woods. Rog's story, in text 6.3, first moves to a state of closure with the retracing of the footsteps, but this ending is crossed out and a new twist introduced which leads quite literally into the unknown. The fate of the dog in text 6.4 is likewise unresolved, with a possible new episode added as an afterthought. Rog's story already employs more narrative conventions, in naming and briefly describing the main character and providing a setting for the tale.

In the hands of their respective 'authors', the two drafts are changed, but it is text 6.3 which is most dramatically transformed in an way that, I would suggest, brings it more firmly into line with traditional nursery tales. The motif of the lone adventurous cat is rewritten as *The Little Kitten that Got Lost* (text 6.5), and the androgynous Rog has definitely become a boy, complete with mother and siblings. The potential of exciting adventures in the woods is contained in the frame of moral obligation, 'don't go too far and don't get lost. Will you promise me that?'. Far from being free to wander off alone, the small kitten learns the lesson of his temerity in the 'big, dark unfriendly forest', where he is tormented by thorns in his coat and thoughts of home, until he is fortuitously rescued by the big tabby cat.

Text 6.5 Girl's story — final version

The Little Kitten that Got Lost

One day as the sun rose over the hills and the morning came to a start, Mrs Peacock the cat woke up. 'Oh, what a lovely day it is!' she said as she woke her kittens up. 'Come on, it's a lovely day. Wake up lazybones'.

One of her kittens was called Rog and Rog said to Mrs Peacock, 'Mum, can I go for a walk?'

'Yes dear' said Mrs Peacock. 'Of course you can. But don't get too far and don't get lost. Will you promise me that?'

'Yes, I promise mum,' said Rog. 'I'll be off now. Goodbye!'

Rog left the cosy warm hole and set off for a nice brisk walk. It was quite a cold morning and the ground had a slight frost. It made a crunching sound under his paws as he walked along. He saw a little grey rabbit run across the field. Being very curious he decided to run after it. As he ran the rabbit ran as well. What a lovely game this was! Such fun! for hours they ran over hundreds of lush green fields till at last the little rabbit scurried down its hole.

'That was a nice run,' Rog thought, half out of breath. 'I think it's time to go home. Er, which way is home? Oh no, I think I'm lost.' The poor little kitten began to cry but he soon cheered up at the thought of getting back. He tried to think of the way he had come but he had no idea of which way to go. He decided to plod on.

Soon he came to a big dark unfriendly forest. He walked into it, thinking how nice it would be to be in front of a cosy log fire, drinking nothing but fresh, cool milk, sweet and refreshing. He licked his lips at the thought of that. He could hardly see anything in the wood because it was so dark. He walked on for what seemed like hours, tripping over the roots of trees and getting lots of sticky burrs stuck in his coat. Then at last he came to a clearing where he saw a big tabby cat having a drink of milk.

'Hallo,' said Rog. 'Do you know the way to Elm Tree Close please?'

'Yes, I certainly do,' said the tabby. 'If you get on my back, I'll take you there.' So Rog hopped on the other cat's back and they were on their way. Rog would have loved to have been able to run like the tabby. He run like the wind. Soon they came to the hedgerow that Rog knew so well. He would soon be home now. Rog got off the cat's back and waved goodbye. 'Thanks ever so much,' said Rog politely. Rog rushed down his hole as fast as lightning. His mother kissed him and told him off for being so late. After that he went to bed.

Text 6.6, the final version of text 6.4, is a much less complicated affair in which the first draft is basically given a lick and a polish.

We might notice that part of the rewriting effort is directed to bringing into the story local descriptive details — name of character and setting — of the sort that were present in the girl's draft from the start. The older boy evidently feels no compulsion to elaborate either setting or motivation beyond the minimum necessary for comprehension, and appears to be quite at home with the ongoing saga of adventures connected just by virtue of Lucky's involvement in them; the finished story ends with only slightly more resolution than the initial draft. There is almost complete consonance between writer and reader here, save for the telling omission of one detail from draft to final version. At first, the dog swimming towards the burning bank admits 'I was afraid'. In the revised version he is most decidedly 'the brave dog' who is immune to any emotion and rewarded accordingly with a new collar and grateful thanks.

Text 6.6 Boy's story — final version

The Brave Dog

I am a dalmatian dog and I am called Lucky. One day I was going for a walk in the woods. It was very shady and damp. I had gone a little way when I saw a red squirrel playing in a rotting tree. I tried to climb the tree and catch it. But the tree was so old that the branch snapped and I fell into a pond. I tried to swim to the other side but there was a blazing fire on the far bank. The fire was started by two cars that had a collision and they were going to blow up.

So I swam back and ran to tell my master. I bumped right into him. I barked and made him follow me to the woods. The fire was coming nearer to the village. My master run to the nearest phone box and dialled 999 and asked for the fire brigade. Five minutes later they were in the wood and had put out the fire. My master gave me a new collar and kennel for being a brave dog.

The next day there was knock at the door. My master opened it. It was the woman next door. A thief had stolen all her riches. So I set off north to catch him. The thief was heading to a cave on Black Hill. I could just pick up his scent. The thief had got to the cave. I was right behind. It was dark and damp in the cave. I heard a noise. I had found him! I chased him right into the village and into my house. We had caught the thief. The woman got her money back and said thank you. The thief was taken to jail.

On the evidence of these two stories, we might be inclined to say that their writers have learnt something about the exercise of power. My guess is that the real lesson lies in the subliminal rehearsal of gendered stereotypes for the edification of younger children: the more competent writer, as always, has the power to control the text, and to persuade the reader who commissioned it in the first place that the outcome is even more desirable than the sketchy brief. Looking at the lengths to which the girl writer has gone in writing up the given draft, we might also be inclined to say that such projects are a trap for girls. Girls' intimate acquaintance with traditional fiction provides ready models for story writing in the nursery genre; instead of being set the task of displaying this knowledge by emulation, they could well be encouraged to explore the larger context of printing and publishing which guarantees the circulation of stories scarcely superior to their own.

For boys, on the other hand, there is possibly a different case to argue, and it has to do with understanding a range of fantasy other than that derived from contextless threats or challenges. The prospect of a long-term project in which boys and girls not only wrote for each other, but wrote differently in different genres, would be one way of getting out of the impasse of reconfirming the stereotypes. The value of such a project would depend on highly skilled teacher intervention and a determination to continue the 'process' of writing and reading beyond the point where a 'product' is handed over to its apparently unique reader. The pedagogy which confers on children's texts the status of adult compositions ought not to back off from questions of adult scrutiny.

Gender skewing in children's writing: 12-year-olds writing for 7–8-year-old readers

In this section, I shall discuss some stories written by 12-year-olds for readers of the opposite sex aged 7–8, because of what is revealed in them about children's underlying preconceptions of gender/genre appropriateness.

Many of the stories written by girls for boys and vice versa show signs of gender skewing as their authors struggle to elaborate a given storyline to suit the presumed demands of the younger reader. Interestingly, although the children were conscious of the problem posed in working with unfamiliar/uncongenial subject matter when questioned about preferred audience, their notion of linguistic difficulty was conceptualized only in terms of vocabulary and sentence structure, 'finding words that they would understand', 'writing it simpler than I normally write'. Yet when we look at how the stories are elaborated, we can see that major revisions and interpolations have been made to the familiar genres of children's fiction.

Girls writing for younger boys

In the hands of girl writers, science fiction and piratical adventures acquire an overlay of domesticity and morality; a boy hero, soon to be the intrepid rescuer of his football club's trophy, is firmly controlled by his house-proud mother, for whom he spares an anxious thought in the midst of his night of Bond-like exploits. The extracts quoted in texts 6.7–6.9 illustrate these features.

Text 6.7 was written by a girl who commented, 'I didn't know a thing about robots and I didn't like the subject'.

Text 6.7 Extract from story by girl writer for younger boy reader (reduced size)

CHAPTER 9

Tail-break got to Electron and
Camero (who was still on the floor) safely.
Electron was in the middle of the oper-
ation.
Bomber-bot took to the air
firing downwards at Camero. Tail-bre-
ak shot back to protect them.
Then something awful happened
bomber-bot started falling to the ground

The shots had hit him and the robots were looking very scared. Murder was a criminal offence and they didn't want Tail-break to be put in prison. 'Oh no,' he cried 'What have I done? I aimed so I would not hit him.'

No-one was blaming it on him but the facts were Bomber-bot had been hit maybe killed and the shot had been fired by Tail-break.

The girl author of text 6.8 stated 'I know more about what young girls did than about boys'.

Text 6.8 Extract from story by girl writer for younger boy reader (reduced size)

By now Captain Nick's crew were on the deck. They knew Dark Mark and his men were trouble so they planned to get them off their ship in the quickest way possible.

"This is your last chance! Give me that map or we will fight you to the death!" screamed Dark Mark.

"Then we shall fight you, and you will loose." There was

a fight then, but only a small one
because Dark Mark's crew got scared. They
ran off Captain Nick's ship onto their own
and hid.

It seems to me that what is revealed here is the resistance which girls feel to the traditional elements of boys' stories, as well as their fear of contravening the strictures of their own gender, the guardian figure of which in most cases is the mother.

Girls don't like to write about mindless fighting and killing — the resistance is captured in the deliberately retarded action of the wounded body which 'started falling to the ground', not 'slumped' or even 'fell' — and consequently seek to minimize such episodes in their stories, going so far as to invoke legal sanctions against wrongdoing. Domestic sanctions against disruptive behaviour are similarly close to the surface as text 6.9 shows, and throughout these stories the male heroes are depicted in uncharacteristically self-reflective, even self-doubting, moods, a long way from the free-floating careless adventures of classic boy-oriented fiction.

Text 6.9 Extract from story by girl writer for younger boy reader

I walked home and as soon as I walked through the gateway, my Mum saw me. She went mad, absolutely mad and I was not surprised. My football kit and tracksuit were filthy, my whole body was caked in mud and I had walked all over her nice clean carpet and dripped mud all over it. Oops!

Mum sent me straight upstairs for a bath while she got the dinner ready. After my bath I crept downstairs and sat in front of the TV. I thought she hadn't heard me come down but she had and she stormed into the living room.

'I want a word with you,' she said. 'Next time you go training, I don't expect to see a single bit of dirt on your tracksuit, alright?'

'Sorry Mum,' I answered meekly.

(Later, at the crisis of the story:)

'Gosh!' It's morning and I was supposed to be home by 6 o'clock last night! My mum will be mad. She'll kill me!' I wailed.

(The trophy is finally recaptured and the boys are taken to the police station:)

. . . our parents were waiting and we poured out the whole story over a nice hot cup of tea. They all said that we were very brave but we shouldn't have trespassed.

In the girls' stories which feature boys as heroes, mothers appear to have far more potential to terrify than the rather unsubstantial villains who populate the tales. The ways in which these girls represent 'mothers' displays the girls' own understanding of language, and in particular of maternal language, as a force of social control which will subdue and regulate the picaresque wanderings of small boys' fantasies. As teachers we need to ask: Do girls need yet another 'dummy run' for their conventional future as keepers of the social conscience? Might not some way be found of turning our knowledge of the voluntaristic structuring of girls' social gendering to alternative forms of empowerment for girls themselves? Texts such as those quoted suggest that boys and girls alike need to be critically alerted to how little the social conscience is a matter for joint construction. A full reading of their writings is an important starting point for raising awareness of this issue.

Boys writing for younger girls

When boys are writing for girls who have suggested an adventure story with a female heroine, they feel no compulsion to lock the heroine into a family context — that is not where they think control lies. One such tale ends with the girl back home in bed only to find her poetry book open at a page which reads as text 6.10.

The little poem encapsulates the tale already told, and holds the promise of further adventures to entice the child across the scary threshold — very different from the containment of cups of tea in the police station. Beyond

Text 6.10 Extract from story by boy writing for a younger girl reader

In the park or in the streets,
Not quite knowing who you could meet.
Going to the local Park.
The ones that's scarey in the dark.
The gates reveal a whole new place,
Just think to yourself 'This is Ace'.

25

THE END

that, the poem contains a frisson of delighted fear, as the boy writer anticipates the anxiety the girl subject presumably feels at 'scary' and 'dark' places made fearful by his own sex (as we might guess he is perfectly aware); thus in his writing he enjoys both threatening and being threatened.

In the stories boys write for them, girls are allowed to participate in practical jokes, such as putting whoopee cushions on teachers' chairs and other varieties of teacher baiting, in a familiar 'Beano' comic style. Such girls take in their stride escapades which endanger life and limb (not to mention clean clothing), and in text 6.11 the mishap of a complete drenching is passed off with a laugh, far from the world of maternal reprimands.

Girls are almost inscribed into boyhood at such moments by virtue of being written into boys' roles. The resulting tomboys are reminiscent of certain adult authors' attempts to write about girls in a more lively way (the adventures of Tyke Tyler or Pippi Longstocking are examples of the genre). Yet in none of the boys' stories is the heroine commanding; her gender is skewed in the direction of masculinity, but no further than the boy writers have been taught to expect or want from their peer group of girls.

Typically, the heroines have to be rescued from magician or peer group gang by *deus ex machinae*, or by total gaps in the narrative; in the boys' equivalent of these predicaments, a hero might be expected to draw out the

Text 6.11 Extract from story by a boy writing for a younger girl reader (reduced size)

Elizabeth mopped her forehead with her hand and quickly launched herself out the window. But she slipped on the ledge and started to fall headfirst. She managed to catch hold of an old flag pole (which is one of those ones which sticks out of a wall) and sighed a sigh of relief. She had sighed to soon because there was a tiny creak and then a crack the pole was nearly in half! It was now hanging on by a thread and Elizabeth could hear her heart thumping now. Suddenly it broke and Elizabeth went hurtling down to earth. There was a gigantic splash as Elizabeth landed in a barrel of water. She spurted a mouth full of water out and clambered out of the barrel.

"Unlucky, Elizabeth!" shouted Helen who was now laughing.

"Ok., Ok. lets get going!" answered Elizabeth.

ray gun or recite some coded formula. Even as 'Elizabeth' and 'Helen' enter the Evergreen Forest on the trail of the promised treasure, they are ambushed by a trio of boys disguised as ghosts (text 6.12).

The ambush illustrates, as did the poem in text 6.10, the entry of the writer as both the threat and the threatened, a sign of the control boys feel they can exert over girls' freedom of manoeuvre. The controlling force or power here is not through appeals to social or moral order but quite simply by assumption of male superiority and physical supremacy.

Text 6.12 Extract from a boy's story for a younger girl reader (reduced size)

> .. The boys then dropped the white sheet down on them and rattled some chairs, just to mock the girls. Still laughing they ran off to find the treasure.

THE PROBLEMS IN REVIEW

First of all, it is important to stress something that is *not* a problem. It is not a problem to find ways of assisting children to become enthusiastic readers and writers, given the kinds of supportive conditions which many literacy projects have created — in Australia, the UK and the USA. More open techniques of classroom management, the practice of group work in composing and redrafting writing, and the encouragement that children receive to take responsibility for their work at all stages of its development, are in principle desirable practices. They have done much to demystify the process of writing, while at the same time serving to create meaningful occasions for oral work as reading and writing is planned and reviewed.

But there is a real danger that the outputs of busily interactive classrooms will not be critically read as anything other than vivid testimonials to the group dynamic. As we have seen from the evidence discussed in this chapter, writing which has many of the hallmarks of success (attentive to a specific audience, carefully executed and presented) can nevertheless be the vehicle for a world view which is restrictive, conventional and ultimately depowering.

The focus of this chapter has been on gender, but the scripts quoted also carry within them the subtexts of race and class. As we read children's versions of nurseryland stories, we might ask: Which culture uses tales of domesticated animals to socialize its young? Which class relies most on women as home-and-hearth bodies, and represents them as such in children's fiction? There is now a growing recognition that books provided for children to read ought to be inspected for bias of gender, race and class — my argument is that the 'free' writing done by children themselves needs similar scrutiny.

The 'new literacy' brings with it additional demands on the teacher. Not only do teachers need diverse managerial skills to sustain changing group structures within their classrooms but more crucially, they must be thoroughly informed about the teaching of writing. Knowledge of teaching writing must also take into account the complex roles of literacy in the wider uses of language in education and society. It is never sufficient to rest content with the notion that children are empowered simply because they accomplish tasks with enjoyment; we have to be confident that the tasks themselves are worthwhile. In the case of language, we need to ask: What purposes are being served by specific occasions of language work in school? How are children being helped to understand, practise and question the forms of language which currently hold sway in our society? Which genres of written language in particular do children most need to control? How are forms of resistance likely to show themselves when children begin to rewrite or reread traditionally gendered texts?

There is nothing new in the suggestion that language is a form of social control, but there is a poignant irony in the fact that when children are encouraged to draw on their 'own' resources as language learners, they may come to identify still more closely with the controlling systems from which we seek to free them. Gender identity is constantly rehearsed and reproduced in language — given precise knowledge of the ways in which this happens, teachers' guiding interventions in children's language development may indeed be powerful.

REFERENCES

Barnes, D. (1987). The politics of oracy. In M. MacLure, T. Phillips, & A. Wilkinson (Eds.), *Oracy matters: The development of talking and listening*. Milton Keynes: Open University Press.

Belsey, C. (1980). *Critical practice*. London: Methuen.

Blanchard J. (1988). 'Glaciation, symmetry etc.': Finding an insider curriculum. *English in Education*, **22**(2), 31–34.

Buswell, C. (1984). Sponsoring and stereotyping in working-class English secondary school. In S. Acker, J. Megarry, S. Nisbet, & E. Hoyle (Eds.), *World yearbook of education 1984: Women and education*. London: Kogan Page.

EOC (Equal Opportunities Commission). (1985). *Girls and Information Technology*. Report of a project in Croydon to evaluate guidelines for good practice in the IT curriculum. Overseas House, Manchester.

ESRC (Economic and Social Research Council). (1988). *Girls and mathematics: Some lessons for the classroom*. London: Girls and Mathematics Unit, Institute of Education, University of London.

Gilbert, P. (1989). Stoning the romance: Girls as resistant readers and writers. In F. Christie (Ed.), *Writing in Schools* (B.Ed. course Reader). Geelong, Victoria: Deakin University Press. Paper originally presented at the ANZAAS Congress, James Cook University of North Queensland, August 1987.

Gorman, T. P., White, J., Orchard, L., & Tate, A. (1981). *Language performance in schools: Primary survey report No. 1*. London: HMSO.

Gorman, T. P., White, J., Orchard, L., & Tate, A. (1982a). *Language performance in schools: Primary survey report No. 2*. London: HMSO.

Gorman, T. P., White, J., Orchard, L., & Tate, A. (1982b). *Language performance in schools: Secondary survey report No. 1*. London: HMSO.

Gorman, T. P., White, J., Orchard, L., & Tate, A. (1983). *Language performance in schools: Secondary survey report No. 2*. London: HMSO.

Gorman, T. P., White, J., Hargreaves, M., MacLure, M., & Tate, A. (1984). *Language performance in schools: 1982 primary survey report*. London: Department of Education and Science.

Gorman, T. P., White, J., & Brooks, G. (1984). *Language performance in schools: 1982 secondary survey report*. London: Department of Education and Science.

Gorman, T. P., White, J., Brooks, G., MacLure, M., & Kispal, A. (1988). *Language performance in schools: A review of APU language monitoring, 1979–83*. London: HMSO.

Gubb, J., Gorman, T., & Price, E. (1987). *International studies in pupil performance. The study of written composition in England and Wales*. Windsor: NFER-Nelson.

Heath, S. B. (1983). *Ways with words: Language, life and work in communities and classrooms*. Cambridge: Cambridge University Press.

Hough, J. (1984). *Deprivation of necessary skills*. Paper presented at The Girl Friendly Schooling Conference, Manchester Polytechnic (mimeo).

Johnson, S. & Murphy, P. (1986). *Girls and physics: Reflections on APU survey findings*. APU (Assessment of Performance Unit) Occasional Paper No. 4. London: Department of Education and Science.

Kaplan, C. (1983). Speaking/writing/feminism. In M. Wandor (Ed.), *On Gender and writing*. London: Pandora Press.

Mahony, P. (1988). *Schools for the boys? Coeducation reassessed*. London: Hutchinson Educational.

Marland, M. (Ed.). (1983). *Sex differentiation and schooling*. London: Heinemann Educational Books.

Martin, J. R. (1985). *Factual writing: Exploring and challenging social reality*. Sociocultural Aspects of Language and Education. Geelong, Victoria: Deakin University Press.

Martin, J. R., & Rothery, J. (1984). *Choice of genre in a suburban primary school*. Paper presented at the ALAA conference, Alice Springs (mimeo).

McNamara, J. (1989). The writing in science and history project: The research questions and implications for teachers. In F. Christie (Ed.), *Writing in Schools* (B.Ed. course Reader). Geelong, Victoria: Deakin University Press.

McRobbie, A., & McCabe, T. (1982). *Feminism for girls, an adventure story*. London: Routledge & Kegan Paul.

Poynton, C. (1985). *Language and gender: Making the difference*. Geelong, Victoria: Deakin University Press.

Spender, D. (1980). *Man-made language*. London: Routledge & Kegan Paul.

Stanworth, M. (1983). *Gender and schooling: A study of sexual divisions in the classroom*. London: Hutchinson Publishing Group in association with The Exploration in Feminism Collective.

Swann, J., & Graddol, D. (1988). Gender inequalities in the classroom. *English in Education*, **22**(1), 48–65.

Wallen, M. (1986). Finding and reaching an audience: Writing and learning 8–13. *Dorset National Writing Project Newsletter, No. 1*. Dorset County Council.

White, J. (1986). The writing on the wall: Beginning or end of a girl's career? *Women's Studies International Forum*, **9**(5), 561–574. Oxford: Pergamon Press.

White, J. (1987). *Pupils' Attitudes to Writing*. Windsor: NFER-Nelson.

Whyld, J. (Ed.). (1983). *Sexism in the Secondary Curriculum*. London: Harper & Row.

7 Literacy for learners of English as a second language

LYNN WALES

ESL STUDENTS

The other chapters in this book are concerned primarily with students who are learners of English as their first language and who will develop literacy skills in English as their first language, from the age of 5. It is of the utmost importance to note that for such monolingual children an introduction to literacy, with all that that involves, presupposes five years already spent in the process of natural language acquisition. Some of the pertinent features of the first language acquisition process are: it occurs when children are very young and receiving maximum personal attention; it is oral language which is acquired; it is acquired through human interaction — there is input from speakers to the child and the child itself participates, responding or initiating; the interactions are communicative and functional in focus.

Through daily communicative interaction over five years, with many examples and repetitions, the child internalizes sets of interrelated rules, phonological, morphological, syntactic, semantic, and pragmatic, and uses them productively. The child's internalized rules may not always be the same as those of the adult speaker but gradually the adult system is acquired, the child apparently adjusting and reorganizing its grammar as input is stored and analysed. While acquiring the rules of the language in this way, the preschool child is, of course, also utilizing what is acquired to advance cognitively. Normal literacy development in western societies is thus based on prior native speaker competence (i.e. internalized knowledge of the rules) in the relevant language.

This chapter, however, is concerned with the teaching of literacy in

I should like to acknowledge the invaluable information given to me in the preparation of this chapter by Chris Davison, La Trobe University, Bundoora; Jennie Medley, Collingwood Language Centre; Ann-Marie Bortoli, Inner City School Support Centre, Melbourne; Paul Jackson, Heidelberg High School; and M. A. Clements and N. Ellerton, Deakin University, Geelong.

English to those Australian students who, during their primary and secondary school years, are endeavouring to acquire English as their second language (ESL). They are ESL students.

The multicultural, multilingual nature of Australian society is of course more obvious to some educators than to others, for demographic reasons. Newly arrived migrant families, for example, tend to settle where their native tongue is spoken. This means that some areas have high density non-English-speaking background (NESB) populations, whereas others will have relatively few families whose home language is not English. Nevertheless, there is a very real likelihood that Australian teachers will have smaller or larger groups of ESL students in their classes in the normal course of their careers.

Who is an ESL student? The most obvious category of ESL students comprises those who have just migrated to Australia from an NES country. These students may be of any school age, educational background, or language experience. For example, they may be children ready to enter prep grade but speaking little or no English. Alternatively they could be older, with the same minimal experience of English but having missed early schooling in their own country for some reason. They are therefore illiterate in their first language. Such students may be of primary age or already in their adolescence. Other older students may have had early schooling and embarked upon literacy in their first language, but for some reason their schooling was interrupted. They may therefore be only semiliterate in their first language.

Another category is that of older students who have had the same amount of uninterrupted schooling in their first language as their English-speaking Australian peers. They are literate in that language, and therefore understand the purposes of print and the processes of reading, but the orthography of their language may be very different from that of English, and they may have no knowledge of spoken English. To these categories can be added that of refugees who, in age and linguistic and educational background, could be in any of the groups described above but who have had particular traumatic life experiences in addition to the other difficulties that migrant children face. All new arrivals will of course vary in their experience of spoken and written English, the extreme being no experience of either, and all have come from cultures which differ to some extent from the dominant culture in Australia.

Some ESL students are not new arrivals in Australia. A number of them, though born overseas, have been in Australia for some time and have undergone previous schooling here. Such students may be illiterate or semiliterate in their first language and be less skilled than their monolingual peers in written English, while being orally proficient in English for social purposes.

Other ESL students have been born in Australia in NESB families. These include Aboriginal children who speak their tribal language as their native tongue and learn English as a second language. A second major group consists of children of NESB migrants whose home language is other than English (LOTE). There are enormous variations in the amount of exposure such children have had to English in their preschool years, depending on parental language policy and/or ability in English. They may speak a non-standard variety of English. They also differ in the extent to which their environment has assisted them to develop in their first language. Some are able to communicate fluently in both languages, some are dominant in one language or the other, and others perhaps have a restricted use of both.

Some general considerations

Where students cannot cope at all with English in the classroom, many authorities provide intensive ESL classes in Language Centres, or in units for withdrawal classes within schools themselves. Some schools also have transition programmes that assist ESL students to learn the specialized skills and procedures needed for school education. In some areas there may not be much specialized intensive assistance with English and the responsibility for the students' language and learning development is left with the mainstream teachers. It is advisable that class teachers in such a position seek all possible information and assistance from specialist ESL consultants, so that they understand the nature of the learning task that their ESL students face and how they as teachers can facilitate these students' language development and school learning.

Even where Language Centres are provided, the time ESL students can spend in them is usually not long enough to accomplish the enormous task of thoroughly preparing second-language learners for the language and learning demands of school life. Adapting to a new language and a new culture is much more complicated and formidable than the native speakers of the host country can appreciate. Reports such as those of Campbell *et al.* (1984) and Campbell and McMeniman (1985) indicate that the intensive ESL provision for Australian students is directed, not surprisingly, at those who have minimal oral skills. The observations made about ESL students' development in language proficiency indicate a 'preliminary growth spurt, followed by premature cessation of growth' (Campbell and McMeniman, 1985:28). Moreover, the so-called second-phase learners — those ESL students who have been in Australia for a number of years or who were born here — are characterized by apparent oral fluency, particularly in the speech variety spoken by their monolingual peers, but by minimal skills in the use of the more formal language (spoken and even more so written) needed in the classroom, especially in the later stages of postprimary education.

A disproportionate number of second-language learners can be found in the slow or basic streams (in schools where streaming pertains). They are often perceived as slow learners and/or as having behavioural problems, rather than as having language problems. While ESL students can, of course, have the learning and behavioural problems common to all children or adolescents, it is particularly important in their case to consider the language factor since in this respect their life experience is very different from that of their monolingual classmates. Williams (1986) and Tsolidis (1985) indicate some of the difficulties faced by second-phase learners and their teachers, confronted with the demands of school learning. Clearly, without further assistance to both students and staff, such students will continue not to reach their educational potential and to be disadvantaged particularly in the area of literacy. Williams (1986) and Campbell and McMeniman (1985) include some quotations from NESB students and from teachers which reveal something of the disaffection and demoralization which students experience when the educational system fails to help them meet the demands it imposes, with subsequent implications for career expectations. Again, mainstream teachers and ESL specialists need to collaborate so that their different areas of specialization can be combined to produce an effective curriculum.

Some principles of approach

It will be apparent from the foregoing descriptions that each ESL student should be considered as an individual, since background experience and consequent understanding of, and attitude towards, the tasks of learning English and of learning through English differ from student to student. A first principle in ESL teaching is to obtain as much information as possible about each student. Students' progress in English is affected by such factors as: level of oral competence and literacy in the first language; stage of education reached in the first language; previous experience of English and of second-language learning; age, sex and socioeconomic status; general intelligence and self-esteem; attitudes towards fellow students, teachers and learning English; teachers' attitudes towards them and their first language; teachers' and parents' expectations of their progress; parents' attitudes towards learning English and towards the school community; and the attitudes of fellow students.

The teacher needs to understand as much as possible about the students to be able to help them in the learning task. If a student has received intensive ESL teaching, important factors such as those described above will have been noted where possible and the information, perhaps in report form and including recent development in English, should be readily available. Otherwise class teachers should ascertain as much as they can, with support from ESL specialists, in order to understand what is required for the students' future development.

CONFIDENCE AND MOTIVATION

A second principle in ESL teaching is that language learning requires confidence and motivation in the learner. The class teacher needs to do everything possible to build confidence in learners that they *can* learn English. The main way of building such confidence is to demonstrate to learners that they have learned and are learning a great deal all the time, and this can best be done by encouraging them to *use* the language in communication. Thus the prevailing view of effective second-language acquisition is that it is accomplished in much the same way that children acquire their first language — that is, the spoken language is acquired first, and is acquired through massive exposure to it over five preschool years of daily meaningful communicative interaction.

Policy towards errors

An implication for building confidence is that the students' utterances are accepted as efforts to communicate, so that what is said is more important than the way it is expressed. Children learning their first language are encouraged to communicate and their listeners seek the meaning in their utterances regardless of their so-called errors of form. The children's overt attention is upon the issues that interest them and the persons with whom they communicate. The rules of the language are acquired gradually and subconsciously over a number of years. The approach in ESL teaching reflects this process.

Communication is all-important: so-called errors are indications that the learner is hypothesizing about English language forms, and the important aspect of the utterance is what meaning the speaker wants to convey. Standard procedure in ESL classrooms is therefore to encourage students to talk as much as possible, and to ignore speech errors. As long as learners continue to learn, their speech, if frequently exercised, will continue to move nearer in form to that of the target speech community. Error correction itself tends to have an inhibiting effect upon communication, and upon learners' desire to communicate, as does the ridicule of their peers.

Affective issues

Confidence and motivation are apparent in the average young child learning its first language. Typically, children communicate because they want to — because they love their families and therefore desire to communicate. Moreover, they have a developing interest in the universe around them, and a healthy set of needs that they wish to have met. They are therefore motivated to communicate out of interest and out of need.

Thus, to summarize the hypotheses of Stephen Krashen (1982), language is best acquired through talking in a relaxed atmosphere to someone you like about things that interest you.

Class teachers can assist language development in ESL students by establishing a caring, supportive and stimulating classroom atmosphere in which ESL learners feel confident and are motivated to communicate in English. Plentiful opportunities to communicate with their peers in group work are especially important, particularly where the work is of a problem-solving nature which promotes the need to communicate.

Teachers can raise ESL learners' self-esteem and increase their classmates' respect through their perceived attitude towards the learners' first languages and cultures. It is easy to assume that, because the learners' competence in English language skills is far less developed than that of their English-speaking monolingual peers, they are suffering from a deficit of language *per se*. This, however, is not the case: NESB students do have *language*: it is just that the language does not happen to be English.

The mainstream teacher can do a great deal to build the ESL learners' self-respect by encouraging the use of the first language. Where there is more than one speaker of a LOTE, for example, students may assist one another in grasping new ideas, words, etc. by means of discussion in their first language. Early written work can be in the LOTE and pieces later translated by the student or by a teacher aide. Language consciousness can be developed for all students by doing language comparisons, helping English speakers to learn expressions (e.g. colour terms, numbers) in the other relevant languages, having labels in the LOTEs alongside the English words, inviting NESB parents to assist with multicultural activities, etc.

In short, rather than viewing ESL students as an additional teaching problem, class teachers can utilize the linguistic and cultural resources offered by the presence of such students in the class in a way which boosts their morale by allowing them some opportunity to show who they are and what they know, and which at the same time broadens the linguistic and cultural experience of their classmates.

AN INTEGRATED APPROACH TO LANGUAGE DEVELOPMENT

In ESL literature, a distinction is drawn between the four macroskills of listening, speaking, reading, and writing, and the activities in the ESL classroom may be designed to focus on one or other of these skills at different times. In theory and in practice, however, the four macroskills tend to be viewed as interlinked and mutually reinforcing. Thus oral and aural skills are considered to be prerequisites for the development of literacy skills, not just in a global sense — i.e. learning to speak comes before learning to read and write — but continually, in that discussion should sometimes accompany, but always preface and follow, literacy work.

Talking about texts directly assists the acquisition of literacy skills but it also assists indirectly, since oral skills underlie literacy skills and it must be remembered that ESL students lack the previous massive exposure to spoken English received by their English-speaking classmates in the preschool years.

On the other hand, literacy gives access to complexities of the language that may not be perceived through the spoken language; it allows backtracking, and it assists in reinforcing the learners' understanding of the underlying structures of English. It also expands the vocabulary, taking readers into wider domains. The reinforcing effect of continually utilizing the four macroskills in an interrelated manner is extremely important for ESL students. They have had fewer years to acquire English than their monolingual peers, they may have more limited access to spoken English outside school, and as there are more gaps in their knowledge of the language, linguistic opportunities need to be intensified.

The considerations listed above are by no means exhaustive, and readers who would like to examine these issues in more detail are referred to the works suggested for further reading at the end of this chapter, which also offer practical advice on useful strategies.

APPROACHES TO LITERACY

The principles outlined above, when applied to the teaching of literacy skills, suggest that effective approaches for ESL students involve:

- Proceeding from the known to the unknown in terms both of students' language and of their knowledge. This is why it is important to know as much as possible about the students' linguistic and experiential background.

- Continuing opportunities to increase and expand competence in listening and speaking skills, especially as students take up new subjects and more advanced phases of work. Increased literacy skills for ESL students — and thus their learning in all other academic areas of the curriculum — depend upon commensurate expansion of oral skills, as students learn to adopt formal registers.

- Providing massive exposure to the printed word so that students receive a rich literature programme. Cambourne (1986) indicates that preliterate ESL learners in schools utilize the print they see around them. It appears therefore that access in classrooms to books, charts, posters, labels, etc. is very important. The literature programme needs to include not only good quality fiction, but to provide good models of the various non-fiction genres so that students can learn the conventions of different types of narrative and of expressive writing (e.g. poetry, reflection, stories), and of expository writing (e.g. recipes, reports, newsprint, textbooks). (For advice on several of these genres, see chapters 3, 4 and 5.) Also, just as the teacher and other students are resources for the development of oral skills, so they can provide models for the act of writing, as the teacher scribes students' dictations, engages in composition herself, or encourages students to share their written work with each other.

- Accepting that students' efforts at written communication are more important for their intended meaning than for their technical accuracy. This means viewing errors, many of which will disappear as competence in literacy increases, as indications of language development, so that students can build up confidence and experience in their writing, uninhibited by fear of making mistakes. Technical refinements can be made as confidence develops.

- Making the learning of literacy skills both enjoyable and relevant. It is most important that students should want to read and write. They need to understand the purposes of the written word and see these as relevant and beneficial to themselves. Teaching effort therefore needs to be directed at ensuring students' rapid success, sense of personal progress, and enjoyment of the enterprise.

Reading

Following in the wake of the analysis-by-synthesis model of speech perception, models of the reading process advocated in the last two decades (e.g. Goodman, 1970; Steinberg, 1982; Smith, 1973, 1984) emphasize the readers' interpretation of the graphophonic cues in the text by means of their pragmatic, semantic, and syntactic competence in the language. Thus successful readers bring their own concepts of the world, their own understanding of word and sentence meanings and their own knowledge of the language structures to bear upon the visual cues of the text, interpreting, indeed perceiving, the latter by means of the former.

Fluent reading depends upon the ability to anticipate what is to come in the text, to predict words, phrases, etc. and this ability depends upon developed pragmatic, semantic, syntactic, and phonological competence in the language. There will be reading difficulties to the extent that competence in these areas in unequal to the demands of the text, and this is true for all readers, since, for example, a technical article is beyond the comprehension of non-specialists (Zimmerman, 1983).

If we accept that to read a text means to comprehend it — that is, to reconstruct the author's intended meaning and to understand that meaning — then clearly the higher order processes — the semantic and syntactic — are crucially important in the reading process. Where the reader is still acquiring the language in question as a second language, special assistance needs to be given if the text is to be comprehended, for the reasons which I will now further describe under the headings of: concept of print, world knowledge and meaning, rhetorical organization and syntax, hearing the written word, language-oriented activities, and materials.

Concept of print

Students who learn literacy through a second language have first to develop the whole concept of the printed word, of how it relates to and differs from the spoken word. They have to understand that there is meaning to be wrested from the printed symbols, and they have to develop strategies for grasping that meaning. (For discussion of differences between speech and writing see chapter 2.)

The point has been made often in ESL literature that there is a world of difference between students who have a concept of the printed word — what its purpose is and how to utilize it — and those who lack this concept. To try to grasp the concept of print in a language in which one is not strong orally is obviously much more difficult than to do so via the first language, more particularly if students come from a culture where the printed word is not relevant to everyday life in the community. This is true of communities where the language is not yet in written form or has only been given a written form in recent years. (Some of these matters are discussed in chapter 1.)

Students who are already literate through their first language understand the reading process and can transfer the process skills to reading in English.

They have to adapt, however, to a new set of sound–symbol correspondences, and may have to adapt to a new script, different punctuation formulae, and possibly to a different direction of eye movement, depending on the conventions in their first language.

World knowledge and meaning

Word meanings are culturally constrained, and the world's speech communities differ in both the aspects of the perceived world they encode in their languages and the manner in which they choose to encode them.

Where ESL students have built up concepts of the world in their first language, these concepts will be correlated with the way in which that language encodes perceived realities. Such encoding may or may not coincide with the way in which English speakers refer to the world they perceive. Cross-cultural differences of this sort have to be learned by the ESL student and an understanding of what words, phrases, idioms, etc. mean to the native speaker of English is crucial for understanding texts written by such speakers. The teacher therefore needs to be keenly aware of cultural differences in semantics, and of possible gaps in ESL students' knowledge of English that will make comprehension of the text difficult.

These differences apply first at the level of words and sentences taken in isolation; English speakers, for example, refer to one type of flora as a *bush*, to another as a *tree*. In other languages these two may not be so differentiated, or there may be, for example, a range of words denoting different *bush* types, but no word for *bush per se*. ESL learners have to understand how such reference in English differs from that of their first language, and what the gross and fine distinctions are within English itself between, for example, *tree* and *bush* on the one hand, and *bush* and *shrub* on the other. Knowledge of this sort will assist the reader to understand the meaning of a sentence like 'the bird is not in the tree, it's in the bush'. However, mere knowledge of how English speakers in general refer to such flora will not help the ESL learner to comprehend a sentence such as 'Stop beating about the bush'. Moreover, in Australia one needs to understand a different use (or meaning?) of the word *bush* in order to comprehend a sentence such as 'She's living in the bush'. Lack of understanding of words and sentences and their range of meanings, which vary in relation to textual and cultural context, can thus impede the ESL reader from making informed predictions in the reading process. Much discussion is needed, therefore, before the reader comes to the text, to ensure that the content is thoroughly familiar to and well understood by the ESL learner, both globally and in the details. Secondly, the overall meaning and the details should be discussed after (or, if need be, during) the reading of the text, and general points brought out where appropriate. Again, much of the task of comprehension can be facilitated by group work and discussion.

Rhetorical organization and syntax

What is meant here by *rhetorical organization* is the way in which the logic of discourse is shaped in a particular language, that is to say, how the interrelatedness of thoughts or ideas is given expression in the language as the speaker or writer moves from one thought to the next. Clearly, an understanding of the rhetorical organization of the text is crucial for a grasp of the author's meaning.

Second-language learners, however, are still in the process of acquiring such an understanding, and many texts could contain features of rhetorical organization (such as complex clauses, or logical connectives) which they have not yet mastered. Gaps of knowledge in this area, as in that of semantics, hamper the ability to predict and thus to read fluently.

The rhetorical organization of the written language differs from that of the spoken language in a number of important ways, and native speakers of English must appreciate this if they are to be fluent readers (see chapter 2).

When ESL students are literate in their first language, they will have learned that written language differs from spoken language, and will have begun to master the conventions and — more importantly — the rhetorical organization of that written language. Their predictive skills for reading that language will thus be based on their knowledge of its written structures.

In learning literacy in English they do not have to learn again that there is a difference between the spoken and written language, but they have to learn to control a different type of rhetorical organization; that is, an organization which differs not only from the written form they already control in their first language but also from the spoken form they are learning to control in their second language. It follows that even for these students, attention has to be given, where appropriate, to general and particular structures they encounter in the written language, which they do not understand. Some of these may appear simple and self-explanatory to the native speaker, but teachers need to be aware that they cannot assume knowledge of written English structures in the ESL students, even the most advanced, and so a careful monitoring of students' comprehension of texts needs to be part of literacy training.

Logical connectives were referred to above as a specific area of syntax that has to be brought to the attention of ESL learners. Examples of other observed areas of difficulty are the anaphoric use of pronouns, and the tense and preposition systems. Teachers can assist by seeking advice and information from the professional consultants on the characteristics of a student's first language which are at variance with typical features of English, so they can anticipate when a given student is likely to have difficulty with a text for reasons of differing rhetorical organization and syntactic features. Needless to say, similar monitoring is needed with those whose grasp of the reading process *per se* is not as strong. Assisting students in these areas requires language-oriented discussions and activities with individuals, groups or the whole class at various times when working with texts, so that students can develop an understanding of the kind of language to expect in a given type of text.

At the graphophonemic level, any student who has embarked upon literacy in a language other than English may have to learn some different conventions in print, as mentioned previously. At one extreme, this may mean learning a completely new writing system if the orthography in the first language is other than the Roman alphabet. In other cases it may mean, for example, learning that capital letters are used only at the beginning of sentences or for proper nouns, not for all nouns. Punctuation conventions may differ. More importantly, the direction of the written words may not be from left to right in the first language. These are aspects of the ESL learners' culture which obviously affect their encounter with literacy in English, and of which classroom teachers can easily be aware, with help from consultants.

Many ESL students have difficulties with English spelling because the sound system and orthography are not in a one-to-one correlation. According to the model of the reading process described earlier, fluent reading depends not on the examination of each incoming graphic cue, but upon the readers' own construction of what is meant, and consequent prediction of what is to come. In this view, word recognition would depend more on prior understanding of structure than upon a piecing together of sounds or letters.

Effective strategies for reading utilize the higher order processes of semantics and syntax in order to identify the phonemes or graphemes. This suggests that emphasis should be placed initially on these procedures, the analysis at word level into sounds or letters being left until these more basic strategies have been mastered. For this reason many ESL teachers have abandoned the phonics or spelling approach to identifying words, preferring to use a whole-word approach at least in initial stages. (In writing, the 'look, cover, write, check' method of practising spelling has been found very effective with ESL students.)

As confidence in reading and writing are established, teachers can direct students' attention to word-building patterns in English and the various rules of spelling which can be learnt.

Hearing the written word

First-language learners often receive regular opportunities to become familiar with the written form and conventions of the language through having stories read to them. As ESL students have not had these opportunities in their preschool years, it is important that they are presented with them in school even though they may be acquiring literacy in later years. The teacher reading to students provides them with a good reading model and allows them to apprehend differences between spoken and written modes. Many poor readers proceed on a word-by-word basis rather than perceiving the larger phrases and sentences of which the words are a part, so access to a good reading model can assist on this issue.

Shared Books combine aural and visual perception for the learners. Taped stories to accompany books are another useful aural/visual resource and have the advantage of allowing repetition of the experience. Teacher and students reading aloud together can take place with Shared Books but can also be set up as an exercise with individuals. As students embark on new subject areas, the subject teacher can assist comprehension of texts peculiar in style and content by reading material aloud in a stimulating and explanatory way.

Language-oriented activities

Based on a text that students are reading, various activities can be used which offer practice in prediction, so that students learn to adopt this strategy in their reading. Several of the books suggested for further reading contain ideas for such activities, so I shall restrict the description here to a reference to cloze exercises.

In these exercises, selected items are excised from a text so that readers have to guess the missing item. Clearly, they must use their knowledge of the text to do so (progression can be made from known to unknown texts, provided the context is sufficiently understood by the student to make a principled guess — otherwise the exercise is self-defeating), and hence this activity promotes utilization of semantic and syntactic processes, or of graphophonic processes if letters are excised.

Materials

Overall, the most effective approach to reading for ESL students requires input from teachers on the cultural context of the text, on word or phrase meanings (idioms need careful attention), on the logic of discourse and on syntactic features, wherever students need such knowledge to comprehend a text. A delicate path has to be followed between explaining what is necessary and overexplaining as though the students know nothing.

Similarly, general reading materials have to be chosen with great care. Many commerically produced materials tend to be culturally biased. (This may be true also of texts in subject areas.) Material needs to be relevant to students' ages, interests, and experience of life, expressed in language which lexically and syntactically does not present too many unknowns but which is not below their level or merely at their level, so that it offers a challenge and an opportunity to advance. Choice of materials is particularly difficult for students beginning literacy at an older age. For teachers, this may often mean creating their own material that is tailored to the needs of a particular group or class.

Writing

The controversies which have arisen in the teaching of mother-tongue English on issues such as the merits or otherwise of process writing, the language-experience approach, or the functional approach, have had their counterparts in ESL circles, and ESL teachers can be found who heartily endorse one or another approach or who combine various approaches to suit particular groups.

A process approach to teaching writing is seen by its advocates amongst ESL teachers as being in keeping with natural language acquisition since the student's own communicative intentions and forms are the starting point. Students are encouraged to write expressively on topics of their own choice, uninhibited by fear of making errors, and to self-correct in the editing process rather than have their work corrected by the teacher. Adjustments to grammar or spelling made in later drafts are understood to be in the interests of clarifying meaning for an audience, a procedure which emphasizes the communicative purpose rather than being a criticism of the author's efforts.

Process writing also encourages volume of writing, which is in keeping with the need for ESL students to have maximum experience of the target language. And its individualized approach is particularly appropriate for the disparate interests, levels of ability and rates of progress among ESL students. Student control over the process again harmonizes with the ESL teacher's aim that students should take control over their own learning.

Conferencing is an opportunity for ESL students to converse with their teachers on a one-to-one basis and to sort out their individual confusions. Student conferencing provides opportunity for the peer-group collaboration considered so helpful to ESL students. For various reasons such as those outlined above, process writing has been considered an appropriate method to use with ESL students (Turner, 1985; Davison, 1985).

However, while process writing has been seen as a good way to encourage students' expressive writing, ESL teachers — perhaps because they are acutely aware of their students' literacy needs and of the wide-ranging demands that will be made upon their reading and writing skills as they advance to higher grades — tend, as the following quotations show, to advocate the provision of written language models, and the teaching of a range of written registers and conventions, alongside the use of conferencing and drafting:

> Don't adopt process writing as 'the way' to the exclusion of class or group writing sessions where the ESL student sees the new language demonstrated. Surround your student with books, books, books. (Turner, 1985:9)

> Although such input [i.e. the teachers' input in conferencing] is very valuable in an ESL classroom it obviously has to be accompanied by more formal instruction in the structures of language and the conventions of writing. Still, the editing process does give the teacher an excellent idea of future directions as well as providing feedback on what has been learned. It also helps to pinpoint individual weaknesses and strengths. (Davison, 1985:16)

It is therefore possible to see ESL specialists advocating the teaching of written genres alongside an approach to students' writing which incorporates the more beneficial aspects of process writing such as the practices of conferencing and redrafting. There is an eclecticism in ESL methodology which is promoted by consideration of the various principles of approach described earlier, one of which, it may be recalled, was the need for exposure to the target language. It is a commonplace of current thinking on natural language acquisition that the learner needs input, and that the kind of language learnt will depend upon the kind of input received. Even on the assumption (which to my mind is considerable!) that reading and writing are natural processes — all the peoples of the world have spoken language, but by no means all develop written language — the second-language teacher would be aware of the need in natural language development to provide appropriate input. Thus, in the learning of literacy skills it would follow that appropriate exposure or input is required if students are to learn a range of registers.

The language-experience approach

The language-experience approach to beginning literacy has been found by many ESL teachers to be particularly helpful for their students. Typically, the process begins with the learners' own experiences, and so the content for literacy sessions comes from the learners themselves and is thoroughly familiar to them. The experience may be collective — some activity the class has just engaged in, such as an excursion, cookery, a scientific experiment or the reading of a story. Or it may be individual — the student's perspective on a collective activity or some experience from his or her own life.

The first transition is from experience interlaced with talk to discussion about the experience. Students and teacher talk about their experiences and such sessions are intended to assist students in formulating, sharing and extending their ideas, answering some questions, raising others, helping individuals to describe, define, clarify, inform, etc. There are then various ways in which discussion can lead in to writing.

Students can collaborate on a group text, or individuals can take turns to dictate a text. With the teacher acting as scribe, the words are written up on the board for all to see, with correct spelling. The teacher can then initiate group discussion of the text, so that by collaboration it is adjusted where necessary to form a grammatically orthodox piece. The text, which has been drawn from the students, is not alien to them culturally or linguistically, and so it provides ideal reading material. Students can practise wielding a pen by copying the text. (In beginning literacy, copying can be a viable alternative to free writing for practice in manipulation and in volume of writing.) The text can be the basis for further discussion, and for language-oriented activities such as cloze exercises. As words are learnt in context, many teachers organize various kinds of word store for students to keep as a reference.

Proponents of the language-experience approach to literacy attribute its effectiveness to the students' familiarity with the content since they have provided it, and this helps their reading attack; also there is a close relationship and continuity between experience, talking, reading, and writing. The language material is thus strongly reinforced.

For some teachers such as Moraro and McIntyre (1988), who apply a language-experience approach to adult long-term-resident ESL learners, a strength of this method is that unlike process writing it does not expose the learners repeatedly to the sight of misspellings and grammatical errors, the theory being that regular input of standard forms will more effectively aid their acquisition.

Overall, the approach to writing which has the greatest consensus among ESL specialists is one which starts from the students' own experience of the topic and the language involved, moves to group discussion of that experience, and then allows students to formulate the written form first themselves. After students have related to the concepts in their own experience, talk and writing, it is possible for the teacher to expand their knowledge of written expression to develop, for example, different kinds of writing pertinent to the topic, which require more formal or abstract kinds of expression.

Language across the curriculum

Reference has been made at various points in this chapter to the increasingly heavy demands for literacy skills made upon students as they advance to the last years of postprimary education. Obviously, in view of the disparity in their experience of English, NESB students face particular difficulties. These are intensified for new arrivals of postprimary age, especially those who are preliterate (that is, not literate in their first language), and the older the students are, the more acute the problem becomes. However, even the NESB students who are long-term residents in Australia, and who appear to be coping well with spoken English, are seen to be vulnerable in the area of literacy in the postprimary years. The following quotations from recent projects illustrate the need for developed literacy skills if students are to be successful in their school education:

> When planning this unit the language skills for report writing were explicitly taught rather than assumed . . . if students are to achieve academic success and have access to a choice of careers, it is essential that these skills be taught and reinforced. (Victoria, Ministry of Education, 1987:72)

> It is through reading and writing and the talking that accompanies it that we expect students to come to grips with ideas, express their understandings and apply their knowledge. Importantly, much of our assessment of student learning in all subject areas is based on students' reading and writing. (South Australia, Education Department *et al.*, 1988)

As was noted earlier, intensive ESL assistance tends to be concentrated upon new arrivals, which leaves long-term residents less well supported. This in itself places a correspondingly greater responsibility on mainstream teachers. However, as ESL specialists are acutely aware, assistance for NESB students in the English required for the various subject areas requires input from the particular subject teachers themselves since, even if there were a full complement of ESL specialists, the latter would not be sufficiently competent in the specialist language required. Where the educational problems are related to linguistic obstacles rather than to learning difficulties — and as observed earlier, this must always be taken into account with NESB students — subject teachers can, with support from ESL teachers, do much to remove those obstacles. In response to considerations of this sort, a number of projects have been implemented throughout Australia in recent years to develop the concept of teaching English language across the curriculum.

Within these movements there have been differences in approach. For example, the English-language-development-across-the-curriculum project (ELDAC), discussed in chapter 8, was based on the teaching of particular language functions (defining, classifying, hypothesizing, etc.) that prevail in subject areas, and the genres in which these functions characteristically occur, while the Victorian language-across-the-curriculum project (Victoria, Ministry of Education, 1987) was based more on the teaching of relevant language through subject content. What the various projects have in common is the collaborative work of subject teachers and ESL specialists, who together have aimed to design course units that will clarify the languages of the different subject areas to enable students to use the formal register of academic subjects in their spoken language, and to read the textbooks with understanding. It is impossible to describe the many interesting initiatives that have been taken to develop a language-oriented approach to the teaching of the various subject areas of the curriculum, but the following examples will serve to illustrate some of the difficulties faced by NESB students and some strategies adopted to overcome them.

The language of textbooks

Much postprimary teaching relies heavily on the use of textbooks, and some ESL specialists feel that mainstream teachers would do well to examine critically the language of their textbooks in relation to ESL students. Two issues are at stake: the first is that the language of a textbook, while perfectly comprehensible to a native speaker, may contain assumptions, structures, and vocabulary which present difficulties to the ESL learner; and the second is that the textbook itself may not be written very well.

Two interesting projects designed to encourage ESL learners to examine and appraise the language of textbooks are outlined in Garner and Biewer (1983). Particular benefits from the first project were that students, when collaborating in group discussion, were able to solve a number of difficulties they had encountered individually in private reading of the text, and that in rewriting the text for another class, they produced writing that was in several instances more immediate and dramatic than the original. In the second project, students began, through group discussion, not only to admit to their own misunderstandings but to perceive that the text itself had led to some of them. They moved from an unquestioning belief in the validity of the text to an ability to appraise the author, the print and the text structure in an intelligent fashion.

Overall, these two projects show the benefits of reading a textbook out loud, rather than just silently; of group collaboration in understanding the text; and of the students being able to phrase the content in their own words. In using textbooks ESL students need to work towards the language of the textbook, not to begin with it, preferably moving from the concrete, the visual, and the experimental to group discussion; from there to written language in the students' own words; and from there to the language of the text. The plea from ESL specialists is not that subject teachers should use simplified textbooks for NESB students, but rather that the language of the textbook should be taught, and taught effectively, with preliminary activities leading towards that goal.

The topic approach

Evans (1986), working with W. Cleland, has developed 'the topic approach' for ESL students, the principal aim of which is to develop literacy skills in the specialized language of school subject areas. This approach proceeds from visual presentation of topic material (experiments, models, whatever is relevant to the topic) whereby key language elements are learned so that students can describe or explain the visuals in their own words and then in the technical language of the subject areas. A period follows in which students build spoken and written sentences about the visual presentation. Students then proceed to building a reading passage about the topic. This is intended as a bridge between the sentence work and a formal reading passage on the topic which the teacher will introduce later. Students judge between true and false oral statements concerning the visuals, and the true statements are written on cards, arranged sequentially, and joined to form a reading passage. Language work is done on the passage through analytical exercises and activities designed to extend the students' knowledge further.

In the last stage, the students write their own passage based on all they have learnt — in content and language — by working through the topic. A process-writing approach is taken here, the final publications being in class books, wall displays, circulated essays, etc. This method, while initially devised for more recently arrived ESL students, provides a very good illustration of how the overall approach to literacy in ESL teaching described earlier, i.e. movement from experience through talk to literacy, has been adapted to a content-based topic approach for subject areas. In particular, it shows that the approach is moving from students' own concept formation towards the more formal style of expressing those concepts characteristic of writing in the specialist subject area.

The language of mathematics

There are some points about communication in the classroom which may appear mundane but which are important for NESB students. One is that writing by teachers on black or white boards needs to be very clear; the second is similar, namely that teachers' classroom discourse can itself be a cause of confusion if it is delivered too fast or too slowly, and if the teacher's assumptions, structures, and vocabulary are not understood.

With regard to assumptions, again cultural differences are significant. Harris (1980) calls for a mathematics syllabus for tribal Aboriginal children which is suited to their environment and needs, on the grounds that cultural and linguistic differences make it extremely hard to explain alien western concepts to them (see also Sayers, 1983). Dawe (1983) states a need for more research into the semantic differences between the two languages of the bilingual child, which might affect mathematical processes; it is worth noting his classroom observation that when the mathematics teacher gave NESB children a question in English which they found too hard, they translated into their first language to work out the answer. Again, on the issue of assumptions, Thomas (1986) shows some important cross-cultural differences in conventions, such as the marking of decimals and the thousands' separator. Triggs and Jackson (1985) show that some vocabulary used in mathematics consists of everyday words such as *expand* — with everyday meaning *to get bigger* — which can have a technical meaning in mathematics — in this case, *multiply to remove brackets*. Thus in addition to words that are peculiar to mathematics, there are everyday words used in a maths-specific manner, about which students may make wrong assumptions.

While the language of mathematics itself may be difficult, the mathematics teacher cannot even assume that a NESB student will readily understand the natural language employed by teachers to talk *about* mathematics (Thomas, 1985).

Newman (1977, 1981) made a study of errors in mathematical processing by sixth-grade pupils and found that most of the errors in verbally posed problems occurred in *comprehending the language* of the question. It is significant that while NESB students were reasonably close to ESB students in the number of errors made in reading the questions, they had a much higher proportion of errors when it came to *comprehending* the questions. Dawe (1983) argues that children must be taught the scientific and mathematical registers of English, both for the expression of ideas and for reading textbooks. He emphasizes especially the need for students to learn the use of logical connectives in deductive reasoning, a process vital for success at the postprimary level, and the need for them to spend time discussing the meaning of mathematical sentences. He urges moreover, that teachers should encourage the use of the mathematics' register in students' own speech.

On the point of literacy in mathematics, Newman observes:

> Traditionally, reading skills for narrative materials have been taught in a reading lesson, and mathematics' processing skills have been taught in a mathematics lesson. The reading skills for mathematics are usually not included in either lesson. Some teachers, recognizing that pupils do experience problems with the language of mathematics, give fewer exercises in a word form and more symbolic work. Unfortunately for these pupils they lack experience with the language of mathematics. When they do need to understand complex verbal items they are not aware of the types of comprehension skills required. (Newman, 1981:5)

Triggs and Jackson (1985) suggest the importance of testing mathematics abilities in the first language, and emphasize the need to teach the language of mathematics in English explicitly to NESB students, the teacher pointing out other uses of the same vocabulary, and incorporating the use of all four macroskills.

The approaches suggested by, for example, Triggs and Jackson (1985) or Thomas (1985) are, like the other work described above, based on language experience. The initial work is with concrete examples using visual aids such as pictures or diagrams, the concepts being discussed and perhaps written about by the students in everyday language. Then specific vocabulary, structure, and symbols are introduced. Students are given ample opportunity to use the new words orally, and in their own written sentences. Group and class discussion are used as the forum for students to discuss, to formulate definitions, etc.

A good example of the language-experience approach used in mathematics is as follows; a large plastic fly was attached to the ceiling and students had to lie on the floor and, through discussion, work out how to describe the position of the fly. It took them about 15 minutes to work out that something like a graph was needed. The teacher was then able to introduce structured lessons on graphing. The perceived benefits of the approach were that it allowed students to voice their thoughts in a non-threatening situation, and then to write about their thoughts and discoveries in a style appropriate for them. They thus had a chance to read each other's work and to appreciate their own interpretation of the topic before they came to the mathematics textbook (Triggs and Jackson, 1985).

SUMMARY

The descriptions I have given are probably sufficient to illustrate some of the language and learning needs of NESB students in mainstream classrooms. It is clear that the language of subject areas both oral and written needs to be taught, and some very promising whole-school approaches to language across the curriculum have been developed, with encouraging improvements noted in student performance and attitude. Houston (1986:13) notes that those who participated in the ELDAC project, including mainstream teachers, claimed an increased understanding of the language demands placed on students by the requirements of the postprimary curriculum, and that subject teachers commented that the project had also given them insights into ways of assisting their English-monolingual students.

It would not be an overstatement to claim that the presence of NESB students in a school, while posing a challenge for mainstream teachers, is at the same time a catalyst for pedagogical development. Many native speakers of English have difficulty with the specialized language registers of school curriculum subjects and become disenchanted with school. While no doubt other factors contribute to such disenchantment, language could well be significant.

Realizing that the language of school subjects cannot be taken for granted but has to be taught, and finding stimulating and effective ways to teach it, will assist not only NESB students but also many of their English-monolingual peers. If this leads the majority of students to a renewed interest in the postprimary curriculum, then the whole school population will undoubtedly benefit.

REFERENCES

Cambourne, B. (1986). Process writing and non-English-speaking background children. *Australian Journal of Reading*, **9**(3), 126–138.

Campbell, W. J., Barrett J., Joy B., & McMeniman, M. (1984). *A review of the Commonwealth English as a second language program*. Canberra: Commonwealth Schools Commission.

Campbell, W. J., & McMeniman, M. (1985). *Bridging the language gap: Ideals and realities pertaining to learning English as a second language*. Canberra: Commonwealth Schools Commission.

Davison, C. (1985). Process writing and ESL in a postprimary context. *Polycom*, **39**, 12–17.

Dawe, L. (1983). The development of inquiry skills in mathematics and science: Problems for the bilingual child. In D. Blane (Ed.), *The essentials of mathematics education*. Victoria: Mathematical Association of Victoria.

Evans, R. (1986). *Learning English through subject areas: The topic approach to ESL*. Victoria: Ministry of Education.

Garner, N., & Biewer, M. (1983). *Talking about textbooks*. Canberra: Curriculum Development Centre.

Goodman, K. (1970). Reading: A psycholinguistics guessing game. In H. Singer & R. Ruddell (Eds.), *Theoretical models and processes of reading*. Newark, Delaware: IRA.

Harris, P. (1980). *Measurement in tribal Aboriginal communities*. Northern Territory: Department of Education.

Houston, C. (1986). *English language development across the curriculum*. Queensland: Department of Education.

Krashen, S. (1982). *Principles and practice of second language acquisition*. Oxford: Pergamon Press.

Moraro, G., & McIntyre, P. (1988). *Steps in literacy*. Victoria: Adult Migrant Education Service.

Newman, A. (1977). An analysis of sixth-grade pupils' errors on written mathematical tasks. In M. A. Clements & J. Foyster (Eds.), *Research in mathematics education in Australia 1977*. Melbourne: Swinburne College Press.

Newman, A. (1981). Comprehension of the language of mathematics. In J. P. Baxter & A. T. Larkin (Eds.), *Research in Mathematics Education in Australia 1981*. Adelaide: Sturt College of Advanced Education.

Sayers, B. (1983). Aboriginal mathematical concepts: A cultural and linguistic explanation for some of the problems. *The Aboriginal Child at School*, **11**(1), 3–18.

Smith, F. (1973). *Essays into literacy*. London: Heinemann Educational Books.

Smith, F. (1984). *Psycholinguistics and reading*. New York: Holt, Rinehart, Winston.

South Australia, Education Department *et al*. (1988). *Literacy and learning in the middle years*. English Language Arts Project. Adelaide: Wattle Park Teachers Centre.

Steinberg, D. (1982). *Psycholinguistics*. London: Longman.

Thomas J. (1985). Access and success with a language-based approach to mathematics teaching. In P. Sullivan (Ed.), *Mathematics, Curriculum, Teaching, and Learning*. Victoria: Mathematical Association of Victoria.

Thomas J. (1986). *Number ≠ Mathematics*. Victoria: Child Migrant Education Services.

Triggs, V. & Jackson, P. (1985). La Lengua De Matematica. In P. Sullivan (Ed.), *Mathematics, Curriculum, Teaching, and Learning*. Victoria: Mathematical Association of Victoria.

Tsolidis, G. (1985). Towards a definition of a second phase learner. *Polycom*, **39**, 2–7.

Turner L. (1985). Process writing, the second language learner, and the classroom teacher. *Polycom*, **39**, 8–11.

Williams, V. (1986). Second phase learners — An analysis of some issues, expectations and strategies. *Australian Journal of Reading*, **9**(3), 167–179.

Victoria, Ministry of Education. (1987). *The language across the curriculum project*. Victoria: Participation and Equity Program.

Zimmerman, H. (1983). Literacy and ESL. In E. Aird & D. Lippmann (Eds.), *English is their right: Strategies for teachers in the multilingual classroom*. Melbourne: A.E. Press.

8 Literacy in the curriculum: planning and assessment

FRANCES CHRISTIE & JOAN ROTHERY

INTRODUCTION

The principles of assessment adopted for marking students' work and the principles of evaluation adopted for determining the success of a literacy programme depend entirely upon the goals of the curriculum programme. Where the curriculum and its goals are clearly articulated, and where teachers have a strong sense of the role of language in general and of literacy in particular in achieving those goals, then what is to be assessed as well as the manner of its assessment should be readily identifiable. At bottom, what we are arguing is that there is no substitute for having a strong theory of language in the curriculum. It is in language that so much of the teaching and learning activities of schooling take place. It is in language that the meanings and values, methodologies and ways of dealing with experience characteristic of the many school subjects are actually found. While spoken language remains fundamentally important in all the years of schooling, it is also apparent that the further students go in their education, the more and more their success is measured in the written word. Whether the policies adopted are those of continuous assessment or of some other pattern involving summative assessments, including examinations, it is clear that capacity in literacy is an essential requirement for success.

All the previous chapters in this book have argued the value of an explicit concern for the language that students must master to achieve success at school. We argue that teachers should be able to identify and teach the various kinds of text types or genres that students need to both read and write in the subjects they study. We teachers owe it to all our students to

We wish to thank Lee Pledger, of North Sydney Demonstration School, who worked with Joan on a factual writing programme in Lee's composite Year 3, 4 and 5 class in 1985. The Koala Report was written by one of Lee's students as part of this programme.

devise educational programmes in which the goals are clear and in which, therefore, the students' expectations of how they are to use their language are also very clear. We owe this to our students, both as a matter of common justice and as a necessary part of teaching effectively. However, we owe it particularly to those students who, because of life circumstance and opportunity, are not always well prepared to deal with the particular literacy demands of schooling. Such students include many from poor and disadvantaged families, children for whom English is a second language (discussed in chapter 7), and the many Aboriginal children in Australia, for some of whom English is a second language — though others may use Aboriginal English, which is often significantly different from the standard English valued in schools. (Walton, 1986, has recently documented some of the difficulties in literacy learning for young Aboriginal children.)

In this chapter, we firstly discuss some of the principles of curriculum planning and assessment which we suggest should apply in schools. Just as schools should have clearly developed curriculum planning, we argue, they should also have well-planned, coherent planning for assessment, so that students can move up the school, passing from one teacher to another in primary school, or from one set of teachers to another in secondary school, understanding the kinds of assessment principles that apply. Secondly, we offer some discussion of contemporary concerns with 'standards' in literacy, and with examinations and other forms of assessment, most notably continuous assessment.

THE NEGOTIATED CLASSROOM AND ASSESSMENT

In recent years more than one writer has argued the merits of the negotiated classroom — one in which the students take a significant role in shaping the course their learning takes — and the kinds of outcomes that emerge (e.g. Boomer, 1982; Gray, 1983). We argue that good curriculum planning and assessment always involve negotiation, so that through skilled teaching the students are involved both in exploring the topics appropriate to the various subjects they study, and in examining and discussing the genres in which such topics are built up to form the 'content' of the subjects. Defining the curriculum objectives, including the range of topics to be considered over a week, a semester, a year, remains a teacher's responsibility, as does deciding the range of genres that students need to use to deal with the topics successfully. However, negotiation should be integral to the way students are taught to engage with the content of the various subjects and to identify, discuss and model the various genres they must read and write in learning the subjects. Learning to handle and manipulate the genres of the various school subjects, adapting and modifying them for different purposes, is important not only because it is a necessary part of learning the content of the subjects, but also because it is a necessary part of learning the ways of reasoning and organising the different aspects of experience that are characteristic of the different subjects. Such matters, as Cope and

Kalantzis have suggested in chapter 5, should quite properly be the subject of debate and discussion, and not merely a matter of unthinking acceptance.

Over a series of lessons, as the teacher and students explore and negotiate the topics to be dealt with and the sorts of resources to be consulted for information, as well as the various outcomes they plan for, they should establish the kinds of genres they will need to read and those they will need to produce. In establishing these two requirements in particular, they will actually be identifying the criteria for assessment. Some examples will demonstrate how the principles for teaching and learning which we are describing might work. We will begin by taking as an example a possible unit of work in the science classroom.

A unit in the junior science classroom

Students in either the primary or the junior secondary school might undertake a unit of work on the Australian marsupials. Initial investigation of the subject might well begin with a class discussion directed by the teacher, intended to establish what students already know about marsupials. This provides a necessary point of departure. Such an introductory discussion should lead to an initial list of possible problems and/or questions that students need to investigate in order to go further into the subject. Such questions should be jointly negotiated, perhaps in teacher/student whole-class discussion, or in student small-group discussion, or in a curriculum sequence in which both kinds of discussion are used. Once questions or problems have been established and written down, some criteria to guide reading will be clear.

This is an important matter to note, since the reading strategies to be adopted when consulting sources of factual information are very different from those that apply when reading a novel, a recipe book, a telephone book, or a car driver's manual, all of which genres we commonly read. In our example, the students will no doubt need to consult reference books — everything from encyclopaedias to textbooks of various kinds, though they might also view appropriate videos or films to obtain information. Whatever the sources of information they use, students will need to make efficient notes, and note making is an important though often underestimated skill. With their teacher's assistance, students will need to establish some principles by which to make notes as they work. Even a set of notes constitutes a genre that has to be taught. Significant numbers of students get to university, by the way, very poorly equipped to take notes efficiently.

To return for the moment to the reading strategies to be adopted in consulting reference books of various kinds: students will need guidance in handling the tables of contents, the indexes at the backs of the books, the various chapter headings and subheadings within chapters, and the points at which, perhaps, matters are summarised in different parts of the books. All these aspects of the genres of scientific textbooks are worth explicit discussion in the classroom, not only to produce efficient readers who can 'find their way' around the books, but also because students will learn something of the ways in which those who provide scientific information organize it into the various discourse patterns of science. Learning these things is part of learning what it is to 'behave scientifically'. Examination of the reference books should in addition take in several other matters: the use of any pictorial information showing marsupials in their natural habitat; perhaps a map of Australia showing where the various types of marsupials are to be found; perhaps any tabular or graphical material, quantifying information about marsupials.

The very discussion and identification of the various characteristics of factual books, as a guide to intelligent reading, also provides the criteria by which the success of the reading will be judged. Thus, for example, students can be questioned by the teacher in ways intended to elicit information about the subjects under review, and the general standard of their oral responses will provide the first evidence of the success with which they have read. Alternatively, students may be encouraged to elicit information from each other, in itself a very useful strategy in that it involves students in assessing and considering the fruits of each other's work. The strategy works very well, by the way, where the unit of work (in this case, Australian marsupials) has been deliberately broken into subunits, so that each group or pair of students is investigating a different aspect in some detail — perhaps different types of marsupials. Oral questioning of each other about what has been learned is an excellent means of assessing students' progress, providing the teacher (who both listens and participates where need be) with useful feedback, not only about what has been learned, but about the skill with which particular students have read the books consulted.

Once students have begun to amass some of the information they sought about the marsupials, they can begin to work over the set of questions they started with, expanding some, reducing others, and slowly clarifying those matters to be written up in some permanent record. At this point, they will need to discuss with their teacher the kinds of genres they will have to write to do justice to the subject in hand. Here again recourse to the models of the textbooks will often provide a basis for discussing the possible genres for writing. In their chapter on literacy in the social sciences, Cope and Kalantzis noted the all-too-frequent pattern, especially in the secondary school, of having students merely copy long tracts straight from the textbooks. Martin, too, commented on the tendency to copy extensively in the science classroom. We certainly do not advocate copying, for reasons which hardly need expansion here since it is obvious it does not develop independent readers or writers, but merely encourages unthinking dependence.

However, we do suggest that some discussion of the various genres found in textbooks, of the kind discussed by Martin, would be a valuable aid in identifying the genres students might need to write. Everyone relies upon the models of others in writing, a point made by Gilbert in her chapter on writing in the English classroom, and it is a quite dangerous misconception, sometimes found in schools, that students must themselves 'invent' or 'create' the linguistic patterns they use for the various subjects they learn. Another and equally dangerous myth, as Martin has also suggested, is the one which proposes that children write scientific information in the form of stories or other 'imaginative' or 'self-expressive' genres, on the grounds that they enable students to use 'their own language' in writing science, presumably graduating — at some never clearly specified point in the future — to writing the 'harder' genres of science.

One of the dilemmas of the contemporary classroom is that many of the school textbooks available do not offer very good models for writing. Teachers need to be alert to this problem, sometimes writing alternative models where they feel able, and — what is often better still — going to the world of 'real scientists', selecting from the scientific magazines and textbooks appropriate genres for discussion. An issue to be stressed in choosing appropriate genres for writing is that the choices to be made are not arbitrary but selective, not a matter of 'free choice' on the part of the learners, as some curriculum guidelines would seem to suggest. On the contrary, they are determined by the requirements of the field or content area, and by the manner in which one needs to deal with that content. As Martin noted in chapter 4, the genres of science have evolved as the most functionally relevant ways in which to build up scientific information, and it is for this reason that scientists write the genres they do. Of course the genres change over periods of time, for they are not fixed but, like everything else in language, subject to modification as new forms of scientific information emerge. An education in science involves some initiation into the various genres in which the knowledge of science is built up.

To return then to our unit on marsupials, and with the criteria for assessment, among the commonest of the genres useful for writing in science are the report and the explanation, discussed in chapter 4. An example of a report — about koalas — is set out here in text 8.1. It was written by Sharon when she was in year 5.

Text 8.1 Report on koalas by Sharon, year 5 (reduced size)

Koalas

Description
A koala is a stub-tailed arboreal marsupial with large furry ears, black leathery nose and long strong claws. The koala's thick woolly fur is grey on the back and white or yellowish on the underside. Its limbs are remarkably long compared with the body and the hands are large. The foot is short and broad. In adult form they weigh 7 to 13 kg. Normally they are under 3 feet long.

Habitat

Koala colonies extend from north Queensland through New South Wales, Victoria and Tasmania. They are now extinct from South and Western Australia. Koalas favour the trees both east and west of the Great Dividing Range.

What They Eat

The koala eats most exclusively on eucalyptus leaves and a few species of smooth-barked eucalyptus that are suitable food trees. There are three species that alone are suitable food trees. They are the forest red gum, gray gum and manna gum. The koala eats 500 grams daily. The gum leaves contain sufficient water for total requirements. If it is hot or there is a drought the koala drinks water if there is any available.

Mannerisms

Koalas are slow animals that sleep normally by day. They have a home range of 14 or 15 trees. They usually have one tree in which they spend a third of their time. They only come to the ground when they want to change trees. Except when they have babies they like to be by themselves in their feeding area. Their feeding occurs two hours after sunset. For 19 hours of the day the koala rests in the fork of the tree without any shelter.

Baby Koalas

When a baby koala is born it is an inch long and it weighs less than 0.5 grams. The baby koala stays in it's mother's pouch for 175 days

When it's nine months old it no-longer goes to its mother's pouch, and from then on it goes or its mother's back until its 12 months old. It is fully grown at 2 years of age and lives till 20 years of. age.

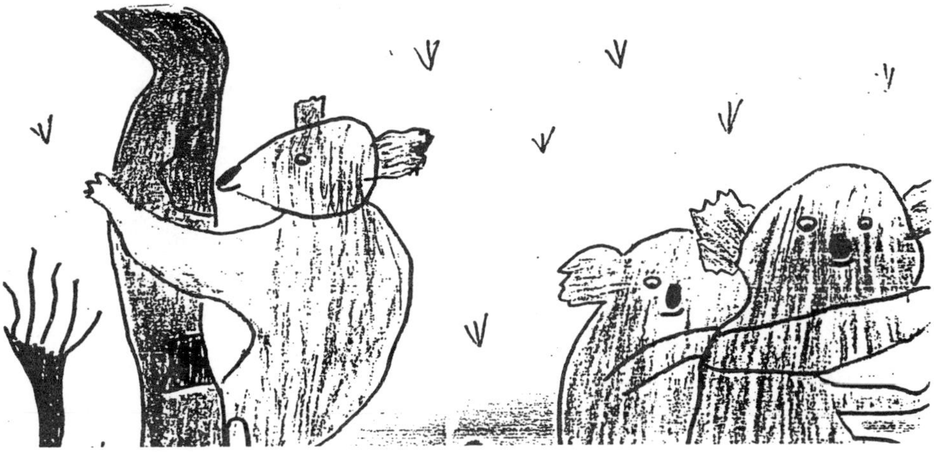

By any standards, this is a well-organised report genre, in which the writer demonstrates very successful control both of the technical language relevant to the field or topic under discussion, and of a clear generic structure. The series of subheadings she adopts helps to build the structure of the genre, but note also the way that Sharon builds general classification to begin: 'A koala is a stub-tailed arboreal marsupial', followed by subsequent description: 'with large furry ears, black leathery nose and long strong claws. The koala's thick woolly fur . . .'. In fact, the whole of the rest of the text constitutes description — of habitat, eating habits, and so on. Overall, the genre is very well organised and quite detailed in its information.

Capacity to write such a genre depended partly upon effective teaching, during which Sharon was enabled to establish very clearly the genre she needed to write, and partly upon Sharon's careful researching of the subject, so that she had something of substance to say about koalas.

There is a number of ways in which report-writing abilities can be developed and assessed. One way is in respect of the field or subject matter of the report. To begin with, junior secondary students may focus on specific marsupials such as the kangaroo, wallaby or marsupial rat, all recognised as belonging to a subclass of mammals. From that, they may go on to deal with a particular type of marsupial, such as the arboreal ones, adapted to living in trees. This group includes koalas and the various types of possums. Eventually students may undertake a wide-ranging report on all the types of marsupials. In this aspect of developing the field or subject area, the scientific taxonomy of marsupials will be built up in a more comprehensive way.

Another aspect of report-writing development is in the way students handle each stage of the schematic structure of the genre. For example, in the primary school or the first year of secondary school, the general classification element may be short and relatively simple as far as technical terms are concerned: this is the case in text 8.1. However, as students progress through the junior secondary school, the general classification element becomes more detailed, in the sense of developing an increasingly precise placement of the animals considered in the taxonomy of marsupials. As a result there will also be increased use of technical terms, the meanings of which students must clearly understand. In fact, using technical language appropriately constitutes an aspect of assessment in its own right in many areas of the curriculum. Students need to learn the meanings of technical terms which are crucial to the different areas of the curriculum. As command of the field grows, more technical terms are used, and it is essential that teachers ensure they are used with understanding.

Students will also develop the descriptive aspect of their reports more comprehensively as they develop as writers, gaining increasing control of both field and genre. What this means of course is that reports will inevitably become longer as students develop their writing abilities. Incidentally, it is not that length *per se* is important, but that developing control of field and genre will inevitably lead to longer texts, in the case of a report genre in particular.

In our imagined unit of work an important explanation genre might well be written to explain why marsupials are found in Australia. Generically, this would involve firstly the phenomenon element — stating the fact that marsupials are found primarily in Australia; secondly, it would involve an explanation element, developing an account of the factors believed to be responsible. Unfortunately, we cannot provide an example of such an explanation dealing with marsupials, but we suggest its model would be very like that in text 8.2, which explains why deserts are dry.

Text 8.2 An explanation genre

Explain how deserts remain dry
There are three possible reasons why deserts remain dry. These are high mountain barriers, cold ocean currents and high pressure systems.

Mountain barriers
When wind passes over the ocean it picks up moisture in the form of water vapour. As this moist air travels over the land, it rises to pass over mountain ranges. When it begins to rise, the air cools and this causes the water vapour to condense into droplets which fall as rain. When the air reaches the other side of the mountain barrier, it has lost all its moisture and so the other side of the mountain remains dry.

Cold ocean currents
Air passing over cold ocean currents is cooled and therefore is unable to pick up and hold much moisture. When this cold air mass reaches the warm desert, any moisture in the air is evaporated and so does not fall as rain and so the desert remains dry.

High pressure systems
In a high pressure system, the air is dry and moving downwards. In this system, moisture is more easily taken in rather than released.

A further development in our imagined unit on marsupials would no doubt explore the various issues of conservation, which often arise in an examination of such animals. A movement into conservation issues would, by its very nature, require entry to a quite different type of genre — one in which argument and debate would have to be handled, and the students would need to be prepared for this very early in their work, so they could understand the kind of information they must collect and the manner in which they should treat it. Koalas are often said to be an endangered species, though some scientists challenge this belief; similarly kangaroos are said by some to be endangered, though others dismiss them as pests, deserving systematic culling if not extermination. Our students could research all the vexed and often controversial information about such claims, beginning much as we indicated above: by raising questions worth exploring about the life of, and possible risks to, the various marsupials in contemporary Australia. Having once identified these, they would go on to consult various sources of information; then they could discuss the results of their findings in the classroom; finally, they would plan and develop the appropriate written genre. In this case, it would involve exposition, having elements of proposition and argument (see chapter 4).

Overall, we argue that in our imagined unit of work on Australian marsupials, an explicit sense of the manner in which language works to build the meanings particular to the subject drives the whole curriculum activity: the teaching and the learning, the assessment of the students' work, and the overall evaluation of the quality of the programme. Guided discussion, guided reading and guided writing are all built up around explicit negotiation both of the matters explored and of the matters written up. The criteria for assessment and evaluation are clear, and the students have a realistic sense of what it is they are expected to do in language in order to be successful in their learning.

Negotiation and assessment in other areas of the curriculum

The model for negotiating the curriculum and for assessing students' progress in their learning as we have outlined in some detail for science applies with equal force to any other area of the curriculum. Some brief examples will illustrate something of the possible range of genres for the different subjects. Thus, procedural genres, such as recipes or sets of instructions to guide the making of objects like toys or tools, are found to be useful in such subjects as health, home economics, and arts and crafts. But procedural genres are also found in the science classroom, in the sets of steps provided to guide the undertaking of certain experiments; they may even be found in the manner in which a reproductive cycle is set out, or perhaps in the series of steps in which a star comes into being and subsequently dies.

Reports and explanations, while certainly a feature of the science classroom, are also used in the social sciences. The social sciences, like the natural sciences, are concerned with classifying, explaining and interpreting aspects of the world — in this case, the social world: for example, social institutions such as types of government, the nature of urban settlement, or the nature of the family. Reports are used to collect and store information about such matters; explanations account for their coming into being, and expositions and discussions take up particular issues to be argued about them.

Narrative genres are associated with the reading of literature, in the sense of examining novels and short stories, while other literary genres such as the many poetic text types can be systematically examined. Myths and legends have a role both in the literature classroom and in aspects of the social sciences, where students examine the manner in which the peoples of different cultures offer differing accounts of the emergence of the world or of other natural phenomena. Argumentative genres, involving expression of opinion and provision of evidence in support, can be used in most subjects, and we suggest they should be more commonly introduced and taught to students, who often remain very uncertain of what is actually involved in successful control of argument.

ADOPTING A COMMON CURRICULUM AND ASSESSMENT POLICY IN A SCHOOL

The principles of curriculum planning and assessment we have briefly described can be shown to apply with equal force in all content areas. Such principles, once adopted in a school, can form the basis of a common curriculum and assessment programme, providing a firm basis for a 'language-across-the-curriculum policy'. For some two decades, in fact, schools have been encouraged by many writers on language in education to pursue language-across-the-curriculum policies, for the importance of language as a principal resource in learning has been argued many times before this. However, we believe that while often accepting the general advice about the significance of language in learning, teachers have frequently felt at a loss in deciding what best to do in developing language, especially capacity in literacy. In particular, they have lacked the tools both for explicit teaching about language, and, more importantly, for assessing their students' growth.

Encouraged as they often have been by curriculum guidelines (see chapters 4 and 5) to have children write personally expressive and narrative-type genres in curriculum areas in which they can be quite inappropriate, teachers have unwittingly tended to narrow the range of genres they teach their students. In the English programme, where narrative-type genres, among others, do have a role, many of the desired characteristics of creativity in writing have remained unclear, as Gilbert has shown.

We need school policies that focus upon what it is to be successful in all areas of the curriculum, which involves addressing the kinds of genres students need to master in order to deal with the contents of each school subject. Different genres have evolved, in the life of our society, to achieve particular goals — goals that are closely associated with working and learning in the subjects in question, and hence too, goals associated with successful participation in the life of the community once children have left school. Real success in literacy can only be measured accurately by examining students' performance in all subjects, for literacy does not stand in isolation from art, craft, science, mathematics or the social sciences, to mention only some school subjects. Furthermore, development in literacy cannot be assessed on the basis of reading and writing narratives alone, as at least some curriculum advice to teachers today would seem to suggest.

Once schools frame their curriculum planning and assessment policies in the manner we have been suggesting, they will be able to assess the range of literacy abilities their students develop. These will constitute the literacy goals of the curriculum, and clear formulation of such goals will be of immense benefit to students, who will then know what it is they are expected to do, and hence the criteria by which they will be assessed.

We know of at least one independent school in Sydney — namely Knox Grammar School — in which the head of the English department, Martin Gooding, successfully co-opted his colleagues in all other subjects into developing a literacy-across-the-curriculum policy (see Rothery and Gerot, 1986: 164–72). The policy emerged from Gooding's concern to help his students deal with the demands of writing in subjects other than English, about which they sometimes complained to him. This led him initially to study the projects, assignments, essays and reports that students were set by their teachers, and in time his investigation led to the development of a school policy in which the various subject departments cooperated in clarifying the literacy standards they required. The result was a well-articulated school policy with very explicit criteria for assessing students' progress as they moved up the school.

Another successful literacy-across-the-curriculum policy was developed by Houston (1986a; 1986b) and her colleagues in Queensland, working initially to clarify the literacy demands for second-language learners studying the various school subjects especially at the secondary level. Houston and her colleagues began by considering the question, 'What do students need to be able to do with English to enable them to cope successfully with the demands of learning at high school?' (1986a:2). So successful was the project, developed originally at Oxley State High School, that it rapidly involved mother-tongue as well as second-language teachers, and led in time to a well-planned policy of literacy teaching and assessment across the whole curriculum. The process took teachers of all subjects into quite close and detailed examination of the patterns of language needed in all areas of the curriculum, and it meant that, firstly, the teachers themselves became more confident with what they were attempting, and secondly, the students enjoyed the benefits of clear advice and assessment of their work.

At present, many schools lack clear goals for literacy development so that the directions they are taking remain a source of confusion to both students and teachers. Very often, in consequence, little or no development occurs over quite long periods of time. In a study of a primary school in Sydney undertaken by Martin and Rothery (1984), a disturbing picture emerged about the development of writing abilities. Children over the school, from year 1 to year 6, all tended to be writing the same kinds of genres: normally simple reconstructions of personal experience involving the writing of personal observations sometimes including an evaluative comment. Such genres, incidentally, they called observations (see Rothery, 1984), and our subsequent experience working with teachers (Christie and Rothery, 1989) has shown that, once they begin to investigate writing in a purposive way, teachers begin to realize both how commonplace is the observation genre in schools, and how limiting and limited it is as a genre for writing. Text 8.3 is an example of an observation written by Zoe in year 1.

Text 8.3 An observation genre from year 1

> Yestday Zoe's Gramdma and Grandpa came to stay for two nites. Thay gave us a lot of presents. Thay gave us lots of loles. Thay gave us a jur [jar] of loles. Thay gave us lolepops. It was Grandpa's birthday. Instead of a cack he had a bowl of ice crem with baby food and three candoos on it. he was 70. He got a tin of chockles. They wor yumm.

This is a defensible genre for a child in year 1, though as Kamler (in preparation) can demonstrate, the child in question wrote very few other types of genre in nearly three years of schooling. Text 8.4 is another observation genre, this one written by a boy in year 5. While the two texts differ markedly in field or subject, the point we are stressing is that both involve some very simple reconstruction of the child's familiar experience or knowledge, and as such they do not challenge the young writer to handle new experience or to build some of the significantly useful other genres that so much school and life experience require.

Text 8.4 An observation genre from year 5

> **Racing cars**
> I think racing cars are unreal. They usually go real fast but it is unusual that they are slow and most have tinted windows and they look like this [*a picture accompanies*]. The people in the car can see through it when the people outside are trying to look in. There are things like mags that are tough tyres and most people that drive sports cars have mags on the back of them. Farrys [Ferraris] have big motors.

Overall, we find all too little evidence of effective planning for the teaching of a range of genres across both the primary and secondary schools, with the lamentable result that when students enter years 11 and 12 and face significant assessment prior to leaving school, they are often worked very hard indeed. Christie (1989) has recently done a case study of Daniel, a senior secondary student in Victoria, and of the considerable number of written genres he was required to write for his year 12 studies. Like many other such students, he found years 11 and 12 very pressured — needlessly so, in our opinion, because had he been better prepared by his previous education for the various writing tasks needed, he would have been able to cope more readily, and would have enjoyed his senior school studies very much more than he did. McNamara (1989), whose work was referred to in chapter 4, working with a group of secondary teachers in Melbourne has shown just how many written genres students need to learn to be successful in their secondary studies. It was an enlightening experience for the teachers of science and history who worked with McNamara to identify the genres they wanted, and it enabled them to teach those genres much more confidently than they had hitherto.

Preparation for writing the many genres valued in our culture should start in the primary school, for learning to write is really a necessary part of coming to terms in a challenging way with the contents of the various school subjects. In our experience, students at both primary and secondary levels are gratified when they feel their capacities to be challenged, their potential as learners and thinkers extended and enriched. One year 3 boy, participating in a genre-based writing programme in a Sydney school, told Rothery that he liked researching and writing the reports he prepared 'because it's the kind of writing that grown-ups do and it makes me feel like a grown-up'. Daniel could also say, once his year 12 studies were over, that though he had found the last two years of schooling much too pressured and hard, he did believe that he had gained a lot in terms of developed capacity to take a point of view and sustain it: to that extent, he felt both enriched and empowered. How much more enriched he could have been if the pressure had not been so great, so relatively late in his school career!

LITERACY, EXAMINATIONS AND CONTINUOUS ASSESSMENT

Contemporarty educational discussion around Australia about policies of assessment is, as always, reasonably lively. Some state educational systems have abandoned public examinations, while others maintain policies which combine school-based assessment with the use of public examinations. We hold no particular brief for public examinations administered by the state since, on the one hand, systems as small as that of the ACT and, on the other hand, as geographically large and scattered as that of Queensland have both demonstrated that they can successfully administer alternative assessment procedures for students leaving school at year 12. However, we do suggest that where examinations continue to be used, whether within schools or within large publicly administered education systems, there is an absolute responsibility upon teachers to prepare students to deal with the very considerable demands of responding to examination questions requiring answers written under pressure.

Such preparation, like that for handling any other genre, should be carefully undertaken in schools, teachers guiding students into an understanding of the very wording of sample examination questions, as well as of the most efficient methods of planning essays for writing under significant time constraints. Our advice, both from students who have recently completed year 12 and from students currently undertaking tertiary studies, is that they were often left 'to work it out for themselves'. Given that students' whole futures depend so significantly upon the results with which they leave school, this seems most regrettable. It is in our view quite wrong — indeed often most unfair — that so much of a young person's future life and career prospects can depend upon satisfactory completion of one examination at the end of year 12. However, where examinations continue to be used, it is clear that schools must have constructive policies to help students prepare adequately for them.

Policies of continuous assessment, generally proposed as a desirable alternative to examinations, do have much to commend them, providing for students' performance to be assessed over sustained periods of time. Folders of students' written work can be kept, and students, equipped — as we have argued — with clear criteria for watching their own growth, can be encouraged to present the best examples of their written work in all the subjects that they study. Such policies are among a number recently suggested by the Australian Association for the Teaching of English (1987), and they should apply not only in the upper secondary school, but be introduced from the earliest years of schooling.

The only cautionary observation we offer about continuous assessment as it is currently applied, is that it can create a lot of work for students. This is probably because teachers, especially in the upper secondary school, feel the need to keep their students 'up to the mark' by having them work all the year around rather than immediately before the examinations (as allegedly happens in schools and systems relying wholly or in part on examinations). The result is that students are often worked very hard indeed. There is no need for continuous assessment to take such a demanding form as far as literacy is concerned if it is implemented from the earliest years of schooling. If, as we have suggested, students keep a writing folder of representative pieces of their work in the different genres for their various subjects, this folder can accompany them from year to year. In this manner, students can build up a most valuable record of their own progress throughout all their years of schooling, so that their own development is apparent to them. At the same time, particularly at the beginning of each year, the writing folder can provide teachers with a clear picture of the stage students have reached, so they can immediately plan work that takes this as the starting point for future development.

Nowhere would the writing folder be more important than at the transition from the primary to the secondary school. Very often secondary teachers underestimate the capacities of their junior students. As a result, the students quite often become bored after entering secondary school, and their work in literacy regresses rather than develops. Writing folders would demonstrate what students could do and would put responsibility on the teacher to take the students' development forward.

STANDARDS AND GRADING

There is no aspect of education that attracts more heat than the perennial problem of 'standards' in literacy. Journalists like Max Harris (1988) often lament the alleged decline in standards as a matter of national urgency: literacy is 'in peril', he writes, and he encourages the reader to 'join the fight for a resurgence in the nation's classrooms'. In an article which is disappointing for a number of reasons, Harris goes on to quote the British radio broadcaster Frank Muir as saying, 'Teaching children English without teaching grammar is like giving somebody a soup spoon to change a 13 amp plug'.

We do agree that there are grounds for concern with the quality of literacy both in our community and in our schools, and we believe that schools have a major responsibility to take steps to improve the quality of literacy education, though whether in fact there are grounds for believing that standards are in decline is debatable. For reasons argued at some length in chapter 1, the world is now so different from even the recent past, that it is difficult to see how one might compare present standards of literacy with those that once applied. Literacy today is a different thing from what it was, say, even ten or fifteen years ago, so that a comparison is rather meaningless. In any case, in our view it serves little purpose to lament an allegedly golden past: what is more to the purpose is what we might usefully do in our present circumstances.

Like Boomer (1987) when, in his capacity as chairman of the Schools Commission, he called for a 'national strategy for literacy', we deplore the fact that many teachers' efforts to develop literacy are 'fragmentary, piecemeal, relatively uncoordinated and often contradictory'. We would suggest that the fragmentary nature of many policies for developing and assessing literacy in the schools is a direct consequence of the kinds of problems initially discussed in chapter 1 and subsequently explored in detail in the other chapters. That is to say, the problems are born of a curriculum tradition, now well established in our schools, that regularly underestimates language, and consequently its quite critical role in the organization of meaning in the various school subjects is simply overlooked.

Policies concerned with 'growth' and 'process' in language since the 1960s in particular have left many teachers deskilled and unconfident in at least two important ways: firstly, in recognizing the differences between speech and writing — discussed in chapter 2; secondly, in recognizing the kinds of genres in which the various school subjects are built up or realized — discussed in other chapters. The effect of both these problems is that teachers currently often have difficulties planning coherent literacy programmes of the kind we have argued for in this chapter.

The solution, however, does not lie in the courses of action that Harris and others like him propose with their apparent return to traditional grammar teaching, and their quite simplistic notion that learning the various parts of speech will somehow produce persons competent in reading and writing across a wide range of school subjects, and in the many contexts in which they will need to participate after leaving school. In fact, so far are we from agreeing with Frank Muir in his observations about school grammar teaching that we would quote instead Halliday (1969), who some years ago wrote that 'teaching the do's and don'ts of grammar to a child who is linguistically unsuccessful is like teaching a starving man how to hold a knife and fork'. That is to say, traditional grammar teaching, with its preoccupations with the parts of speech and the rules of syntax of the written sentence, is simply not relevant to a good many children in our schools. In general, the more disadvantaged and unhappy the student is at school, the more irrelevant such practices of teaching language are. Functionally relevant approaches to the study of language start with issues of meaning and with corresponding issues of text organization of the kinds discussed at some length in several parts of this book, and lead to the development of various genres. Ultimately, such studies take students into examining a great deal of the language, including no doubt its parts of speech and the syntax of its written sentences. But these should never be the primary focus of language studies in the school because, as many years of school practice testify all too well, where these matters become the main focus of interest, considerations of meaning and the wider issues of rhetorical purpose in using language simply disappear, leaving many children disadvantaged.

Like Boomer, we believe the articulation of nationally held principles for teaching literacy is desirable. Explaining his envisaged model of a 'national standard', he writes that it would be:

> a quite extensive 'rich' book of exempla, accompanied by notes on criteria and diagnoses, of the kinds of achievement which would represent suitable competent performance, not a unidimensional marker. (Boomer, 1987:11)

We suggest that such a model is in many ways in accord with the one we had in mind for schools to follow in developing their literacy curriculum and assessment policies: the examples from the work of Gooding and Houston alluded to indicate that some schools have already demonstrated ways of developing such policies. These policies, dedicated to identifying and teaching the genres required for competence in the various subjects across the years of schooling, would provide a fundamental curriculum framework for defining curriculum goals, within which to promote and assess developing competence in literacy in students.

Where curriculum goals are clearly articulated, and where the expectations for performance in literacy are made explicit to students, then it makes some sense to talk of 'standards' — criteria for judging proficiency in students and assessing their progress. Teachers owe it to all their students to assess their work carefully, giving them explicit advice about both the strengths and the limitations of their writing. Without a clear sense of the kinds of genres their students should be striving for, teachers will be handicapped in their efforts to offer such advice.

All this brings us to the issue of grading, a matter which inevitably arises in discussions of assessment. In recent years, such is the changing manner in which students' progress through schools has been viewed that teachers have been encouraged to abandon numerical scores and to adopt instead what are sometimes called 'descriptive methods of assessment' and sometimes 'methods of non-graded assessment'. We agree that providing assessments which describe aspects of performance carefully is desirable — indeed essential — since it is through detailed responses to their work that students are enabled to progress. We would, however, make two observations about descriptive assessment, as it is often discussed in Australia. Firstly, teachers will not be in any position to provide helpful advice of the kind advocated — at least, with regard to literacy — unless they have articulated clear curriculum objectives and clear goals for performance in literacy. School programmes based upon a detailed identification and description of the range of genres to be read, discussed and written are thus essential. Our second observation is about the curious view that descriptive assessment is in itself more desirable than the various forms of assessment by numerical scores, on the grounds that it does not grade students. Any form of assessment by definition involves grading, and it is a serious misconception to suggest otherwise. The point is an important one here since it relates to some fundamental responsibilities of schooling.

Assessment is intimately a part of the whole curriculum process, so that where teachers take their students and their students' learning seriously, they necessarily regard assessment as an important responsibility. To *assess* is to *grade* — to 'match up' students' efforts, especially their written work, with those produced earlier, and to compare them for evidence of improvement. Where a method of assessment was used primarily to have students try to 'out-do' each other in a competitive manner, then we would agree that such a method was not very useful or helpful. But graded assessment need not have this effect, especially where teachers encourage students to watch their own progress, comparing their present performances in writing with their earlier efforts.

The most serious objection we can see to conventional graded assessment is that it often makes exclusive use of a numerical score, leaving students to deduce from that what they can about the quality of their work. This is clearly an inappropriate method of assessing, since it offers students little useful information to guide their future endeavours. But where a numerical score (or any other grading) is offered in association with a careful statement about what the score represents as a measure of achievement, it can be very helpful. That is because it can provide students with some measure of 'where they are at', and some corresponding sense of 'where they might go'.

In general, we suggest that students are grateful to have their work examined and critiqued seriously. They want advice about the quality of what they have done, as well as directions about the things they might do in future to improve their work. Where work merits a failure, then it is as well to say so, always supplying, of course, as much constructive help as possible about ways to improve the quality of future work. Equally, where the work is of real distinction, then again we should say so, awarding a result accordingly, and pointing the way to possible future directions that might be pursued. Finally, where the work shows evidence neither of great distinction nor of disappointingly poor effort, we again owe it to our students to indicate this in the manner in which we award results, and to offer helpful advice about how to progress.

PUTTING IT ALL TOGETHER: LITERACY FOR THE TURN OF THE CENTURY

We began this book with a discussion of the way in which literacy has changed and continues to change as our society grows and diversifies. As we look to the end of this century, we can have no certainty about many of the future challenges and problems that Australia, in common with other nations, will need to confront. We do know, however, that in an increasingly complex and technologically advanced world, the demands upon our language will grow as we strive to deal with new situations and inventions, new social and political developments of many kinds. The nature of knowledge, like the nature of society itself with its industry, commerce, government and legal system, is changing very rapidly, and we need a community equipped to deal with significant social changes, flexible in responding to problems, and courageous in confronting challenges of many kinds.

One significant measure of the changed nature of our society is the fact that the written mode is in many ways more important now than it was in the past. Thus, whatever the measure we adopt for what constitutes genuine literacy, it must be understood as a complex many-faceted matter, developed in children across a wide variety of learning situations and an equally varied range of text types, and as a necessary preparation for participation in a demanding world. Effective participation in a democracy, like effective participation in the workplace, involves capacity both to understand what is going on and to change it, where change is a desirable and important thing. Those people who leave school unable to handle the written mode satisfactorily are in important ways disempowered, for they lack some of the most significant skills with which to enter their world and to achieve fulfilment both in a personal sense and in the sense of playing a full part in a democracy. We owe it to all our students to plan comprehensive literacy programmes: programmes that will equip them to take their full and rightful place in the modern world.

REFERENCES

Australian Association for the Teaching of English. (1987). *The teaching of English in Australia: A national position paper* (with a separate statement on assessment). Adelaide: Australian Association for the Teaching of English.

Boomer, G. (Ed.). (1982). *Negotiating the curriculum: A student-teacher partnership*. Gosford, NSW: Ashton Scholastic.

Boomer, G. (1987). Organising the nation for literacy. *Proceedings of the 13th Australian Reading Association conference on language and learning*. Sydney: Australian Reading Association and Ashton Scholastic. Plenary paper presented at the conference, 11–14 July, Sydney.

Christie, F. (1989). Writing genres. In *Writing in schools* (B.Ed. course Study Guide, section 1). Geelong, Victoria: Deakin University Press.

Christie, F., & Rothery, J. (1989). Exploring the written mode and the range of factual genres. *Writing in schools* (B.Ed. course Study Guide, section 2). Geelong, Victoria: Deakin University Press.

Gray, B. (1985). Helping children become language learners in the classroom. In M. J. Christie (Ed.), *Aboriginal perspectives on experience and learning: The role of language in Aboriginal education*. Geelong, Victoria: Deakin University Press. Paper originally presented at the Annual Conference of the Meanjin Reading Council, Brisbane, May 1983.

Halliday, M. A. K. (1973). Relevant models of language. *Explorations in the functions of language*. London: Edward Arnold. (Reprinted from *Educational Review*, November 1969.)

Harris, M. (1988, 23–24 April). Literacy in peril. The *Weekend Australian*.

Houston, C. (1986a). *English language development across the curriculum*. Queensland: Division of Special Education, Department of Education.

Houston, C. (1986b). English language development across the curriculum. *Seven papers presented at the national conference, ESL in mainstream education: Access and equity*. Canberra: Commonwealth Schools Commission.

Martin, J. R., & Rothery, J. (1984, August). *Choice of genre in a suburban primary school*. Paper presented at the Annual Congress of the Applied Linguistics Association of Australia, Alice Springs.

McNamara, J. (1989). The writing in science and history project: the research questions and implications for teachers. In F. Christie (Ed.), *Writing in schools* (B.Ed. course Reader). Geelong, Victoria: Deakin University Press.

Rothery, J. (1984). The development of genres — primary to junior secondary school. In F. Christie (Ed.), *Children writing* (B.Ed. course Study Guide, section 3). Geelong, Victoria: Deakin University Press.

Rothery, J., & Gerot, L. (1986). Writing in the junior secondary school. In C. Painter & J. R. Martin (Eds.), *Writing to mean: Teaching genres across the curriculum*. Occasional Papers Number 9. Sydney: Applied Linguistics Association of Australia.

Walton, C. E. (1986). *Aboriginal children learning to write: Kriol and Warlpiri speakers in an English-speaking classroom*. Unpublished M.Ed. thesis, University of New England, Armidale, NSW.

Suggested further reading: an annotated list

CHAPTER 1 LITERACY IN A CHANGING WORLD

Butt, D. (1985). *Talking and thinking: The patterns of behaviour*. Geelong, Victoria: Deakin University Press.
Here an attempt is made to address questions of the ways in which language builds thinking processes. Butt sets out the discussion in the form of a dialogue between two people, one a psychologist, the other a linguist. Several traditions of scholarship — linguistic, psychological and philosophical — are drawn upon to develop the discussion.

Christie, F., & Rothery, J. (1989). *Writing in schools*, Sections 1–2 (B.Ed. course Study Guide). Geelong, Victoria: Deakin University Press.
For readers who are interested in pursuing notions of written genres and their teaching, these two sections of the B.Ed. course on children's writing from Deakin University will provide an appropriate introduction.

Lemke, J. L. (1988). Towards a social semiotics of the material subject. In T. Threadgold (Ed.), *Working Papers Vol. 2, Nos. 1–2*, Sydney: Sydney Association for Studies in Society and Culture.
For those interested in pursuing the notion of language and its role as a 'semiotic', this paper provides a useful discussion. In particular, it considers the question of how we can reconcile a view of people's 'individuality' with a view of human experience as socially constructed, very considerably through language.

The Newbolt Report. (1921). *Report on the teaching of English in England*. (The report of the Departmental Committee appointed by the President of the Board of Education to enquire into the position of English in the educational system of England.) London: HMSO.
For those interested in tracing something of the history of patterns in teaching the English language, especially in the nineteenth century, this report provides a helpful account. The enquiry on which it reports was the first ever held in England, or indeed, probably any other part of the world.

Ong, W. J. (1982). *Orality and literacy: The technologizing of the word*. London: Methuen.
Of the many publications Ong has produced on the impact of literacy upon western cultures, probably this one offers the best relatively brief and comprehensive discussion on the subject.

Tannen, D. (Ed.). (1982). *Spoken and written language*. Vol. IX. In Roy O. Freedle (Ed.), *Advances in discourse processes*. Norwood, New Jersey: Ablex Publishing Corporation.
This volume offers a set of interesting papers reflecting in varying ways upon the differences between speech and writing, and upon the importance of both in different contexts and cultures.

CHAPTER 2 IS LEARNING TO READ AND WRITE THE SAME AS LEARNING TO SPEAK?

Christie, F. (Ed.) (1984). *Children writing* (B.Ed. course Study Guide and Reader). Geelong, Victoria: Deakin University Press.
Sections 1–3 of these two course books, which were written for Bachelor of Education students at Deakin University, provide a clear and comprehensive explanation of an approach to literacy development which incorporates a recognition of the importance of mode differences. They include theoretical and practical perspectives.

Gray, B. (1985). Teaching oral English. In M. Christie (Ed.), *Aboriginal perspectives on experience and learning: The role of language in Aboriginal education*. Geelong, Victoria: Deakin University Press. Paper originally presented at the Annual Conference of the Meanjin Reading Council, Brisbane, May 1983.
This paper gives an account of a language programme developed for Aboriginal students in Alice Springs. The programme focused on both oral and written language development of the students, and incorporated explicit teaching about language. It was an extremely successful programme, which demonstrated how some of the principles discussed in this chapter might be put into practice.

Gray, B. (1987). How natural is 'natural' language teaching? — Employing wholistic methodology in the classroom. *Australian Journal of Early Childhood*, **12**(4).
This paper critically examines 'natural' theories of literacy development. In particular, it examines the assumption of such theories as that learning to read and write involves the same process as learning to speak. The paper discusses Bruner's notion of scaffolding and its implications for development of both spoken and written language.

Halliday, M. A. K. (1985). *An introduction to functional grammar*. London: Edward Arnold.
This book explains the systemic-functional approach to analysis of grammar. It has provided the theoretical basis for the analysis of mode differences developed in this chapter. Most of the other writers listed here have drawn upon the work presented in this book in one way or another. Consequently it is central to the discussion in this chapter.

Hammond, J. (1987a). Process or genre in teaching ESL children to write? *Proceedings of the 5th ATESOL Summer School*. Sydney: ATESOL Association.
This paper compares the effectiveness of 'process' and 'genre' approaches in the literacy development of young ESL children. It suggests that although the 'process' approach has some positive features, ultimately it fails to take sufficient account of mode differences, and hence does not provide sufficient explicit knowledge about how language works. The 'genre' approach, it is suggested, does this.

Hammond, J. (1987b). An overview of the genre-based approach to the teaching of writing in Australia. *Australian Review of Applied Linguistics*, **10**(2).
This article outlines what is meant by the 'genre-based' approach to the teaching of literacy, and traces its development. It argues that what principally distinguishes this from other approaches, such as those using 'process writing' or 'growth models' of teaching English, is its development of an explicit understanding of the role of language in the educational context.

Kress, G. (1982). *Learning to write*. London: Routledge & Kegan Paul.
This book looks at what it is that children learn when they learn to write. It suggests that because writing is produced in different contexts and for different purposes from talk, learning to write involves learning a very different way of making meaning. Consequently, a very significant part of learning to write is learning the differences between spoken and written language.

CHAPTER 3 AUTHORIZING DISADVANTAGE: AUTHORSHIP AND CREATIVITY IN THE LANGUAGE CLASSROOM

Gilbert, P. (1988). *Writing, schooling and deconstruction: From voice to text in the classroom*. London: Routledge & Kegan Paul.
A critical reappraisal of popular writing pedagogy, and a discussion of alternative approaches to the teaching of writing from a post-structuralist point of view. The book uses an Australian case study in its discussion.

Hart, K. (Ed.) (1988). *Shifting frames: English/literature/writing*. Geelong, Victoria: Centre for Studies in Literary Education, Deakin University.
A challenging collection of papers, and responses to these papers, from the one-day conference *Shifting Frames* held at Deakin University in 1987. The papers present contemporary critical perspectives on the teaching of writing and of literature.

Kress, G. (1985). *Linguistic processes in sociocultural practice*. Geelong, Victoria: Deakin University Press.
A helpful introduction to concepts of discourse, genre and text, and a very useful discussion of the way in which ideology operates through texts.

Piper, K. (1983). *Curriculum style and English language*. Hawthorn, Victoria: ACER.
The report from a research project which attempted to document and analyse current curriculum practices in the teaching of English in Australian schools. The report provides one of the few available accounts of the differing perspectives of teachers and students.

Reid, I. (1984). *The making of literature: Texts, contexts and classroom practices*. Australian Association for the Teaching of Literature.
An excellent account of the way in which contemporary literary theory might well inform current classroom practice in writing and literature study.

Reid, I. (Ed.) (1987). *The place of genre in learning: Current debates*. Geelong, Victoria: Centre for Studies in Literary Education, Deakin University.
A thought-provoking collection of papers which addresses the question of whether, and how, generic forms might be taught in classrooms. Contributors include John Dixon, Frances Christie and Gunther Kress.

CHAPTER 4 LITERACY IN SCIENCE: LEARNING TO HANDLE TEXT AS TECHNOLOGY

Lemke, J. L. (1983). *Classroom communication of science*. Arlington, Virginia. (ERIC Document Reproduction Service No. ED 222 346).
Lemke, J. L. (1985). *Using language in the classroom*. Geelong, Victoria: Deakin University Press.
Two texts which look at scientific discourse as it is used by teachers and students in science classrooms.

Martin, J. R. (1985). *Factual writing: Exploring and challenging social reality*. Geelong, Victoria: Deakin University Press.
Provides a basic introduction to non-narrative writing.

Martin, J. R. (1987). *Working Papers in Linguistics No. 5: Writing project report*. Department of Linguistics, University of Sydney.
A more detailed analysis of writing in history and geography in junior secondary school.

McNamara, J. (1989). *Writing in schools* (B.Ed. course Reader). Geelong, Victoria: Deakin University Press.

Morris, A., & Stewart-Dore, N. (1985). *Learning to read from text: Effective reading in the content areas*. Sydney: Addison-Wesley.

Painter, C., & Martin, J. R. (1986). *Writing to mean: Teaching genres across the curriculum*. Occasional Papers No. 9. Applied Linguistics Association of Australia.

Rothery, J. (1986). *Working Papers in Linguistics No. 4*. Department of Linguistics, University of Sydney.

The best applications of the socio-semantic perspective are to be found in the above four publications, which converge from a psychological point of view.

CHAPTER 5 LITERACY IN THE SOCIAL SCIENCES

Cope, B. (1986). Traditional versus progressivist pedagogy. *Social Literacy Monograph No. 11*.

This paper sets out a detailed critique of the progressivist position discussed in this chapter.

Cope, B., & Kalantzis, M. (1988). Facing the challenge of 'back to basics'. *Social Literacy Monograph No. 28*.

As the title suggests, this paper reviews the challenges and problems of current 'back to basics' moves in education.

Kalantzis, M., & Cope, B. (1987). *Social literacy: An overview*. Sydney: Common Ground.

This volume provides an overview of the Social Literacy Project. It may be obtained from the Common Ground Publishing House, Annandale, Sydney.

CHAPTER 6 ON LITERACY AND GENDER

Acker, S. (1983). Women and teaching: A semi-detached sociology of a semi-profession. In S. Walker & L. Barton (Eds.), *Gender, class and education*. Lewes: The Falmer Press.

A 'must' for all teachers who have ever wondered how they came to fill the role in life they do . . .

Harding, J. (1985). The making of a scientist? *Culture, Education and Society*, **40**(1), 55–62.

A suggestive article which opens for question the differences underlying girls' and boys' orientation towards, or away from, science.

McRobbie, A., & Nava, M. (Eds.). (1984). *Gender and generation*. London: Macmillan Education.

A collection of eight studies of the lifestyles of adolescent girls and boys, including Valerie Walkerdine's 'Some day my prince will come'. Multifaceted insights on language use.

Moss, G. (1989). *Un/popular fictions*. The Education Series (General editor, Jane Miller). London: Virago Press in association with the University of London Institute of Education.

Gemma Moss explores the ways young writers use the genres of popular fiction in their own writing. In doing so, she demonstrates how young women use the genres of romance fiction to raise and examine many questions about social identity.

Stanworth, M. (1983). *Gender and schooling: A study of sexual divisions in the classroom*. London: Hutchinson Publishing Group in association with The Explorations in Feminism Collective.

Exposes the 'myth of meritocracy' through observational and interview data from seven year 12 mixed-sex classes. A good starting point for discussion among teachers.

Swann, J., & Graddol, D. (1988). Gender inequalities in classroom talk. *English in Education*, **22**(1), 48–65.

A careful analysis of videotaped oral exchanges in the classroom (children aged 9–11). Very revealing about the patterns of gender bias in all aspects of teacher/pupil talk, and the implications of this for literacy behaviour.

Finally, two collections of stories:

Lee, H. (Ed.). *The secret self: Short stories by women.* Vols 1 & 2. Everyman Fiction. London: Dent & Sons Ltd.
Although Lee discounts any attempt to search for a 'psychological sentence of the feminine gender', the study of how women writers use *genre* is a meaningful undertaking. This two-volume collection of short stories by women provides rich data to inform such a study, and many of the stories will be enjoyed by secondary age pupils.

Riordan, J. (1984). *The woman in the moon and other tales of forgotten heroines.* London: Hutchinson Publishing Group.
The heroines in these 'forgotten' tales were always there — unlike modernist retellings of legends which simply switch male/female roles. These stories would be accessible to primary school children.

CHAPTER 7 LITERACY FOR LEARNERS OF ENGLISH AS A SECOND LANGUAGE

Lock, S. (1985). *Second-language learners in the classroom: Some considerations.* Victoria: Education Department.
Draws attention to general principles that school staff need to consider when teaching ESL students.

Moore, H. (1987). Process, outcome, and language education: A discussion. *Australian Review of Applied Linguistics*, **10**(2), 128–162.
Probes the reactions of Australian educators to pedagogical movements developed overseas, and the place of the teacher in theories of autonomous learning.

Bortoli, A. M., Campbell L., & Mitchell, J. (1983). *Literacy for ESL students.* Victoria: Child Migrant Education Services.

Garner, N. (in collaboration with Biewer, M.) (1985). *Otherwise it could go on forever. Language, science, and second language learners.* Victoria: Education Department.

Mansfield, J., & Hajislava, L. (1986). *Do it with experience — Language development and awareness through an experience-based approach.* Victoria: Multicultural Education Services.

Mansfield, J., & Pledge, S. (1986). *No English.* Victoria: Multicultural Education Services.

These last four works offer practical ideas and suggestions to teachers who want to assist ESL students in mainstream classrooms.

CHAPTER 8 LITERACY IN THE CURRICULUM: PLANNING AND ASSESSMENT

Australian Association for the Teaching of English. (1987). *The teaching of English in Australia: A national position paper* (with a separate statement on assessment). Adelaide: Australian Association for the Teaching of English.
This paper sets out some useful principles for curriculum planning and assessment, especially with respect to English studies in schools. As such, it is a helpful guide for teachers planning the English curriculum. Its statement about assessment, in particular, will be of value to teachers in all areas of the curriculum. Copies can be obtained from the AATE.

Boomer, G. (1987). Organising the nation for literacy. *Proceedings of the 13th Australian Reading Association conference on language and learning*. Sydney: Australian Reading Association and Ashton Scholastic.
This paper provides a useful overview of recent trends in language education in Australia, and discusses the implications of such an overview for changing views of curriculum planning and assessment with respect to literacy.

Christie, F. (1988). *Language and education*. AATE Studies in English No. 2. Adelaide: Australian Association for the Teaching of English.
This paper, originally written in consultation with several teachers and curriculum consultants in Victoria, offers, in the words of the president of the AATE, 'a sound and lucid exposition of the nature and role of language in education'. As such, it is intended as a policy-planning document, and schools may find it helpful in planning their literacy programmes. It is available from the AATE.

Directorate of Studies, NSW Department of Education, & Literacy and Education Research Network. (in press). *Writing 3–6: Genre, grammar, evaluation. A support document for writing K–12*. (Prepared by Mary Macken, Mary Kalantzis, Gunther Kress and Jim Martin with assistance from Bill Cope and Joan Rothery.)
This document has been prepared for the NSW Directorate of Studies to provide a support document for teachers who are implementing the new writing curriculum guidelines in that state. It will be helpful to teachers planning literacy curriculum elsewhere.

Houston, C. (1986a). *English language development across the curriculum*. Queensland: Division of Special Education, Department of Education.
This publication both reports on the writer's activities in developing language-across-the-curriculum policies in helpful ways, and offers good advice to practising teachers on ways to implement similar policies in their own schools.

Houston, C. (1986b). English language development across the curriculum. *Seven papers presented at the national conference, ESL in the mainstream education: Access and equity*. Canberra: Commonwealth Schools Commission.
This paper provides a less detailed account of the work described in Houston, 1986a, but it offers the reader some additional information of interest to both the mother-tongue and the second-language teacher.

Piper, K. (1988). *English language in Australian schools: Towards a practical framework*. Australian Education Review No. 27. Hawthorn, Victoria: ACER.
While the main thrust of this monograph is to review various models of language and its teaching with respect primarily to the English classroom, the substance of the discussion is nonetheless of interest for considering policies on language, its teaching and assessment in all areas of the curriculum.

Rothery, J. & Gerot, L. (1986). Writing in the junior secondary school. In C. Painter & J. R. Martin (Eds.), *Writing to mean: Teaching genres across the curriculum*. Occasional Papers Number 9. Sydney: Applied Linguistics Association of Australia.
This paper provides an account of the method of planning the writing-across-the-curriculum scheme adopted by Martin Gooding and his colleagues at Knox Grammar School. As such, it provides some suggestions that teachers in other schools may wish to follow in planning their policies.

Notes on the authors

Frances Christie is Foundation Professor of Education at Northern Territory University, Darwin. Prior to that appointment she was a senior lecturer in Education at Deakin University, chairing the course teams responsible for the Bachelor's course in Writing in Schools, as well as the two Master's courses in Language and Learning and Sociocultural Aspects of Language and Education. She has research interests in classroom discourse as well as in writing in schools, and has conducted a study investigating the relationship between spoken classroom discourse and writing development. She has also worked at the Curriculum Development Centre, coordinating the national Language Development Project; she has served on several language advisory panels advising both the Commonwealth Curriculum Development Centre and the Victorian Institute of Secondary Education; and she was an expert witness before the Senate Standing Committee on Education and the Arts when it undertook an enquiry into a National Language Policy for Australia in 1984. In addition to her own publications, she has edited a series of ten monographs on *Language Education* which were published by Oxford University Press in 1988.

Bill Cope is a research fellow in the Centre for Multicultural Studies at the University of Wollongong. Together with Mary Kalantzis, Stephen Castles and Michael Morrissey, he is co-author of a book on racism, nationalism and multiculturalism, *Mistaken identity: Multiculturalism and the demise of nationalism in Australia*, published by Pluto Press in 1988. He is also a co-author of the Social Literacy materials.

Pam Gilbert is a senior lecturer in Education at James Cook University of North Queensland in Townsville. She is particularly interested in the teaching of writing and of literature in schools, and in gender issues related to these areas. She is the author of two books released in 1988: *Coming out from under: Contemporary Australian women's writing* (Pandora Press, Routledge) and *Writing, schooling and deconstruction: From voice to text in the classroom* (Routledge). She is currently working with a research team from James Cook University on a project evaluating early literacy programmes in Australia, and on a booklet for the Australian Reading Association to be entitled *Reading, Writing and Gender*.

Jennifer Hammond is a lecturer in Professional Development at the National Centre for English Language Teaching and Research, Macquarie University, a position to which she is seconded from the University of

Wollongong. Her main research interests lie in the application of systemic-functional theory to language education, particularly in the spoken and written language development of students from English and non-English-speaking backgrounds. She is currently engaged in developing literacy programmes for adults, and hitherto was researching the language development of children from both English-speaking and non-English-speaking backgrounds. She has also been involved in inservice and consultancy work in NSW and the Solomon Islands in the area of literacy development and ESL education.

Mary Kalantzis is a research fellow in the Centre for Multicultural Studies at the University of Wollongong. She has worked in education for ten years, teaching at primary, secondary and tertiary levels, conducting research and writing and publishing curriculum materials. Her published research has included work on multicultural education, languages other than English, and basic literacy. She has also co-authored the Social Literacy materials (social studies/social science materials covering years 4–12) and is currently working with the Literacy and Education Research Network (LERN) on genre, grammar and evaluation materials in support of the NSW Department of Education *Writing K–12* syllabus.

Jim Martin is a senior lecturer in Linguistics at the University of Sydney. Since 1979 he has worked with Joan Rothery on the development of children's writing. His main research interest is in functional grammar and discourse analysis within a systemic-functional linguistic framework, and the ways in which these tools can be developed to intervene in political processes. His book *Factual writing: Exploring and challenging social reality* (Deakin University Press) was published in 1985; and *Learning Language, Learning Culture* (Ablex), which he co-edited with Ruqaiya Hasan in honour of M. A. K. Halliday's retirement as professor of Linguistics at the University of Sydney, appeared in 1988.

Joan Rothery is currently working as a language consultant in the Disadvantaged Schools Programme in Sydney, and also assisting with the writing of a genre-based support document for the *K–12 Writing* syllabus in New South Wales. She is finishing a PhD on children's narrative writing in the Department of Linguistics at Sydney University, where she worked for some years in the Writing Research Project with Dr J. R. Martin. In the 1970s, Joan Rothery was a lecturer in Education at the University of Sydney, and she subsequently lectured in Language Arts at the Catholic Teachers' College, Sydney. She has published a number of papers contributing to the discussion on language learning, especially the written mode.

Lynn Wales was born and educated in the United Kingdom. She has an honours degree (London) in Latin and Greek and a Master's degree (Edinburgh) and PhD (Monash) in Linguistics. Her teaching experience includes six years teaching secondary classics and English in Scotland, and eleven years at Australian universities, teaching Linguistics, Psycholinguistics, and Language Education. Prior to her present position of senior lecturer in Applied Linguistics at the University of Queensland, she was a lecturer at Deakin University. Her interest in Applied Linguistics began in 1983 with research in the area of English as a second language, and has also included preschool bilingualism and the teaching of languages other than English.

Janet White was born in Australia, and took her first degree at the University of Melbourne. For the past ten years she has worked at the National Foundation for Educational Research in Slough, England, where her principal employment has been as a member of the Assessment of Performance Unit (APU) research team, commissioned to carry out twelve national surveys of the language performance of children aged 11 and 15. Since 1986 she has also been involved in a collaborative study with the Schools Curriculum Development Council (SCDC), evaluating the work of the National Writing Project. Apart from her contributions to APU and SCDC reports, she has also published papers in the area of her research in journals and edited volumes.

Index